Mourning Men
A Journey Through Grief

Clifford E. Denay, Jr.

For Nathaniel and Nick

INTRODUCTION

Men grieve differently than women.

We tend to withdraw while women reach out to others for help. Maybe they are on to something. A Swedish proverb teaches, "A joy shared is doubled; a sorrow shared is halved." It is true. Sharing our grief will lighten our burden.

Grieving the death of a loved one continues long after the funeral service ends. But with the help of family and friends, the sharp edges of our sorrow will begin to soften, like broken beach glass eventually worn smooth by the action of endless waves. Our journey through grief is the shortest path to healing.

This book was born from my own losses, the most heartbreaking being the death of my twenty-seven year old son, Nathaniel, and his friend, Nick Lightfoot, in a boating accident on Little Traverse Bay in Lake Michigan on April 25, 2010. On a beautiful Sunday afternoon two young, vibrant men were suddenly gone. Life as I had known it ceased to exist. I was thrown into a world of chaos and grief unlike anything I had ever experienced. I was a traveler in a foreign land without familiar landmarks. Fortunately, family and friends reached out to me and kept me from sinking into oblivion. And they encouraged me to reach back to them. You can choose to do the same.

You are not alone. My wish for you is that these short daily readings instill hope in your heart and help ease your suffering.

Petoskey, Michigan
January, 2015

❧ JANUARY ❧

JANUARY 1

"Life has to end," she said. *"Love doesn't."*

– Mitch Albom

So who am I to walk beside you, dear brother, in your hour of despair? I am, like you, a broken-hearted man in the throes of grief. We have both suffered a grievous loss, the death of someone we love, perhaps more than life itself. Yet, we live.

We men are the survivors.

I write from a Christian tradition, but the death of my son has thrown me into great questioning and confusion. So when I use words like "prayer" and "faith," please know that I mean no harm. You see, I write for men of all faiths and men comfortable without faith. I write for every man who has joined the brotherhood of broken dreams. I write for men fearful of their lost future. I write for men full of regrets for their past. I write for men who cannot sleep at night. I write for men who cannot concentrate during the day. I write for men who wonder if life is still worth living. The answer is yes.

I write for you.

Come walk with me down this new and strange healing path. It is a twisting trail, one filled with tears, and, surprisingly, much joy. Thank you for joining me on this journey. I wish you well.

JANUARY 2

I thought I could not
Go any closer to grief
Without dying
I went closer
And I did not die...

– Mary Oliver, *Thirst*

Sages through the centuries have all taught the importance of working *through* grief rather than trying to step around it or keeping it stuffed inside. We men have a long history of not talking at important moments, like at the death of a loved one. But it's not too late to learn. We can put our feelings into words and help ourselves heal. We can call or text someone we trust.

Today.

Somewhere on the other side of this unspeakable loss there is a new land awaiting our arrival. It does not look familiar now. We need to give this journey as much time as we need. Healing a loss of this magnitude will not happen tomorrow. Be assured though. Grief is a journey that has an end. We will not suffer forever. Be patient with yourself. And as we travel through our grief, we can choose companions along the way who love and care for us.

We will not die. In time and with work on our part our wounds will heal, but there will always be a scar. Regardless, be assured. Joy will return.

This death is a staggering blow. I will reach out to those who love and care for me. I trust they will help me stand tall again.

JANUARY 3

No regrets.

– Emily Jasperse

This journey through grief stirs up all kinds of feelings for us men. Regret, for example. We may find ourselves wishing we had said or done things differently while we still had the chance to do so. Now, we think, it is too late. Our loved one is dead, gone. Our old relationship is over. This is the end of what used to be.

But today is also the beginning of new possibilities, what we have now.

For example, now I often find myself talking with my dead son when I take my daily walks. I carry on a conversation with him, speaking his words in response to my comments. We even laugh together. He had a wonderful sense of humor and I often share my newest puns with him during our talks. He called my puns "groaners." He "speaks" to me in this way, and I find it brings me great comfort. I feel closer to him in spite of his absence.

Other men I know write letters or poetry to their beloved dead, play favorite music they shared, plant trees in their memory, start flower or vegetable gardens, prepare special meals, brew beer, and compete in athletic events in their honor. The list of options can be long.

The love we make in the lives of our loved ones can continue after their death. We have another chance.

The love I give and take with my beloved one can reach into eternity. It's my choice.

JANUARY 4

"I don't need very much now,"
said the boy,
"just a quiet place to sit and rest.
I am very tired."

— Shel Silverstein, *The Giving Tree*

We men may not hear much about the fatigue that mourning brings. We feel tired regardless of the time of day. A simple walk is a challenge. Household chores seem beyond possibility. Aerobic exercise may hold no interest.

We may need to rest for a while until we regain our strength.

The death of a loved one throws us off balance. The world has suddenly changed. The solid ground we stood on before has shifted. Nothing may feel certain any longer. The age-old advice of not making any major decisions within the first year of our loss still holds true. We most likely are not thinking clearly even though it feels like we are. We are like a man who has had too much to drink but still believes he is functioning normally. We need time to reflect on our loss and consider how our life has changed as a result. No wonder we are so tired. Change takes a lot of work.

After my son's death, we were tempted to sell our house right away. As we had been preparing to build a new house, selling seemed logical. However, cooler heads prevailed. Friends came forward and encouraged us to hold back on the sale and wait until we were certain of our decision. We were grateful for their wisdom.

I am tired. Simple movements take great effort. But like my grief, this too, in time, shall pass.

...and, when the time comes to let it go... let it go.

– Mary Oliver

Perhaps we will learn to do nothing more difficult in our lifetimes than this: to let our loved ones go.

Those of us men who are parents know this truth intuitively. Still, admitting it is another story. Especially in front of our guy friends. If we have lost a son or daughter, letting them go when they die changes our parental role from being in charge to being left behind, from a sense of power and authority to being powerless and speechless. In the early days after our child's death, we may be filled with rage, angry at an unjust God. We search for someone or something to blame.

It takes time for the reality of the death to sink in. Perhaps it will never completely do so.

Traditional death wisdom teaches the importance of giving our loved ones permission to leave, to travel into their new life, wherever and whatever that may entail. Some faith traditions teach that a "heavenly paradise" awaits us. Others teach that we become "one with the universe." Still others teach the idea of reincarnation, being "re-born" into a new human body for another chance at life.

Regardless of what you believe about life after death, each of us is required, ultimately, to let our loved one go.

I pray for the courage to let my loved one depart in peace. I can speak my goodbye, write a letter, sing a song, think a silent prayer, or scream permission into the universe for him/her to leave. No one prepared me for this grim task. I'll do the best I can.

JANUARY 6

It ought to be remembered that there is nothing more difficult to take in hand, more perilous to conduct, or more uncertain of its success, than to take the lead in the introduction of a new order of things.

– Niccolo Machiavelli

When a loved one dies, part of the work of grief involves the introduction of a new order of things, especially if this has been the death of an immediate family member. A link in the chain that held us together is now missing. A familiar voice sounds no more. A face is missing. Familiar footsteps are silent.

A "new order of things" will be required to help us pick up the pieces of our broken lives together.

Where do we start? With me?

Sometimes. And sometimes the responsibility is shared between all family members. Often this decision is reached in silence, as when a household task is shared equally between the members of the family who are present to do the work at hand. In other families, this "perilous" responsibility is talked through and each family member agrees to his or her new role. If the death was a child, both parents may let the "new order" evolve gradually as both struggle with their own grief while trying to stay attentive to the needs of the remaining child (ren).

There is no handbook for how to do this, but we can tap the wisdom of other men who have suffered before us and succeeded in establishing a new order of things after the death of a family member. The leader of a local grief recovery group may be able to put us in touch with one of these men.

What is one thing I can do today to help establish the new order in my family?

JANUARY 7

We are brothers after all.

– Chief Seattle

Perhaps the hardest question we men have to deal with from friends and neighbors after the death of a loved one is: How are you doing? It is an impossible question to answer. We are devastated after our loss, trying to find a map of sorts in this foreign land of grief. The question is common and any response will be painful and inadequate. We often hesitate to answer.

Men are seldom taught how to explain the devastation of being left behind, lost in a wilderness of despair without a compass.

Still, every now and then, the question comes from people who really want to know. You can tell. Perhaps it's the look in their eyes, the way they are standing, the soft touch on your arm, their willingness to sit and listen, the unhurried demeanor, the questions about your lost one, their own stories of loss and despair. Their tears.

At the recycling station I see a friend whose father has died just weeks before. I tell him I am sorry, that I have no other words to share that might bring him comfort, that I am happy to see him. Tears fill his eyes. "You're the first man to say anything to me. I have never been so lonely in my life." Tears fill my eyes. We talk more.

There is a brotherhood of loss. I will welcome more men into this fellowship of grief. My invitation may lighten my own sorrow.

JANUARY 8

*We know very little about death...the moment of death.
What do we see? How does it feel? We don't know.*
— Ken Untener

It is hard to be a man in this world and say "I don't know," in answer to any question. Any yet, death forces us to admit the unknowable. What is death? How does it feel? Where do we go? Who, if anyone, will be there to greet us when it is our turn to die? Mothers? Fathers? Children? Grandchildren? Grandparents? Spouses? Workplace friends? Animals we have loved?

Is there a heaven? If so, is it in the sky? If there is no heaven, why not? Isn't there supposed to be a reward for a life well-lived?

The questions continue on and on and on. There are few if any answers. Our faith traditions may offer consolation and suggestions about what is to come in the afterlife. If you find comfort in your faith, grab it and hold on tight. Whatever gets us through the day is fair game. Perhaps acknowledging that our loved one is now safe in the arms of a loving God is enough. No more suffering. No more agony. No more tears. Just peace and infinite solitude. Security. Safety. Warmth. And love. Inexplicable, never-ending love.

There is a lot about this world that I do not understand, especially death. I'm not even sure about the existence of heaven. But I have faith that my loved one is safe wherever he or she may be.

I walked into a store. The ordinariness of what I saw repelled me...How could everybody be going about their everyday business when these were no longer ordinary times?...Do you not know that he slipped and fell and that we sealed him in a box and covered it with dirt and that he cannot get out?

– Nicholas Wolterstorff

My father died on May 21st, the very heart of spring. I recall leaving the hospital room where his body lay and walking out into the sunshine, the blue skies, the white, billowy clouds, and the warm, fresh, springtime air. The lilacs were in full bloom, their fragrance astounding. A robin sang. I remember thinking that my father would never again smell the extraordinary scent and hear the sweet robin's song. The blooming lilacs seemed impossible.

My father is dead, I thought, how can the world still be turning?

I drove to my parents' deserted home. I changed into one of dad's t-shirts and slipped into the rest of my running gear. Although not yet a runner of any distance, I drove to my old high school track a few miles away and started jogging the quarter-mile loop. I didn't stop until I had finished six miles, a record distance for me at that time. I didn't know what else to do.

My loved one is dead. I have no power over death, but I can still choose how to live today's life.

JANUARY 10

*We cannot change the cards we are dealt, just how
we play the hand.*

– Randy Pausch

We may be surprised by this death. Caught unaware. Unprepared. Even if we had the good fortune to see it coming, the actual death still catches many men off guard. We may be thinking that our loved one cannot possibly be dead. This is a nightmare from which we will awake and everything will be the way it was before. Our mind is trying to protect us from the truth.

But life, as it turns out, is not a game.

At some level beyond our overwhelming grief, deep down inside, we may realize that we can "play the hand" we are dealt. Two choices appear in the fog of loss. We can steer our sorrow inside, lock it up, and pretend that all is well, that this is no big deal. Or, we can look into the eyes of friends and family members, recognize that we share this astonishing loss, and accept the love and consolation they offer. We can hug them, hold them, comfort them. We can explore our grief with our hands and hearts, like a potter holds and molds a new portion of clay. We can begin to shape a new life without our loved one.

This is the "work" of grief.

We can come out on the other side of grief if we are willing to walk through the forest of sorrow. This is not easy. But others who are familiar with the path will help show us the way.

*And now we welcome the New Year. Full of
things that have never been.*

– Rainer Maria Rilke

Everything seems new in the wake of our loss. This may be a
new year, but for us, it is a new life. We have not walked in this
valley before. All things once familiar seem to have faded into
the background.

What is a man to do?

Perhaps we rediscover one simple activity from "before" that
may once again be possible in this new "after." For me, it was
a return to walking. The rhythm and psychological rest that
walking provides has always been comforting for me. The exercise is also helpful. Before this loss, I enjoyed walking during
my lunch hours on the nature trail behind our local community
college. Nature has always been healing for me. When I found
myself once again walking on my familiar trails, I felt the wel-
coming presence of the animals, birds, and trees, a kinship that
is hard to describe but comforting for my troubled soul.

Or, as Rilke suggests, perhaps a new activity is called for now.
What would bring some measure of relief back into our world?
That vacation, too long-postponed? Volunteering in a local
charity, civic organization, or school? The hobby long-ago
researched but never started? Ham radio operator? Woodworking? Gardening? Writing? A stint in the local community
orchestra? The possibilities are endless. Today may be a good
day to start.

*Today, I will consider the beginning of a new activity that
may bring me some comfort after my loss. Or, I will return
to an activity that I used to enjoy. I ask for the strength to do
one or the other.*

JANUARY 12

I have been where you are now, and you will be where I have gone.

– Italian Graveyard Headstone Epitaph

Where do our beloved dead go? And where will we be when we finally join them? This may be life's most important question and greatest mystery.

The truth is that no one knows.

If we are men of faith, we may believe that our beloved one is waiting to greet us in a heavenly realm after our own death. Or, if we do not believe in an afterlife, we may feel that after death everything ends except eternal silence. Many of us are simply not sure. We have heard convincing arguments to support both points of view. Most of us, though, may want to believe that something is on "the other side" of this life.

Every major world religion teaches that an afterlife awaits us all. One day, we will finally know.

In the meantime, how shall we live? It seems that doing what we can to make this world a better place to live, to foster more compassion, more love, more justice, more caring, and more attention to the pain and suffering of others might be a good place to start. Reaching through the mist of sorrow to take another's hurting hand may ease the pain of our own loss. Perhaps we can let the future take care of itself.

I will trust that wherever my loved one is now and where I will be when I die, is a place of goodness, mercy, and eternal love.

JANUARY 13

*...no good thing ever vanishes. It is carried
forward from generation to generation.*

– Pam Brown

Three days before my father died, I walked into his hospital room and he greeted me with these words: "Hi, Cliff. How's the family?" He was dying, but through his pain and suffering he still chose to ask about the welfare of my family instead of focusing on his impending death.

Where did he learn how to love like this?

I don't have to look far for the answer. His parents, my Grandma Josephine and Grandpa Henry, were known in their part of the countryside for their hospitality, friendship, concern for their hungry neighbors, and for protecting the area's farm animals from cruel treatment at the hands of their owners. My father had wholesome mentors in his parents, and he learned to pass this compassion on when it became his turn to be a parent.

In spite of our sorrow, can we look back at some of our own male role models, men who taught us how to be a man in the best possible way? A man who can love, care, show emotions when necessary, is compassionate, kind, and loving? A man with the courage to not run away from death, but to walk into its great mystery in spite of our fear?

I am a product of generations of strong men who lived before me. I am grateful for the lessons of love they shared by faithfully living their values. (If these words do not describe my experiences, I am strong enough now to break from tradition and make my life an example for the generations that will follow me.)

Let's talk of graves, of worms, of epitaphs;
Make dust our paper and with rainy eyes
Write sorrow on the bosom of the earth.
Let's choose our executors, and talk of wills...
For God's sake, let us sit upon the ground
And tell sad stories of the death of kings.

– William Shakespeare, *Richard II*, Act III

We men are story tellers. And when a loved one dies, we have to tell our stories again and again and again. Endlessly, it may seem. This is what grief does to us. It pushes us toward repeated explanations of this inexplicable tragedy in the hope that someone, anyone, possibly even everyone, might have some idea of the pain we are suffering.

This giving words to our sorrow may be new to us who are used to being men of few words.

Yet our grief often sidesteps our discomfort. We long for understanding, perhaps to be held. We may want to cry. We want someone to tell us that the world is still a safe place. We may feel afraid. We're not used to being afraid.

Through our own "rainy eyes" we search the eyes of those who dare approach us, pushing through their own fears of death to touch our near-mortal wound. They come to help us heal. We are amazed at their courage. We may be surprised that their courage gives us hope. We are grateful.

If my grief is fresh, raw, and overwhelming, I may feel compelled to "...write sorrow on the bosom of the earth" by telling my stories time and time again. This is a normal part of the grieving process and will, eventually, help me to come to terms with the death of my loved one.

JANUARY 15

All journeys have a secret destination of which the traveler is unaware.

– Martin Buber

This journey through grief certainly qualifies as a journey with a "secret destination." Who knows where the road ahead will lead? The death of a loved one takes us into unchartered territory. The road signs telling us which way to go are missing. We are flying blind. This is not the way most guys like to travel.

And this is a journey we did not choose.

When my son died unexpectedly, I told friends and neighbors that I felt like I was trying to walk through Jell-O. I knew where I thought I needed to go, but the effort it took to simply move was almost impossible to summon. I felt numb. My head was in a fog. Thinking took great effort. Friends steered me through necessary tasks. I did what I was told to do.

We men are not used to traveling without a map of some sort. Our technological devices usually lead us to where we want to go. But now we need more than devices. Now we need each other. Now we need never-before-experienced amounts of love and support. Now we need sensitive and kindly loving care.

Now we need tolerance for our outbursts of anger and rage.

Now we need to grieve.

Now we may need to hold and be held.

I did not ask for this journey. But, here I am. I hope for the strength to walk into the unknown land of grief with as much courage as I can muster. I cannot see the road ahead. But no one else can either. I'll do the best I can.

JANUARY 16

*He sought his former accustomed fear of death
and did not find it. 'Where is it? What death?'
There was no fear because there was no death. In
place of death there was light.*

– Leo Tolstoy

We may have heard stories about near-death experiences. One theme in common with all of them seems to be the presence of a "light." Many people near death report seeing a light of indescribable beauty. Often the light beckons and they are drawn toward it. Most folks who survive a near death experience say they were reluctant to come back because what they had seen was so beautiful and peaceful.

What is the light?

Some would say the light is God. Others might argue the light is a physiological phenomenon that occurs in the brain when the body is shutting down. We may have heard additional explanations. Regardless of which we believe, those who have been through these near-death experiences now report being unafraid of dying because of the beauty that awaits them.

These few words above from Tolstoy's *The Death of Ivan Ilych* come near the end of Ilych's life, just moments before he dies. In the story, Ilych suddenly stirs and proclaims, "So that's what it is! What joy!"

In the midst of my dark grief, I hope that my loved one was greeted by a peaceful and beautiful light. I hope for the same for myself when it is my turn to die.

JANUARY 17

Some of us may embrace the concept of "rebirth," the belief that those who die are reborn into new bodies and return to earth for a second chance at life. This may be a comforting thought in light of the death of our loved one. Still, many of us may find this concept strange.

Who knows? A... traveled soul... may appreciate life even more.

Or perhaps we have heard others tell stories about departed loved ones returning in the form of birds or animals. One woman saw a bald eagle flying above her son's grave. She felt he had been resurrected in the form of the eagle and that he was telling her he was okay. A pair of mourning doves has visited our home repeatedly since my son and his good friend died in a boating accident. Are the doves the dead boys in... new flesh... reassuring me all is well?

On the day my son died, his sister-in-law learned she was pregnant with her first child. When their daughter was about six months old, she started pointing at our son's picture on the fireplace mantel at her parents' home. Once, our son's mother-in-law brought his picture to her and she reached for it and kissed the picture on my son's lips. They were amazed. In the months to come, she kissed his picture repeatedly, once in front of my wife and me. We were stunned. How could this baby, who had never known our boy while he lived, love him so after his death?

There is much I will never understand.

*What you cannot see with your eyes, see with
your faith.*

– Phillips Brooks

In the face of overwhelming grief, we men often cast aside anything we cannot see with our own eyes. Often, but certainly not always, and depending upon the circumstances surrounding the death, whatever faith we had before our loved one's death may be shredded. Tattered. This might be especially true if the death was unexpected or accidental. Or, if our child has died.

Our "faith" may have died along with our loved one.

I was a man of faith before my son died, but I felt that faith shatter. Yet I still found myself touched by the beauty of the world, as if I was being lifted up. I believed in God and did not believe at the same time. How could this be? Then the love of family and friends caught me just when I felt I was falling into an abyss. Is this how God works? Through the compassionate hands and hearts of those who love us? Maybe this is what faith is: a belief in the goodness of fellow human beings in good times and bad. Maybe this is what Brooks meant when he said, "...see with your faith." What I saw was real.

*We cannot see love, yet do we doubt its existence? Perhaps
there is more to this world than I can see. Today, in spite of
my sorrow, I will try to see the world with whatever faith I
may have that still remains. It may make a difference.*

JANUARY 19

Surely there're some other children
Who've died, to come play with me. They're
always dying...
— Rainer Maria Rilke

Statistically, about ten percent of all fathers and mothers have children who die. So if we have lost a child, we have a lot of company. Not that companionship makes our grief any lighter. Perhaps it even exacerbates our sorrow. Who's to know?

But knowing we are not alone with the worst possible loss may help us on our healing journey.

How could I have guessed that the man who greeted and held us in his arms at the hospital the night our son died was a father who had lost a daughter himself? And how would I have known that the men who turned to look at me when I walked into my first meeting of The Compassionate Friends were also fathers who had lost children? Had I passed those same men on the street, I would have never guessed. After all, they looked normal to me.

Parents with dead children look just like other parents. The only difference is in their eyes. When you look at them, you notice something deeper inside. Deeper compassion. Deeper empathy. Deeper understanding. Deeper love. Deeper appreciation for living in the moment. Deeper gratitude for the opportunity to have shared their life with their child. Deeper tolerance for life's sorrow. Deeper joy for knowing us.

I am grateful to know other parents who have lost children. Now I do not feel so alone in my grief. And I have someone to call or hug when I need to talk.

In loving the spiritual,
You cannot despise the earthly.

– Joseph Campbell

Some of us may be living this life like it is less significant than the grandeur of the world to come. Others are living like there is no tomorrow, no new world after death. And some of us may be comfortable in not knowing, or caring.

For all of us, though, this death brings cause for reflection on what we believe will happen after we die.

When we lose someone we love, we are reminded of how precious life is. The one we mourn today may have brought joy and encouragement to many lives. This loved one's voice and spirit is already missed, his or her absent smile mourned. Countless lives were likely enriched because our loved one lived.

A friend talks wistfully about her dead son's absence. "I miss him horribly. He liked to work in the kitchen with me, experiment with new recipes, make his homebrew, bake cakes, play music, and just hang out. He was my friend and companion. Now it's so lonely here. So quiet. I look for him everywhere in the house."

Our life experiences shape our beliefs. And regardless of what we believe, as long as we are alive, we can choose our attitude in the face of this death.

I loved you while you lived. And while I live, I'll keep on loving you.

JANUARY 21

We were in no way prepared for this dreadful thing.
We were a happy family, we had been happy from
the beginning; we did not know what trouble was, we
were not thinking of it nor expecting it.

– Mark Twain

Perhaps the unexpected that Twain writes about is true for many families. Things are going well. Children are growing up. We are getting older. We have our family spats, but nothing serious. We are taking care of aging parents, worrying about the lack of money, thinking about retirement, but for the most part, we are happy. And then, death intrudes. Unannounced. Unexpected. Unimaginable. Unwelcome.

Not us, please. Pick on some other family. Leave us alone. We don't deserve this.

But who does? Before this death arrived at our own doorsteps, we may have felt we were successfully handling family affairs. We may have even imagined that our own power had something to do with how well our family was doing, how well we got along, what a happy group we were. But the death of our loved one has taught us differently. We now know how little we control, how powerless we can become, how quickly we can be pushed to our knees. After my son died in a boating accident, one of my students said to me, "You used to be the happiest man I have ever known." I replied, "I still am. Only now my son is dead."

I may have had no way to prepare for this death, so I am preparing, today, now, this moment. I will even ask for help when I need it and will not desert my remaining family members. They need me more than ever now.

JANUARY 22

In my beginning is my end
In my end is my beginning

– T. S. Eliot

It has been said that there is no such thing as "lost," that wherever we are, even if we do not know where we are, the place is someone's home. Therefore, it is impossible to be truly lost. This may be good news to us men who prefer to find our way without asking directions. We may simply be in a place that we do not recognize. There may be no familiar landmarks, no street signs to point our way. A cul-de-sac at the end of every one-way street is just a place to either turn around or continue on into unfamiliar territory.

The death of a loved one marks both the end of the known and the beginning of the unknown.

After arriving in Budapest, Hungary, for Christmas vacation a number of years ago, my family and I first boarded a train and then transferred to a bus to take us into the city center. Had I not known the name of the city, I would have declared us lost. Nothing looked like home. The street signs were written in Hungarian. Billboard advertisements were equally unintelligible. I felt like a stranger in a strange land, but I knew I was not "lost." I just needed a map.

Grief is unfamiliar territory. It has a beginning and an end. I will be kind to myself while I learn to find my way. When I feel "lost," I will ask for help, perhaps from a friend who has been here before me. I can even call _____ today, now. He knows how this feels.

I come to tell my story
As a gift to those who follow –
You can survive the death of your child
By living not in yesterday's sorrow.

– Clifford E. Denay, Jr.

Is there a greater loss for parents than the death of a child?

After the death of my son, I could think of no reason to continue living. Nothing meant anything to me. All I could think about was the enormity of my loss, the unspeakable horror, the unimaginable absence of this young man who gave so much to the world, who loved so deeply, cherished friendships, laughter, love, and sleeping under the stars. And children. How he loved children and they loved him!

Grief pulls us backward into yesterdays and pushes us forward into tomorrows. But, we can only live in this moment. It's all we have.

Grief will try to prevent us from standing in the present moment. Men especially wander in the land of "what ifs" and also "what will become of me now without him or her?" We lament our fallibility. We berate ourselves for not being a better protector. And yet... yet, we did the best we could to prevent the death. We are not all powerful. We are human.

One of the songs played at our son's wedding was entitled "Be Here Now." He and his bride chose this song as a reminder to themselves and to all in attendance that we can only live in the present, not the past or future. Not yesterday. Not tomorrow. Just today.

We played the same song at his funeral.

I will try my best to live in this day. If I remain stuck in yesterday's sorrow, I will ask for help. I might start writing in a journal, putting my feelings into words.

The biggest question I had as a child was, "How would I leave my mark on the world?"

– Dale Rogers

Perhaps at no other time do we consider our own death as much as we do when a loved one dies. Losing someone so close to us may even feel like a near miss. We may wonder why we are still alive while our loved one is now gone. We may even feel guilty for still being here. This is the protector in us coming out of hiding. It's a guy thing.

So in addition to our grief over the death of our loved one, we may also be wondering what our legacy will be when it is our turn to die. This is a big deal.

Death is not a topic usually discussed in social gatherings in our culture. We live in a youth-orientated society and tend to put death as far away from our reach as possible. It is not until we have no other choice in the matter that we will talk about our final leave-taking. This death may be an unexpected opportunity to ask ourselves what most of us care deeply about: What will I leave behind when I die? How do I want to be remembered? Or, as Dale Rogers put it, "How would I leave my mark on the world?" On what accomplishments would I want my fingerprints to appear?

It is not too late for me to decide how I want to leave my mark on the world. Maybe I already know. If not, I will talk with someone who will listen without judging or criticizing me.

In all things we learn only from those we love.

– Goethe

As we struggle with the death of our beloved one, our thoughts may turn to a recurring question: what have I, as a man, learned from this person who was so dear to me and is now gone from my sight? In the face of my overwhelming grief, this question may surprise me. Where is the question coming from? Why now, so soon after the death? What am I supposed to do with the answer, if indeed I have an answer? Aren't there more important things to worry about?

Yet, what can be more natural than to think about what we have learned from people we love?

In the midst of my grief after my father's death, I found myself telling stories of his sense of humor, his propensity for barber-shop jokes, (He was a barber for more than 60 years) and his ability to straddle the fence on issues involving religion and politics so as to not offend his customers. When my mother died, my stories turned to her willingness to help us children with homework, to encourage the improvement of our spelling skills, and always to her expectations that we would go to college. Many of these skills are now my traits.

And since my son's death, whenever I am faced with a vexing problem, I find myself asking: How would Nathaniel solve this? What would he do? I want to be more like him. One friend remembered our son for his "...uncanny ability to make tools from all sorts of things."

Love is a great teacher.

My God, if our only prayer throughout our lives is "Thank You," that would be enough.

– Thomas Merton

It is tough to think of saying "thank you" when a person so precious to us has been taken away. A more likely response from a man would be anger at the injustice of life, at a God who would either take our loved one away for unknown reasons, or, worse yet, stand idly by while our beloved dies.

Either way we lose, huh? We men do not like to lose. Death, however, has the ultimate say.

But, when it comes to death, thinking in terms of winning or losing may not be helpful. Perhaps we will feel some small portion of relief if we consider the love and joy that was brought into our life as a result of our loved one having lived. This is hard to do when we are overwhelmed with grief. Gratitude may be the last thing we want to express.

When my son died, I asked my counselor if my son would be returning. This, of course, was a question that made no sense. Yet I had to hear "no" with my own two ears. Her answer, as full of horror as it was, opened the possibility of admitting gratitude for his life. Not at that moment, but later on, when I began to think more clearly.

I am grateful for the life of _____. In spite of my unspeakable sorrow, deep down inside I acknowledge my gratitude. Dear world, thank you!

Therefore, I will not keep silent; I will speak out in the anguish of my spirit. I will complain in the bitterness of my soul.

— Job 7:11 (NIV)

How do we stifle our rage after the death of a beloved family member or friend? After all, aren't we men of action? How do we repress the urge to do something, especially when the wrong person has died? All of the people who deserved to die are still alive, we may protest. What kind of world is this? Why do the good ones seem to die first?

If I was in charge, wouldn't different decisions be made? More just decisions, for starters?

But, I'm not in charge. And never before have I felt like such a helpless bystander. At moments like this, God is an easy target. Just ask Job. And the injustice of an untimely death may especially provoke us into unpredictable rages, against God, or anyone else for that matter.

Fortunately for me, after the most recent death in my family, I made a beeline for my woodpile and began splitting wood like an automated machine. My splitting maul fell ten, twenty, a hundred, a thousand times, who counted? When I was wet and exhausted, when I could no longer lift the weight of the maul, until I began, once again, to sob, to fall to my knees and rage at the universe, I stopped.

If this has been an unjust death, I have a right to my rage. But, I will reach out for help about how I can channel my anger so no one around me will have to suffer.

*One of the darkest undercurrents of the glaring
statistics is that one suicide in the family boosts future
suicide risks for everyone else in the home.*

– Bill Briggs

Suicide is a permanent solution to our grief and suffering. But, of course, it is not the only solution.

There are still those who love and desperately need us now that our beloved friend or family member is dead. Just ask them.

None of us have experienced identical horrors. In that sense, we can never be completely understood. But most of us have experienced some horrors. Many of us have witnessed death and destruction. Darkness. Fear. Abandonment. Feelings of hopelessness, perhaps betrayal. The list goes on.

And yet if we seek help, we will find help. There are those who will listen and care. They will stand by our side. For those of us who have suffered from the suicide of a military loved one, the Tragedy Assistance Program For Survivors may be an effective resource. Spouses and siblings of military personnel can also use the TAPS program. Suicide can be contagious.

For civilian guys, the Community Mental Health Department is just a phone call or email away. Or your local hospice may offer grief recovery programs, usually at no cost. I found hope in the office of a trauma expert employed by our local hospice. She was kind, compassionate, and competent.

Reach out. Someone is waiting to help.

*Grief and suffering are equal opportunity employers. They
welcome one and all. Suicide is just one ticket out. There are
other, less-painful choices I can make. Today, I hope for the
strength I need to ask for help, to choose life instead of death.
There are those who need me.*

JANUARY 29

Laughter is the sunshine of the soul.

– Murray Banks

It is not uncommon for many funeral ceremonies to include a period of time when family and friends are invited to come to the front and tell stories about the person who has died. Although these stories can be eloquent and full of praise for the dead person's life and accomplishments, invariably, funny stories rise from the ashes of grief.

Ironically, the laughter and joy the person brought into the world may be what we remember the most.

At our son's funeral, his wife's grandfather, Albin, stood in front of the crowded church and told a brief story about the first time they met. The fundraising event required participants to walk laps around the local high school track. He said, "When Nathaniel and I started our walk together, we were strangers. By the time we finished the first lap, we were friends. I loved this young man." He told of Nathaniel's smile, his easy laughter, of how Nathaniel asked questions about his life, how his interest evoked a sense of joy.

Most of all, however, Grandpa Albin spoke of their shared laughter and joy of living.

How can a father forget such a moment?

In the midst of my tears, I will always remember _____, and the joy and laughter he/she brought into the world.

> *"Pooh, promise you won't forget*
> *about me, ever,*
> *Not even when I'm a hundred."*
> *Pooh thought for a little.*
> *"How old shall I be then?"*
> *"Ninety-nine."*
> *Pooh nodded.*
> *"I promise," he said.*

> – A. A. Milne

One fear men may have is that if we ever let go of our grief, we may forget about the one we love who has died. The danger with this way of thinking is that long-term sorrow itself may become a substitute for our beloved dead, something to hold onto, even cherish, in the absence of the one who is no longer present.

None of us want to be forgotten. Ever.

Short of developing dementia, it is as likely that we will forget a departed loved one as we will forget to breathe. Or our heart forgets to beat. His or her picture is indelibly etched in our brain. Think of an unforgettable scene from a movie you may have seen as a child, something you may have recalled hundreds, perhaps thousands of time already. Perhaps you "see" it even at this moment. Will you ever forget it?

Some mornings when my eyelids flutter open, I look at the mental picture album of my life experiences and "see" all those I love who are no longer alive. Just looking at their beautiful faces, as often as I wish, brings me great comfort. So, "...promise you won't forget about me, ever, not even when I'm a hundred?"

I promise!

My dear _____, *I promise I will never forget you. Ever.*

JANUARY 31

"... Lament not, O [father], and be not grieved. I am not of the lost, not have I been obliterated and destroyed. I have shaken off the mortal form and raised my banner in the spiritual world. Following this separation is everlasting companionship. Thou shalt find me in heaven, immersed in an ocean of light."

– Abdu'l-Baha'

If your child has died, this is a message at once horrible and also comforting. Saying goodbye to a loved one is hard enough. Saying goodbye to our child is beyond horror. Beyond comprehension. Beyond our imagination. Beyond any other earthy fear. Beyond any possible words.

And yet, here we are. A father without our beloved son or daughter.

Slowly, our days will turn into weeks, the weeks into months, and the months into years. The reality of our loss will slowly sink into our hearts. And this description of a world to come may bring comfort to a grieving father's heart. We are assured that wherever our child is now, all is well. Given the circumstances, what could be better?

And if we do not believe this or no matter what our faith, we can take solace, even for a moment, in this description.

Dear _____. I sense that all is well with you, wherever you are and whatever you are doing. I wish I could have prevented your death. I did the best I could.

❧ FEBRUARY ❧

FEBRUARY 1

*In fire and water we went under. We died
yet we live...*
                                  – Daniel Berrigan

For many men, the death of our loved one almost feels like
our own death. And it's no wonder. This person was a central
figure in our everyday life. Now, he/she is gone. Like Berrigan,
we may feel like we were the one who "went under."

Yet we live.

And that we still live may surprise us. We are left behind. We
may feel abandoned. Lost. Lonely. Lethargic. We move in slow
motion. Everything we do takes a lot of effort. Old activities no
longer appeal to us. Some old friends no longer seem to "fit"
into our new world of grief. They avoid us. Even relatives may
struggle to speak of our loss. Thankfully, a phone call or text
message to an old or new friend will enable us to tell our stories
repeatedly. Either may be willing to listen. We may have to risk
moving out of our comfort zone to make this contact. Yet one
such friend may become our salvation.

Yet we live.

Our stories help us absorb the reality of death. The "work" of
grieving is to help us accept what has happened so that we can
continue to live. To live, even joyfully, is what our beloved dead
would want us to do.

Yet we live.

*My loved one is dead, but I am still alive. It is my responsi-
bility to honor him/her by the way I choose to live the rest of
my days.*

There is nothing like loving remembrances from one's own family. I especially appreciate it now that one by one the members of my immediate family have left…

– Sr. Mary Ignatius

And so life goes. The author of these few lines, my beloved Aunt Honey, has also now joined her immediate family members on "the other side." All seven siblings are together again. In this letter to me, she was reacting to the deaths of her brothers and sisters, and to a birthday greeting I had sent.

In the agony of our loss, we men also want to be remembered.

Communication from family and friends helps us realize we are not alone. Love is made visible in the faces of others who have traveled this lonely road of bereavement before us. A card or letter, telephone call, email, text message, or a brief in-person visit will certainly gladden our sad hearts. And because we will all have our turn to grieve, we can return the favor when it is another's turn.

Perhaps being remembered is our lifelong, unspoken quest.

Some days there won't be a song in your heart.
Sing anyway.

– Emory Austin

When my father and my brother Mark left my father's house on the way to the hospital that Friday afternoon, my dad reached into his back pocket, pulled out his wallet, turned to Mark and said, "Here, I won't be needing this anymore."

Did he somehow know at that moment that he would die five days later?

Randy Pausch was a computer science professor at Carnegie Mellon University and the author, along with Jeffrey Zaslow, of the book *The Last Lecture*. When he was diagnosed with terminal cancer, he decided to leave his students with the wisdom of his years. The hand he decided to play was a book about living rather than a treatise about dying.

He knew he could control little about his cancer, but had complete control of his attitude toward it.

As men we often think we have a great deal of control in our lives. This death of our loved one may be a hand we have never been dealt before. Choosing a life-affirming attitude and reaching out for help may be steps in a helpful direction on this grief journey.

If I try, maybe I can sing through my tears.

FEBRUARY 4

*...a dream about a late loved one is often a gift.
Don't over analyze it. Accept it with gratitude.*

– Carla Blowey

On the Friday before my son died, he had finished drawing the plans for a new house for my wife and me. The two of them had worked together on the design details over a period of just two and half-weeks. I watched him push away from his laptop and announce to no one in particular and in a gleeful voice, "I love this little house! I just love it."

A week later, through the fog of unspeakable grief, we decided to carry on with the plans to build Nathaniel's house. The house would be built in his honor and memory, a beautiful tribute to his life.

And it is.

One night, halfway through the building project, while the two by four studs were starting to outline the shape of the interior rooms, I had a dream that I saw Nate in the bathroom of the lower level of the house. I had just stepped off the stairs and started to enter the bathroom when I saw his left arm between the studs. I walked around the wall and there he was, looking straight at me. His facial expression was neither sad nor happy.

He just stared at me. "I'm okay, Dad," he said, "I'm okay." Then I awoke.

I do not know what to make of my dreams. But this I do know. Some of my dreams bring me joy and peace. I awake feeling closer to my loved one. I'm grateful.

FEBRUARY 5

Every night, millions of people are visited by deceased loved ones. In dreams, the living and the dead embrace, converse and reach understandings. What are we to make of these encounters?

– Jeffrey Zaslow

There is so much in this world we do not understand. As my mother grew older, she began to answer many of my questions with these words: "I don't know." That was it. No additional explanation. Now that I am older, I am starting to understand. She really didn't know the answers.

Neither do I. And, it's okay.

We men may be too ashamed to admit the contents of our dreams with our departed loved ones because we may not want to be perceived to be weird or "out there." Yet, the dreams may keep coming. What can we do with them?

Perhaps we can simply admit to one trusted friend that we do dream about those we have lost. This person may offer insight that will provide some measure of relief for our anguish, and if sharing our dreams with someone we know is too risky, we may choose a pastor, rabbi, or imam, or even a professional counselor. We need not live alone with our grief. Our dreams help us stay connected with the one we have lost. And even without such dreams, of course, our loved one will never leave us.

We don't have to understand why.

I used to think I knew a lot of answers. Now I realize I know far more questions.

FEBRUARY 6

Everything has an end.

– Tanzania Proverb

Somewhere inside us we know that we will one day die. Men are good at keeping that awareness at "arm's length." It is only at moments like this that our realization of death comes home, becomes personal. My loved one is dead. This is my life. This is happening to me. This is real.

This isn't possible.

Yes, it is possible. Death eventually "happens" to all humans. We each have a beginning, and we each have an end. Our aging bodies remind us of this truth. It's that simple. And saying goodbye to my loved one is brutal.

In Harold Kushner's book, *When Bad Things Happen to Good People*, he tells the story of his son who died of old age at the actual age of 12 years. As a rabbi, Kushner struggles to explain why children die before parents, out of the natural order, and why it would happen in his family. As a father, Kushner's heart breaks while he watches his son age before his eyes. He questions God and comes up empty-handed.

Death is a part of life. And death respects no social, economic, religious, or cultural boundaries. Everyone takes a turn.

Everything has an end. It doesn't matter if I like it or not. The real question for me now is, how shall I live the rest of my life?

FEBRUARY 7

Prayer often brings to the surface what I would rather not remember. I make this a prayer for mercy. For fathers, and sons.

– Kathleen Norris

Death often brings men face to face with prayer. And prayer is not a word that many of us use in our day-to-day vocabulary. Prayer can be a thought, action, or simply silence. When we lose someone we love, prayer might be an expression of rage, helplessness, turmoil, anguish, or hopelessness.

But perhaps our most desperate desire is to finish business with our loved one and so we may turn to prayer even if we have never prayed before.

We bring our shared history with our loved one into our grief over the death. There may be "loose ends" we no longer have a chance to tie together. And we may feel guilty for not being enough. Perhaps today we pray for mercy for ourselves and forgiveness for our inadequacies. No man is perfect.

I pray for mercy for myself. I will remember that prayer does not have to be words. Prayer can simply be a thought.

FEBRUARY 8

Throw out the lifeline across the dark wave.
There is a brother whom someone should save.

– Edward Smith Ufford

Death eventually knocks on every man's door. There are no exceptions. It's just a matter of time. And now that it is our turn, what shall we do? To whom shall we turn? If we are lucky, another man may step into our aching world to lend us a hand. If we are not so lucky, we may have to search him out and ask for his help.

At some point in our lives, we all need a lifeline. And we all take turns being on the receiving end or the throwing end.

When I walk to work each day, I often pass the home of community friends whose son died a few years ago. We are attuned to these deaths because our own son died several years ago and we know the pain of losing a child. Yesterday, I picked up the telephone and dialed their number. "John," I said, "this is Cliff. I'm just calling to tell you that Jane and I think about you and Joan almost every day. We know you lost your beloved Phillip and want you to know you are not walking this journey alone." Brief silence. "Cliff," John's voice hesitated ever so slightly, "we're going to have a memorial service on June 9th. You are more than welcome to come. Thanks ever so much for your call. It means a lot to us."

In spite of my own horrific loss, and when I am able, I will reach out to other suffering men. They are my brothers. We need each other.

FEBRUARY 9

...everything can be taken from a man but one thing: the last of the human freedoms – to choose one's attitude in any given set of circumstances...

– Victor Frankl

When we are grieving the death of someone we love, examining our attitude toward death is the last thing on our mind. Our hearts are broken. A part of us is missing. We walk slowly through the fog of our sorrow. We may be searching the rooms at home, desperately looking for the one who is now missing. It makes no sense, but a part of us believes we have to try.

Attitude? Who wants to think about attitude? Not us. Not now. Not even later. Most likely we are thinking, leave me alone, can't you see what has happened?

But choosing our attitude does not mean giving up our grief. We'll not be denied our grieving. Nor should we. Grief appears suddenly, an uninvited guest, moves into the now empty bedroom, and becomes a family member whether we want it to or not. In this way, grief chooses us. But we have the last say about what we choose to do with our grief. We can choose what we do to help alleviate our pain. We can choose to stay. We can choose to look grief in the eye.

Even in the face of death, I realize that I can choose my attitude. Maybe it will take a long time for me to recognize this power. But, somewhere down the road, I will be able to once again choose my attitude toward this hellacious loss.

...there is purpose and meaning in everything that happens, and that in our most anguished moments may reside the greatest gifts, not only for ourselves but for the world.

– Elizabeth Kuebler-Ross

We spend a lot of time looking for the answers. But when it comes to the death of a loved one, we are often stuck with more questions. This is disconcerting. It is tough to live in our culture and have to admit that we do not know the answer. And when it comes to death, it is harder still to admit that we are not even sure what the questions should be.

No wonder many of us suffer in silence.

How are we to discover our greatest gifts in the midst of our most anguished moments? Isn't it gift enough that we survive this death rather than have to look for some silver lining hidden within our sorrow? The thought that our loss will bring "gifts" may even be repugnant. We don't want a gift. We want our loved one back.

Purpose and meaning can wait.

Perhaps, after the passage of some time, we will be able to look back to this loss and see changes in us that have made our own life and the greater world where we live and love a better place. Perhaps this will happen. But not now. Not today. Not yet. Let's give it some time.

I have spent my lifetime searching for purpose and meaning. This death has me again pondering the purpose of my life and how I should spend my remaining time on earth. Is this opportunity one of the "gifts" Kuebler-Ross was referring to?

FEBRUARY 11

Arriving at her father's sunny hospital room,
Elizabeth pressed her face to his sunken cheeks.
In spite of the indignities of his helplessness and
the noise of the suction machine drawing off pus
from the abscesses in his abdomen, Mr. Kuebler
appeared at first to be in good spirits. But soon
his brow furrowed and he spoke urgently of the
matter uppermost in his mind. He wanted to die
at home.

– Derek Gill

Don't we all want to die at home?

The excerpt above, from Derek Gill's book about Elizabeth Kuebler-Ross, relates the story of her father near the end of his life. When Elizabeth arrives at her father's hospital bedside, his sole wish is to be taken home so he can die in his own bed. Against the advice of the attending physicians, she rents necessary equipment and sets up her parent's bedroom to accommodate his needs. These were pre-hospice days.

Gill adds, "He... rejected her offer of morphine and instead asked for a glass of wine." The agitation that marked his hospital days quickly disappeared and he died peacefully three days later.

I will always regret that my mother died alone in a nursing home bed in the early hours of morning. She too loved her own home, her comfortable bed, the tidy bedroom where all five of us boys were conceived. My older brother Mark who lived in the same community was the one called to her side that day. He later told the rest of us, "I felt her forehead. She was still warm when I got there." Then, his eyes filled with tears.

We all want to die at home. Even us men.

There are hundreds of ways to kneel and kiss the ground.

> – Rumi

Prayer can be a healing agent, but what exactly is prayer? And how shall we pray? Boyhood memories of prayer may no longer appeal to us or if we even believe in prayer at all. But maybe we haven't figured out manhood prayer either, what that might look like. Maybe crying at the death of a loved one is a form of prayer. Or maybe silence. Can anger be prayer? Or laughter? It doesn't matter what we choose.

There may be as many ways to pray as there are men on the face of this earth.

John Berry, a friend from Dublin and also a minister in the Moravian church once said to me, "Prayer is whatever you and your God decide it should be. It is between the two of you." And Thomas Merton, a Trappist monk wrote, "Dear God, I pray better by walking than by talking." For Merton, walking was prayer. For me, being in nature is prayer. The natural world helps me commune with God.

Whatever activity or thought that brings you closer to God is most likely prayer. You define it. You live it. Pray it if it helps.

Prayer is mysterious. It puts us in touch with the other side.

FEBRUARY 13

Only love can keep anyone alive.

– Oscar Wilde

She told me her story on a cold February afternoon. Her five year old son had been jumping on the couch or on the floor near the couch. She wasn't sure. She was busy and felt it safe for her son to be doing his "boy thing." Suddenly, he screamed in anguish, "My eye, my eye, my eye!" She jumped to her feet. He kept screaming. Just as she reached for him, he fell to the floor and lay comatose. She grabbed him and shook him, calling his name, thinking at first that he was teasing her.

But this was no game. She thought he was dead.

She and her husband rushed him to the hospital. By the time they arrived, the boy had regained consciousness and was already acting like his usual self. They were embarrassed, but still frightened by what had happened. They planned future tests. They are parents who love their only child.

We talked about life and death. We both agreed that nothing on earth was more important to we parents than our children. We agreed that the love we shared with family and friends gave us a reason to live. She said she didn't know if she could live without her son. I told her she could, but that it would be the hardest decision she would ever make. She knew that my own son had died a few years earlier. We looked deeply into each other's tear-filled eyes.

It is true. Only love can keep anyone alive. Even beyond death.

FEBRUARY 14

Love recognizes no barriers. It jumps hurdles, leaps fences, penetrates walls to arrive at its destination full of hope.

– Maya Angelou

The love we share for our beloved dead does not stop when they leave this world. We still love them even though we may feel lost and confused because of their physical absence. We will always love them although now we have to direct our love to their new home.

As Maya Angelou says so beautifully, our love recognizes no barriers. Even death cannot stop our love.

Many men believe that reality consists of only what can be seen. But we can take a lesson from the women we love. Women understand that the world also is made up of what cannot be seen. Love, for instance. It is just as real as a tree, but, unlike a tree, we cannot see it, we cannot touch it. We can sense it if we pay attention. And sensing love makes it real.

So on this St. Valentine's Day, let's remember that even though we are physically separated from our loved one, we may be closer than ever to him/her because our love continues to flow like a river and is never-ending. It is indeed full of hope.

Dear _____, *my love for you is real. And, never ending.*

...if you run from a problem, even if you get away for awhile, it keeps chasing you.

– Dan Millman

My friend's son died together with my son in a boating accident on Lake Michigan in 2010. Both young men were experienced outdoorsmen and had climbed several mountains together. But, on a beautiful April afternoon, hypothermia and drowning took their lives. So far, my dear friend has been unable to visit the cemetery where our sons are buried near each other.

I sense that staying away from his boy's gravesite has caused him great pain.

I remember being afraid of the dark when I was a little boy. Actually, I can still get the shivers when I'm walking alone after sunset. I recall stories of the "boogeyman," a mythological character that can still feel real after all these years. Running away at such moments remains appealing.

Because of the love of friends and the help from a mental health professional, I have been able to come face-to-face with my son's death. My boogeyman, my fear of dying, has largely disappeared. My wife and I have planted a flower garden and a bird's nest shrub at his gravesite and we visit often to water, weed, and sometimes weep. I believe my friend's pain could ease somewhat if he is able to visit and create a memorial honoring his beloved son.

Today, if I have been running away from my beloved one's death, I will choose to return with the assurance that I do not have to face this death alone. I will ask for help if I need it.

Where grief is fresh, any attempt to divert it only irritates.

– Samuel Johnson

Well-meaning guy friends may offer any kind of diversion to try to pull us away from our sorrow. But fresh grief will not be fooled. We know what they are trying to do. It is irritating.

Our pain is all we know. Our penetrating pain and our incomprehensible loss.

A few weeks after our son's death, my wife and I had a chance encounter with a member of our church. She and her two young children were out for an afternoon outing in our small northern Michigan community. We both were sure that she knew of our loss, yet her questions about our lives covered most summer topics except the one that mattered most to us.

How dare she not ask about our beloved son's death? Nothing else matters! Surely she knows.

In the weeks that followed, we had similar encounters with other community acquaintances. We soon decided to work our son's name into many conversations. This decision seemed to ease our friend's discomfort and their fear of reminding us of our loss. We tried our best to explain that our loss was always on our minds. We also expressed gratitude to them for asking about us. And, if they told us a kind story about our son's life, we sometimes cried.

We still do.

When grief is fresh, it is like a bleeding wound. We need recognition that we are injured, kind words, and offers to help us while we heal.

FEBRUARY 17

If I truly showed my feelings, the other guys
would eat me alive. It's too dog-eat-dog out there
to be honest about the things that really count to
you. You can't leave yourself wide open like that.

– Michael E. McGill

Even in the midst of our sorrow, we may still struggle with the belief that other men may make fun of us if we show our feelings. And yet, how can we not? Our loved one is dead. We are heartbroken. Is it a sign of strength for a man to live without showing emotions?

Men have often been told to live without showing emotion from their fathers and their father's fathers. Our popular culture tells us this. It is truly brave and necessary to open ourselves to sustaining friendship. Facing death, what else can men do? There's nothing left to lose, right?

Perhaps we all know other men in our workplaces or families that we have hung out with for years but whom we do not really know at all. Our relationships have been at a "surface" level, someplace comfortable, non-threatening. Safe. But how much do we value relationships like that? How important is that man to us? Would we like the relationship to be more meaningful?

Death reminds us that we do not have forever to forge friendships that help sustain us through life. We are time-limited beings. Beneath the mask we may wear in public, don't we long for a true male friend to help see us through dark valleys? Isn't this what most of us want when it is our turn to suffer? Someone who loves us enough to risk being open, to risk being real, about how they feel?

Especially now, in the midst of our despair?

I will risk showing my feelings today. Perhaps a less sorrowful and more meaningful world awaits me.

FEBRUARY 18

*Life breaks us all sometimes, but some grow
strong at broken places.*

– Ernest Hemingway

This idea may be the last thing on our mind today. And the thought that somehow we may become a stronger man because of this death blow may be appalling. What man would want any benefit from the death of a loved one?

But most broken hearts, like all broken bones, eventually heal. And health care providers will tell us that the place where the broken bone heals is stronger than at any other place along the original bone. Nature repairs the break.

Perhaps God repairs broken spirits. Who knows? Something certainly does.

An engineer who works for the small northern Michigan community where I live told me a story about his grief journey after his wife's death. Her death left him with three young daughters. In the weeks following his wife's death, many neighbors and friends dropped off food to help his young family out. As weeks turned into months and the months into a year, one particular woman came by repeatedly to drop off food and offer friendship. Her smile was infectious. Eventually, he invited her in for coffee.

Soon after, he asked her to marry him. She accepted. His broken heart was healed.

I will leave myself open to the possibility that my broken heart will somehow heal and that I may become a stronger man as a result of this death. At the moment this seems impossible, but tomorrow morning's light may bring a glimmer of hope.

There is sacredness in tears. They are not the mark of weakness, but of power. They speak more eloquently than ten thousand tongues. They are the messengers of overwhelming grief, of deep contrition, and of unspeakable love.

– Washington Irving

From the time we were little boys we were told that "big boys don't cry." That message, of course, was not true. However, some of us may still believe it. Yet at this moment, in the heart of our numbing sorrow, our tears may be speaking "unspeakable love" whether we want them to or not. Without saying a word, our tears tell our entire story of love for our lost one.

We need to hear this again: There is sacredness in tears. They are not the mark of weakness, but of power. Power!

Throughout our lives we have watched talented sporting figures cry tears of joy or tears of sorrow depending upon their performance in any number of athletic events. Olympic heroes often fall down on their knees and bury their heads in their hands, tears flowing freely. They are teaching us an important lesson of manhood. We can almost hear them speak: "Who cares what anyone thinks? This is my life. It belongs to me. This is my moment. I will not be denied."

I will cry if I want to.

I refuse to hold in my love. If my words come out in tears, so be it. I will hold my head high.

FEBRUARY 20

He who has a why to live can bear with almost any how.

– Nietzsche

In our hour of need, Nietzsche's words ring true. And clear. In spite of our agonizing loss, we know there are others who still love and need us. Our work here on earth is not over. We have many reasons to continue living, to find our way through the stunning maze called death.

And, we are not being "unfaithful" by carrying on without our lost one.

Our dead wish us well in our remaining responsibilities as grandfathers, fathers, husbands, step-fathers, sons, grand-sons, sons-in-law, friends, workplace role models, and on and on. We do have plenty of whys to live and we will bear with almost any how.

We'll need help of course. And we'll need strength to accept help. Perhaps some of the courage will come from our beloved dead who now reside on "the other side." Why not? Who can say for sure where spirits, both living and dead, dwell? And, who knows how much they influence the activities in our daily lives? We can hope, can't we?

I know the whys. I pray for strength to learn the hows.

Courage is fear that has said its prayers.

– Dorothy Bernard

It will take courage to face this death.

Courage to look upon the remains of the one we love. Courage to walk into the funeral home to make arrangements for the service. Courage to look into the eyes of other loved ones who mourn at our side. Courage to pick out the burial or internment site. Courage to stand at the grave site for the final good-bye. Courage to leave flowers behind. Courage to not run.

Courage to pray.

One of my teachers, Leo Buscaglia, once said, "We fear what we do not know." And we men certainly don't know much about death. So the idea of "fear saying its prayers" may bring us some comfort. If fear can say prayers, we can too. And praying implies the possibility of hope. We hope to honor the life of the one we have lost. We hope for the strength to live up to our responsibilities to those left behind. We hope we can hold our head high even though our heart is also breaking.

We hope that our fear will somehow make us courageous. It's worth a try.

If fear can pray, I can, too. I pray that my fear will turn into courage so I can do what needs to be done.

FEBRUARY 22

Everyman,
I will go with thee,
And be thy guide,
In thy most need,
To go by thy side.

– Source Unknown

What is this presence we often feel in our times of need? And where does it come from? Who knows? Women call it intuition. Men have the right to call it intuition as well. It is just as real for us as it is for them. And in this time of sorrow, we need all the help we can get.

So let us pay attention to these outstretched hands, to whomever they may belong.

Perhaps this guide is the spirit of our departed loved one helping us through our grief and this transition. Why not? This is a reasonable expectation. After my son died, I often felt his presence at the side of my bed in the middle of the night. I would awake and find him there, reassuring me that all was well, that he was okay, and that my wife and I needed to continue on enjoying the rest of our lives without him. His visits were both heartbreaking and comforting.

And if we do not feel the presence of our loved one, we should not be disheartened. It may be they are communicating by other means. There is so much we do not understand.

Putting our faith in the unseen takes courage, but can fill our aching hearts with hope. The mystery of death seems less foreboding knowing that something or someone is out there watching over us.

There is so much I do not understand. Today, though, I will pay attention to my intuitive sense that there may be help available to me beyond my human comprehension. What harm can it do to embrace this possibility? And, it may help.

No ray of sunshine is ever lost but the green that it awakens takes time to sprout, and it is not always given the sower to see the harvest. All work that is worth anything is done in faith.

– Albert Schweitzer

Perhaps one of our greatest sorrows is the death of a young person. So much potential is lost, so many dreams destroyed, a future evaporates in front of our eyes. The time to sprout has been stolen by death. Now, the young sower will never see the harvest.

What is a father to do in the face of such loss?

At meetings of The Compassionate Friends, a worldwide organization for grieving parents, broken-hearted fathers tell story after story of lives ripped out from under their feet, of grandchildren they will never have, of coming-of-age children hitting their stride just before their tragic deaths.

Yet, no ray of sunshine is ever lost.

At the same meetings, these same fathers also repeat stories of their dead children's great love and compassion, of their self-sacrifice in the service to others, of their laughter and dreams shared with those they loved, of their children's lust for life and belief in the goodness of humanity and faith. Of how much their children cared for others.

We will not always see the harvest, but we will still sow in faith.

FEBRUARY 24

So high, you can't get over it,
So low you can't get under it,
So wide you can't get around it,
You must go through that door.

– Frances J. Crosby

These lyrics bring our dilemma home. When we encounter fresh grief, we scan the horizon for some way to avoid the worst of it. We look over, under, and around our sorrow to see if there is a pathway through it without actually having our hearts break.

There isn't.

We must go through the door if we are to come out on the other side as a reasonably whole man. We know men who seem to have made forward strides following horrendous loss. They appear to be happy and well-adjusted. Yet, we also know men who still suffer after years of struggle. They have taken refuge in isolation, drugs, alcohol, sexual promiscuity, or perpetual anger. These guys have attempted the high, low, and wide roads without success. Sometimes they die broken hearted.

Choosing to go through the door of grief is our best chance at surviving the death of a loved one. This means holding our head high and doing what must be done. If we have family members and friends at our side, all the better. They are tangible reminders us that we do not face our loss alone. Sooner or later, we all have our turn.

I will not try to go over, under, or around my grief. I will walk through the darkness knowing that some sort of light is waiting on the other side. I have watched other men do this. I can do this too.

FEBRUARY 25

Comfort one another.

– 1 Thessalonians 4:18 (NIV)

Perhaps we felt awkward when family members, friends, neighbors, and even folks we did not know began to stop by with food, flowers, hugs, and tears of sorrow. Our discomfort may have continued when the mailbox began to overflow with cards and letters of condolences. Even strangers felt our grief and needed to express their concern. From where did this amazing outpouring of love originate?

And we thought no one really noticed. Or possibly, cared.

Here is the love at our own doorstep. Now it is our turn to cry. Hands reach out to us with compassion and concern. They are here to help wipe the tears from our eyes. And they know this will not happen overnight, though we wish it could. We are heartbroken and desperately seek comfort anywhere we can find it. We feel alone, like no one else has been on this journey before, like no one else could understand. We are wrong.

Countless others understand. And sooner than we would wish it to be, it will be our turn to do the reaching out, our turn to comfort, and our turn to show how much we care. Our turn to love unconditionally when their world falls apart. And we will reach out because they have reached out to us.

This much is clear. I am being comforted by others in my hour of need. One day it will be my turn to do the comforting. I will never forget where healing hands are needed the most: around those weeping in sorrow.

*If I am what I have – and if what I have is lost,
who then am I?*

– Erich Fromm

Perhaps the death of our loved one is a horrific lesson in learning to not hold on too tightly to those we love. We men like to be in charge. We like to be in control. Now we know that we do not control as much as we thought we did. We have no control over when souls arrive and when they depart. We only control our attitude about the arrivals and departures.

We don't own anyone.

And it may be helpful to rethink what we possess. Do we think we possess another person, even those we love? Have we tied our identity around those we love? Do we feel incomplete when we are alone? How many times have we heard others say, "I don't know what I would do without you?" Or, "I cannot imagine living without you." Yet, if we live long enough, we may be faced with living our lives without someone we love.

Erich Fromm's question bears repeating. If I am what I have – and if what I have is lost, who then am I?" I am not my possessions. I do not own anyone. I am me. I will survive.

I will not tie my identity to my possessions or even to those I love. Today my heart may be broken, but I will survive. If I need help, I will ask for it.

No one ever told me that grief felt so like fear.

– C. S. Lewis

Feeling afraid was a surprise. After my son's death, the entire world felt alien to me, like I was suddenly living on an unfamiliar planet. Nothing looked or felt the same. I was a stranger in a strange land. Lonely and lost. Abandoned. Without a compass to point me in the right direction.

If my son can die so quickly, my son who was so strong and healthy and wise in the ways of the world can die suddenly, without warning, surely I can die just as quickly. I had a foreboding sense of gloom, a fear that death would strike me or another family member "out of the blue." It was not rational, but my fear was real.

We do fear what we do not know. And those of us who are alive do not yet know our own death.

In counseling I learned about these phenomena. I learned that grief turns our world upside down, shakes us to the core, distorts our perceptions, and often blinds us to the world we knew before the death of our loved one. I learned that death ushers us into a new, less predictable world.

Thankfully, though, I also learned that in time my fear would slowly slip away.

I may be afraid for my own safety or the safety of my family at this moment, but I know this moment will pass away into a less fearful future. My fear is only my grief speaking to me. I can handle that.

*The friend who can be silent with us in a moment
of despair or confusion, who can stay with us in an
hour of grief and bereavement, who can tolerate
not knowing...not healing, not curing...that is a
friend who cares.*

– Henri Nouwen

During the visitation for my father's funeral, I learned Nouwen's lesson about caring.

A few minutes before the service was scheduled to begin, I saw Doug slip in through the front door entrance of the funeral home. He was dressed in a suit and tie, unusual attire for my friend and colleague of many years. He took a seat near the back, a respectable distance from family members.

He had driven one hundred and sixty miles to be there that evening.

After the service when everyone was mingling and sharing stories about my father, Doug quietly approached and said, "I'm sorry about your father, Cliff. I know he was a fine man because of the stories you have shared about him through the years. He reminds me of my own father." I thanked him with a firm handshake and misty eyes. Then he whispered, "Well, I'll be heading home. I've got to work in the morning."

Then, he slowly walked out for his long drive back home.

In times of grief and sorrow, the actions of others often speak louder than their words. Look around. Who cares enough to be here at this moment?

FEBRUARY 29

I'm for whatever gets you through the night.

– Frank Sinatra

Throwing ourselves into a carpentry project may help us sleep in the early days following our loss. Or we may find working on a car, truck, or motorcycle better suited to our skills. Some of us like to write, compose music, or sing. Or maybe we find comfort in walking in the woods or along the riverbank. Many men throw themselves into physical activities, anything that keeps them moving. Still others create works of art. All of us struggle to understand death and to find healthy ways to cope with grief.

Whatever gets us through the night.

We know we will not forget our loss. We could not if we tried. But putting our sorrow into something we can temporarily control eases the pain and gives us a brief break from our sorrow.

After my son's death, my wife resumed sewing and learned how to make quilts. She now uses her hands and broken heart to fashion quilts of breathtaking beauty and comfort. Then, she gives them to surprised and grateful family members and friends. I have joined a small group of like-minded men. We meet weekly for coffee, conversation, and connection. And we encourage each other to stay away from addictive substances.

Whatever gets us through the night.

What will get me through this night? Something constructive? Something that will lead me through my grief and not around, above, or below it?

❦ MARCH ❧

MARCH 1

*All my life I've been like a doubled up fist... Poundin',
smashin', drivin', – now I'm going to loosen these
doubled up hands and touch things easy with them.*

– Tennessee Williams

That's what the death of a loved one does to us men. It gives us
a whole new outlook on life. We become kinder, gentler guys,
filled with a level of compassion we have never lived before.
Now when we touch the things of this world, we touch them
easily and respectfully. We touch them like we are holding a
child's hand.

Reverently. And with a sense of awe and wonder.

This doesn't mean we no longer experience anger. We do. But
our new anger is more often directed at the helplessness we
feel because of the loss of our beloved one. Our old anger was
directed at the injustices of life. There's a difference. Anger at
the world has kept our fists doubled up full-time. Anger at the
loss of our loved one is driven by a broken and lonely heart.
This grief comes and goes like waves washing up at the shore.

*I am grateful for open hands. Now I can hold my lost love
closer to my broken heart.*

Brief is life but love is long.

– Alfred, Lord Tennyson

When does love begin and end? Who knows? The beginnings of love are often hard to define. But, most of us men will agree that love has no end, that it is eternal. That's long enough for us, huh?

Think of loved ones who died years ago. Our love for them endures to this very moment. And this fresh grief, this latest unimaginable loss, well, our love for him or her will endure throughout the rest of our days. And who knows how long afterwards?

Perhaps our sorrow can become a bit lighter when we consider the mystery of why love remains when our loved one's body is forever stilled by death. I can still hear my beloved aunt's voice speaking encouragement and admiration across the barrier of death years after her earthly departure. My father's laughter echoes in these ears long after his last spoken words.

That's what love does. It makes those we love a permanent part of our lives. What a gift to treasure, what a blessing to embrace!

Dear _____, I will love you always. Thank you for loving me throughout eternity.

MARCH 3

*Without you in my arms, I feel emptiness in my soul.
I find myself searching the crowds for your face — I
know it's an impossibility, but I cannot help myself.*

— Nicholas Sparks

Who says men aren't sentimental?

We miss the physical connection to the one we have lost: the passing touch, the brush of the shoulders, the pat on the back, the mussing of the hair. If we have lost our child, we may also be missing the impromptu wrestling match, the high fives, or the jostling that we practiced in place of a hug. Or perhaps we are lamenting the loss of the hugs themselves. The touch of each other's hands.

And, some of us miss shared backrubs.

Before my son's death, he liked to gently tap my leg during our church service, his code for requesting a light back scratch. As he grew older, whenever he returned home for a visit, we started a tradition of giving each other a thorough back rub. Our aching muscles were grateful for the strong hands that massaged them back to joy.

Surely, in the midst of this extraordinary sorrow, there is someone willing to share safe physical contact with you. Who do you have in mind? When will you reach out to that person? Today? Ask for nothing complicated. Just a simple touch.

Dear _____, I miss holding you, touching you, seeing your face, your beautiful eyes. There is no one to replace you. Ever. But today I will call a friend who is willing to touch me, even if it's a handshake, or holding hands. This will help ease some of my pain.

MARCH 4

He is the most beautiful creature I have ever seen and it's not about his face, but the life force I can see in him. It's the smile and the pure promise of everything he has to offer. Like he's saying, 'Here I am world, are you ready for so much passion and beauty and goodness and love and every other word, that should be in the dictionary under the word life? Except this boy is dead, and the unnaturalness of it makes me want to pull my hair out...it makes me want to yell at the God that I wish I didn't believe in. For hogging him all to himself. I want to say, 'You greedy God. Give him back. I need him here.'

– Melinda Marchetta

We can substitute she for he if you have lost a beloved woman in your life. How can we describe our sorrow more completely?

Talk about taking the words right out of our mouths.

But death cannot hold this world's love in its grip. Nor can death bury love with the body. Love always remains. And with luck and a lot of hard work, our rage against God may eventually lighten. Perhaps it never completely disappears. We'll see. But the love, well, that's safely locked away in our hearts. Thankfully, we have the key. And that will have to do for now.

My Dear Beautiful One, where are you now?

MARCH 5

*...the closer you get to what you fear
The safer you are.*

– Connie Wanek

Is it also true that the closer we get to what we fear, the safer we feel? Strange, isn't it? Death used to be the dark dragon, yet now we may have a sense of peace about it. We have acknowledged, 'Well, if my loved one can die, so can we. So will we. That's not news. Just a reminder. What have we been afraid of?'

Wanek's poem speaks of a spent white-tailed buck that approaches her compost pile for food. Usually white-tails avoid places of human habitation out of fear for their safety, like men avoid discussions of death for the same reason. Perhaps, we think, if we do not talk about death, we'll avoid it. What are the chances of that happening?

Since my son died, I have lost my fear of death. My reasoning is simple. I have lost a precious reason for living. I still love life, but if I should die soon, I believe I will be reunited with him somewhere, somehow. Illogical? Well, we'll see.

Death is a hard fact. I'm okay with that. I won't run away.

MARCH 6

What do you do when you lose a loved one too quickly? When you have no time to prepare before, suddenly, that soul is gone?

– Mitch Albom

The sudden death of a loved one stuns us. What we considered impossible has come to pass. All senses fight against the truth of what has happened.

And we men are powerless.

Sudden death is cruel. There is no chance to say goodbye, no opportunity for spoken gratitude or forgiveness, no time for a last embrace, a tearful farewell. No time to hold hands or gaze into each other's eyes. No possibility to do what we said we would do tomorrow.

Tomorrow just ended today.

At approximately 2:00pm on a glorious Spring afternoon, my son Nathaniel was alive and laughing, eager to drink in another early spring afternoon outdoors with his friend Nick Lightfoot. About an hour and a half later, both young men were dead, victims of a boating accident on Little Traverse Bay in Lake Michigan. From life to death quickly, without warning. No words to describe the heartbreak. None.

What do I do when I have no time to prepare before, suddenly, that soul is gone? Hope for strength, lean on friends, and implore whatever powers may be in the universe to help me live when everything within me wants to die.

It sucks that we miss people like that. You think you've accepted that someone is out of your life, that you've grieved and it's over, and then bam. One little thing, and you feel like you've lost that person all over again.

– Rachel Hawkins

That one little thing might be a stranger's gait that you would swear is the same, the tilt of the head, the way the handkerchief hangs from the pocket, a voice so identical you have to look twice, the lyrics of the song you'll never forget, the answering machine message you dared listen to, the tee shirt you've been wearing since after the death. The handwritten note you come across. The books on the shelf.

The tattered and beloved hiking boots you stumble upon in the closet.

One little thing can bring us to our knees. At any time. And we men thought we had this grief stuff under control? Once, when speaking to a group of students about the death of my son, I felt something rising in the pit of my stomach. Not now, please. But it was already too late. As I stood staring at them in disbelief, I began to sob. Then the tears came. I sat and cried and cried. Through my tears, I saw that many of them were crying, too.

When the one little thing comes along, and it will, I will let myself grieve again. Perhaps, at some distant place in time, I will be able to speak of my loss without crying. Until then, I will not be ashamed of my tears.

MARCH 8

Remember me as loving you.

– John Powell

Is there a more important message for us from our departed loved one than John Powell's reminder above? Does anything else on the face of this earth matter more to us men than being loved? Isn't love what life is all about? And are there better words to weave into a parting message?

Remember me as loving you.

A beloved aunt writes this note to her treasured nephew: "When our good and gracious God created you, He put into your generous heart a great capacity to love and serve...I can imagine that everyone you meet becomes your friend because you are so lovable." Isn't this a message we would all like to receive? And isn't this the love note we would like to leave behind when it is our turn to die?

We can. It is not too late. Let's use our own words and expand the world's supply of love. It will only take a few moments, and a treasured someone may find our note years from now and bask once again in the glow of the love we express.

I will always remember you as loving me. Thank you for your love!

MARCH 9

As my fathers planted for me, so do I plant for my children.
　　　　　　　　　　　　　　　　　– The Talmud

Perhaps the last thing we may want to consider is that something good can grow out of the death of our loved one. Especially when our grief is fresh and raw, we may even rage against this notion. And yet, there is something about early spring mornings that gives us hope for the days to come. Why not plant something to nurture that hope?

It is no act of betrayal to our beloved dead when we start to think of the future again. After all, how long would they want us to live in the past? And the thought of planting something to honor a loved one's life is an ancient notion. Let's look around for a moment. Who planted the trees and flowers we see?

When my mother-in-law died, my wife Jane and I planted a white oak tree in memory of her in the front yard of our country home. Today that tree stands tall, proud, and beautiful, a perfect tribute and symbol of her life. And the process of planting her tree helped ease the pain of our loss.

I will consider the possibility of planting something in memory of my loved one. If not soon, then perhaps in the days to come. Until I do, I will think about what I would like to plant. Flowers, a shrub, a tree? If I need any advice, I will ask for help.

MARCH 10

Listen and follow the guidance given to your heart. Expect guidance to come in many forms; in prayer, in dreams, in times of quiet solitude and in the words and deeds of wise elders and friends.

– Lane Bopp, et al.

When a loved one dies, the last thing we may be thinking about is listening for guidance from those who have been down this grieving road before us. We may feel that no one could possibly understand our pain. Yet, if we look around, wise elders and friends who have suffered before us may already be walking at our side.

When my son died, friends from our faith community moved into our home and took over the day-to-day chores. They answered the telephone, washed dishes, greeted those who were bringing food and sympathy, arranged to have our lawn mowed, and protected us from any responsibility other than our attempts to absorb the reality of our loss. They even sent us to bed when we could no longer function.

Expect guidance to come in many forms: in prayer, in dreams, in times of quiet solitude, and in the words and deeds of wise elders and friends. Indeed!

Do not seek death. Death will find you.

– Dag Hammarskjöld

For men, the pain of losing a loved one is indescribable. Poets and sages through the years have tried their best to explain it. Often, though, they admit their words fail in the attempt. But, the pain. The pain. What do we do with the pain?

Some of us fear dying from the pain.

When we decide to love someone, we are making a decision to become vulnerable to that person, to share whatever comes our way together. And in the early stages of love, we are not thinking about the possibility of loss. Instead, we are concentrating on what we are gaining. This is only human. Natural. Death seems a lifetime away. Sometimes it is, sometimes it isn't.

When my mother died alone in her bed in a nursing home, I was thousands of miles away at a conference. She had suffered for thirteen years and no one knew when death would finally arrive. I'll never forget the pain of not being able to be with her in her final hour.

I will not die. There are people who can help: a family member, a colleague at work, a sports buddy, someone at our place of worship, a counselor, anyone I deem trustworthy. Other men have survived the death of a loved one. I can, too.

MARCH 12

...so many of us struggle against acknowledging the possibility of losing a loved one. Loss is too threatening to the ways and the myths of the world around us. It calls into question what we believe to be the security of our lives, and we shrink from this awareness.

– Paul F. Wilczak

With so much pressure in our culture for men to be silent, strong, and tear-free, it is no wonder that we protect ourselves from thinking much about death. We don't want to look weak or, worse yet, out of control. We don't want anyone to see us cry. We learned early on that tears are for sissies. Right?

Wrong. And myths die hard.

With our magical thinking in place, we refrain from discussions about death in day-to-day conversations. And when someone dies, expected or not, we withdraw inside ourselves for protection against the pain of loss. If we keep our feelings about loss inside, how will this affect those we love? They want to know how we feel, if we are caring for ourselves, if we still have hope. If we risk sharing feelings, others will share in kind. We need to stay connected to those we love, including ourselves. Compassion breeds compassion.

A young friend talks about her losses: "My parents both died before I was a teenager. Now, my grandmother who became my surrogate mother has also died. I feel devastated. Neither of my uncles will talk about her or their feelings about her death. I am so lonely. I have no one to talk to."

Today I will choose one person with whom I can share my feelings about my loss. I will no longer accept the myth that grown men must always be strong and brave, even in the face of death.

MARCH 13

Whereas previously our moods seemed simply sad with occasional patches of light, now we may find an unsettling variety in our feelings, as happy times seem engrossing and satisfying, and then we are plunged into sadness again. Perhaps we can learn to accept these mood swings, recognizing the reality of each, knowing light gives way to darkness and darkness to light.

– Martha Whitmore Hickman

Some days do seem lighter than others. Maybe without noticing we have even been gifted with a few good days strung together. An unexpected laugh may surprise us after so much heavy sorrow. Then, out of nowhere, a new day dawns dark and dreaded. The reality of the death brings us crashing back to our knees.

Where did this come from, we wonder? How long this time?

In the first few days after my son's death, I could see nothing ahead but endless years of unbearable sorrow. Now, almost five years later, and with the love of family and friends, I have learned that endless sorrow can change into bearable sorrow, that I can choose to laugh without feeling guilty that I am still alive and my child is dead. I have learned that sunlight still follows moonlight.

I often hear my son's voice encouraging me back to the land of the living: "I'm okay here, Dad. You and mom have a lot of living to do. Go for it, please? I'll be at your side. I'll always love you."

I am learning that joy and sorrow often arrive unbidden. Both are real. Both are temporary. Love is eternal.

She took the things the owl had brought – threads of sunlight fine as silk and cobwebs gray as skulls –and wove them all together into a cloth. And when the owl pulled his story round him, it was so full of woe and gladness, so beautiful and strong, that when he stretched out his new-made wings, people thought he was an angel hovering in a breathless sky.

– Valiska Gregory

When we suffer the death of a loved one, we need to tell our story again and again and again. Perhaps for the rest of our days. And, why not? Is there anything more important on the face of this earth than those we love?

When we love and lose, a weather report or football scores just don't cut it anymore.

When we greet mourning men at a funeral home, what first flows freely from our mouths? Our story of this loss. The details of the dying, what medical efforts were made to intervene or at least to make our loved one's departure comfortable, who we called to come for the final moments, who we wished had been able to make it "in time." We need to tell the story of our ongoing sorrow. Every word. The... cobwebs gray as skulls... our woe and gladness... our hovering in a breathless sky. Our brokenness.

I need to tell my story as often as possible if I ever hope to heal. I will look for receptive hearts and willing listeners on this journey through sorrow. Here's my secret: man to man, I need to share.

*The world is a book and those who do not travel
read only one page.*

– St. Augustine

Death is our final journey. This loss of our beloved one is a vivid reminder that we are here on a time-limited basis. Our existence is not infinite.

Death makes us think about the number of pages of our life we have "read."

I have often described our son's brief life by saying that he lived the lives of three men in his twenty-seven years. He worked enough to travel to many foreign destinations, often with one or two good friends. When my son and his two particular friends traveled together, they referred to themselves as "los tres amigos," the three friends. On a trip to Equador, they landed near the small town of Machachi, about twenty kilometers south of Quito. There they rented an apartment, set up housekeeping, found jobs teaching conversational English in a local school, and spent their free time riding motorcycles and climbing mountains. Does life get any better?

Is there a trip we would like to take while we still have the time? What's holding us back?

MARCH 16

I've begun to realize that you can listen to silence and learn from it. It has a quality and dimension all its own.

– Chaim Potok

Our inclination following the death of a loved one is to talk. A lot. But perhaps the path to healing after loss is to become a better listener. For men, this may be a formidable challenge.

Toby Jones, founder of the Living Vision community in Petoskey, Michigan, shared this story about the importance of listening:

> "Just before he died, long-time ABC News Anchor, Peter Jennings, said that his most memorable interview was with Mother Theresa. And in that interview, Jennings asked her one question that I'll never forget. He said, 'When you pray, Mother Theresa, what do you say to God?' She crumpled up her face in a confused expression and said, 'Say?... I don't say anything. I just listen... I just listen.'"

None of us can grasp the reality of eternal silence. But we can all practice temporary silence from time to time. Silence gives us a chance for introspection, for reflection on the life we are living. The last thing we may want to hear at this moment is that someone's death gives us an opportunity to make changes in our own life. But it is true.

I will practice becoming a better listener. Who can I start with today?

We exist only to discover beauty; all else is a form of waiting.
              – Kahlil Gibran

Maybe death is the only true opportunity that will awaken us to the beauty all around in this world. This morning's sunrise. The new day's light falling across the still-frozen water's surface. The early spring sunrays etching designs into south-facing snow banks. Rivulets of water laughing their way downhill. A robin's syncopated call. Wind blowing through white pine needles. The patter of raindrops. The beauty of silence.

The grace, glory, and glow of a loved one's smile.

What are we waiting for? From 2000 to 2002, my son was a student photographer for the University of Minnesota's newspaper, The Minnesota Daily. For two years he photographed sporting events, student organization activities, individuals who were profiled in special interest stories, and, always, nature. His eyes captured close-ups of glances and gardens, frowns and ferns, laughter and light, personalities and peonies. He saw beauty everywhere he looked and took its picture. So can we.

What are you waiting for? Look around right now. What beauty do you see at this moment? Look at an object, nearby scenery, a picture, a painting, or a person. Imagine that your eyes are new and that you can see for the very first time in your life.

MARCH 18

... Let us try before we die
To make some sense of life...
We'll build our house, and chop
  our wood,
And make our garden grow.

– Voltaire

Yes, let us try before we die to make some sense of life. When a loved one dies, life seems to make no sense at all. And, we like to look for the common sense in the world around us. That's what our culture teaches us to do. So, we wonder, why me? Why now? What did I do to deserve this?

There are no answers. Only endless questions.

We're neither pure nor wise nor good. But we do the best we can. We'll build our house, and chop our wood. Some of us still live this way. By hand. And make our garden grow. Or at least plant our seed, fertilize if necessary, pray for rain, and hope our garden grows.

When someone we love dies, we often reflect on foolish choices we made that hurt the one who is now gone. Regret can eat into our soul and cause anguish beyond description. Sleepless nights become common. But, we can make a healthier choice. We can forgive ourselves as we would offer forgiveness to our best friend. Why not? We all make fools of ourselves. After all, we're human. And after forgiveness, we act, we do something physical like chopping wood, running, walking, hiking, bicycling, kayaking, lifting weights, or playing team sports. Anything that gets us moving. That's when healing can begin.

I did the best I knew. Forgive me if I hurt you. I forgive me too.

MARCH 19

If typical male roles tend to interfere with grieving, why be concerned? Why does it matter? It matters because the wound is real.

– William C. Schatz

Just because men tend not to talk much, does not mean that we don't have a lot to say. We do. Especially when it comes to the death of someone we love.

A death wound cuts deep. Our pain is real.

But we pick our moments to open up, choose carefully whom we will trust. Our egos are fragile, tender, in spite of our outward appearance. We've been taught that "big boys don't cry," but we learned this was not true. Little boys and big boys cry, young men and old. And if our tears are invisible, a sensitive observer will see that we are crying on the inside while waiting for a handshake, a gentle touch, a warm smile. Any sign of love, compassion, understanding, patience. We are waiting for someone with courage enough to approach us.

When my uncle died, I watched his son, my cousin, break down and cry openly at his funeral service. When my parents died, I wept openly, unable to hold back the flood of tears. But when my son died, I was able to speak with composure at his funeral though my heart was breaking. Which male role was "typical?"

Regardless of my outward appearance, my wound caused by this death is real. I will pay attention to anyone who is willing to walk through my veil of tears with me. I need their love, support, and courage.

MARCH 20

Peter's death changed the trajectory of my life... I could never just sit around now that I understand how precious life is... our sadness was so great that just living was difficult... we could barely wake up every day and put one foot in front of another.

– Steve Alderman

The realization of how temporary our lives are may be the greatest gift from the death of a loved one. The awareness may be more acute if this loss is one of the first we have suffered. Until now, perhaps, we may have naively acted like death only happens to others.

But now it has happened to us as well. Now we know. Death is real, and so is our pain.

In the quote above, Steve Alderman is speaking of his son Peter's death in the twin tower tragedy in New York City on September 11, 2001. After Peter's death, Dr. Alderman and his wife Liz decided to devote the rest of their lives helping victims of trauma by establishing the Peter C. Alderman Foundation, a non-profit with a special focus on mental health services.

And now our own story is here in this mourning place. Who is the one you love and has died? How did this death occur? Was it sudden or did you have time to prepare for it? How has it changed the trajectory of your life? How have your values changed? How do you want to live the rest of your precious days?

I will not just sit around now that I know how precious my days are. I will do something to make the world a better place.

I come into the peace of wild things who do not tax their lives with forethought of grief... For a time I rest in the grace of the world, and am free.

– Wendell Berry

Many of us have found some peace in being loved by our pets while in the fog of grief. And the quiet peace of animals in the woods is also healing, as is the small adventures we have with birds who visit our feeders regularly. Some of us are in tune with the rhythms of the animals that move across our land or favorite places. One day in a deer blind, seeing no deer, I bonded with a chipmunk who kept checking on me – I fed him some of my trail mix.

No matter the reason, unconditional love is wonderful.

We have all read stories of faithful dogs awaiting the return of their now-deceased masters. They sit patiently looking out their favorite window toward the entrance to the yard that their master always used. Or they watch for the car or truck that always meant a reunion after a long day of being home alone. Or they curl up around the beloved pair of slippers, the shirt still lying on the bedroom floor.

And cats stretch out on their favorite couch or chair waiting for the familiar neck rub or the belly scratch, hoping for the familiar voice. Or they pace back and forth, crying mournfully. They refuse at first to be comforted. After a while, they may settle down into a restless slumber. Still they gaze silently at the closed door.

I am grateful for the unconditional love I get when I return home at the end of a sad day. For a time I can rest in the grace of the world.

The only cure for grief is action.

– George Henry Lewes

After my son's death, my wife and I started a new tradition for his "death day." We invited family and friends to join us on a bike ride to honor his memory and the memory of his beloved friend Nick who died with him that horrible spring day. Nathaniel loved to recycle, repair, and ride bicycles. What better way to honor his memory?

The only cure for grief is action.

At first, it is difficult to simply move at all. Walking takes a lot of effort. Our arms and legs may feel like they belong to someone else. Anyone else, please. Soon we tend to divide our lives into *before* and *after*. Before seems like a long time ago. After feels strange and new, like landing on another planet. Nothing looks the same. Nothing is the same. We cannot go back to before. Here we are now in after. This will take some getting used to. But we have to move into action.

One of my favorite activities before was _____
_____. Now, afterwards, an activity I
enjoy is _____. I am also think-
ing about trying to_____
_____. It might be fun. The only cure
for my grief is action.

MARCH 23

*Now is the season to know that everything you do
is sacred.*
– Hafiz of Persia

What is there about spring that makes anguished men's hearts rejoice against our will? From where does this vestige of hope come in the midst of our suffering, our great loss? Why does our heart thump, our blood thrum, when the sun's angle begins, once again, to warm our face? When the buds thicken?

Faithful spring! Regardless of our sorrow, it comes.

There is no holding back hope. On the windowsill in our kitchen sits a large vase filled with Red Twig Dogwood branches. My wife Jane brought them into the house in late February on a bitter cold afternoon. The tiny buds were barely visible. The dark crimson branches alone are enough beauty. But the buds looked like they had no intention of opening anytime soon. "I'm forcing the buds," Jane announced. "With any luck, the leaves will start to open. They will be beautiful." I glanced at her, then the twigs, and finally the blowing snow, the single digit reading on the thermometer.

Now, almost a month later, tiny flags of green and miniature flower blossoms herald new life.

Everything we do is sacred. Today is the season.

MARCH 24

...perhaps this very holding back
is the one suffering
you could have avoided.

– Franz Kafka

Men abhor death. We shrink back from the ultimate entry into the other realm, the one we will never understand. We fear what we do not know, so we keep our distance. Let the women do the mourning. We can handle our emotions. They cannot, we think. Yet, in spite of openly suffering, women live longer than men. Do they know something we don't?

Is this holding back the one suffering we could have avoided?

Earlier in my life a favorite guy phrase was "cork it, brother." In other words, keep quiet. Shut up. Stuff it. We don't want to hear it. Say it anyway you like. The message was clear. Hold your thoughts inside. Don't share them. Someone, maybe everyone, will laugh at you or judge you for speaking up and sharing your feelings. Especially your male friends. Their friendships can be ruthless.

But, listen, have any of them been down this death road you are traveling? Those who have understand. Those who haven't will not understand. It's that simple. So, yes, we have permission to hold back from the suffering of the world, our own included, but at what cost? An early death?

I will not hold back from the suffering of the world. Holding back is more painful than the suffering I have been trying to avoid. I hope for the strength I need to do this. I will ask for help along my journey.

To be able to invite pain to join in my experience and not have to control my life to avoid pain is such a freedom!
— Christina Baldwin

In the first moments or days after our loss, we men search for someone, anyone, who might have any understanding of our feelings. The tragic has happened. Whether on the battlefield, the highway, an accident, or suicide, those of us left behind grasp for fragments of understanding. How has this moment arrived? How did we end up in this trance?

Trying to avoid pain takes a lot of work.

Our eyes fly in many directions, searching for clues that we might be next. After all, if death has swallowed up our loved one, then it can happen to us, too. Fear and guilt set in. Why him and not me? Why am I still alive? What could I have done to protect him? Endless questions. Unanswerable questions.

But wait. There are hands reaching for us. Loving hands. Compassionate hands. Understanding hands. Knowing hands. Helping hands. Truthful hands. Forgiving hands. Healing hands. How is this possible? It is hard to believe at first, but others have been down this road before us. They are waiting with open hearts to share our sorrow.

I have been swallowed up by death, yet still I live. It is not my time to leave. I have work to do here. There are others who have been swallowed up by death, too. They need me. I need them. As soon as I am able, I will extend my healing hands.

MARCH 26

*...when we no longer know which way to go,
we have begun our real journey.*

– Wendell Berry

The death of a loved one throws our lives into chaos. If we have lost a companion, a spouse, or, worse still, a child, we are like a sailboat with sails unfurled and lying limp in the sun. Our journey has ended with no land in sight. We thought we had forever. We were wrong. No one has forever.

It may be when we no longer know which way to go, we can begin our real journey.

We may hear stories from other bereaved men about how the death of a beloved family member caused them to re-evaluate the direction of their lives. At first feeling lost and adrift, they discovered their real work was to make the world a better place. Material things lost their importance. Kindness, compassion, and love became a passion. Some men even declare they have awakened as if from a dream. They have a new urgency to live life to its fullest. Isn't it amazing what death can do to us? Here we are now, how can we go on with purpose?

I am starting to sense a new direction in my life. I hope for a clear vision of how I want to spend the rest of my days. I want to begin my real journey.

The highest tribute to the dead is not grief, but gratitude.

– Thornton Wilder

An honest "please" and "thank you" have served us men well throughout our lives. Now is the time for a difficult "thank you" to our beloved one. Although we are overwhelmed with grief at our loss, through our tears we can see clearly how much gratitude we owe to this precious one we have loved and lost.

Here is a partial list of the things I am grateful to my dead son for.

Thank you for the wisdom you shared with me in the years we were together. Thank you for showing me better ways to do the most mundane tasks. Thank you for teaching me the importance of living an earth-friendly existence. Thank you for your exuberance. Thank you for your spells of laughter that often brought tears to my eyes. Thank you for laughing with me, not at me. Thank you for bringing your friends into our home; now they are my friends, too. Thank you for teaching me the value of honesty, for teasing me about my puns, and for your culinary skills. Thank you for showing me how to be courageous. Thank you for helping me become a better father. Thank you for your patience. Thank you for believing in me. Thank you for your tolerance. Most of all, thank you for loving me!

Thanks, finally, for our last kiss, our final embrace. Thanks for no unfinished business between us. Wasn't our life together wonderful?

Now it is my turn. My beloved _____! I thank you from the bottom of my heart for:

Routine is really important. However late you went to bed the night before, or however much you had to drink, get up at the same time each day and get on with it.

– Mark Anthony Turnage

When someone we love dies, it is important for us to stick as much as possible to daily routines. This may be the last thing we want to do. After all, we have lost a loved one. We cannot think clearly. Our whole world has been turned upside down. We are beside ourselves with grief. We may wonder why we should bother with anything, including daily tasks.

Because we can.

Death reminds us how little control we have over most of life's events. Until now, we may have blissfully been under the illusion that we were in charge of day-to-day happenings. Perhaps this is true in our workplace, but not in matters of death. As a grieving friend once said, "I'm okay when I'm on the job, but I fall apart when I get home. I don't know what to do."

Routines help us because we are in charge while doing them. Here's a simple example. Many of us start our morning shave at the same place on our face. We know what to do. We know where to go. We know the process. In this sea of grief, a morning shave, well performed, is a helpful way to start a sad day. Can you think of a routine in your own life that will help you feel better?

In the confusion of these grief-filled days, my daily routine is an important part of my healing journey. I will stick to it as much as I can.

Love... bears all things, believes all things, hopes all things, endures all things. Love never ends.

– 1 Corinthians 13:7-8 (NIV)

Perhaps at the beginning of our relationships with others, we may have been confused about the responsibility and power of love. Many of us thought physical attraction was love. Certainly being physically attracted to someone often sets the stage for true love. But not always. And now in our grief, we understand how losing someone we love breaks our hearts. We have lost a part of ourselves.

When we choose to love, we become fully invested in that person's life. The whole nine yards. No wonder we mourn so deeply. We sometimes hear the phrase, "I knew her as well as the back of my hand." Or perhaps you have heard parents who have lost a child say, "Losing my daughter was like losing my leg or arm. I'll never be the same without her." Losing someone we love is losing a best friend.

To love takes great courage. Love... bears all things, believes all things, endures all things, even death.

Who wants to risk losing it all? Yet this is what we do when we choose to love. To love is to gamble. After a sleepless night years ago, we had a heart-to-heart talk with our son who had stayed out later than usual. At a crucial moment I said, "You and your sister are more important to mom and me than anything else on the face of this earth." I meant every word. He understood.

Love hopes all things. I hope to see you again. Love never ends.

The darker the night,
the brighter the stars,
the deeper the grief,
the closer to God.

– Fyodor Dostoevsky

Losing a loved one is a tough way to dance closer to God. We have observed or participated in a variety of experiences within religious traditions. Some of those experiences have helped us grow spiritually, others have hindered our spiritual lives; some of us attend church, temple, or synagogue services, some do not; some of us believe in God, some of us do not; some of us hope there is a God, some of us could care less.

But when it comes to the death of a loved one, most of us likely think, at least for a while, about the God we envision.

By the close of the winter months north of the forty-fifth parallel, we have taken for granted clear dark skies sprayed into the far reaches of the universe. Seemingly unlimited numbers of stars stretch out across our field of vision regardless of where in the sky we gaze. Our spiritual beliefs notwithstanding, it seems impossible not to think about the origin and reason for this universe. We stand in awe at the magnificence before us. The beauty dwarfs our imaginations. It humbles us. We reflect on where we fit in and wonder why it often takes death to help us appreciate this existence.

Here I am, gazing skyward. Heartbroken. If Dostoevsky's words are true, I have never been closer to God than I am at this moment.

MARCH 31

*Many times a day I realize how much my own outer
and inner life is built upon the labors of my fellow
men, both living and dead and how earnestly I must
exert myself in order to give in return as much as I
have received.*
> – Albert Einstein

Each of us has generations of other men who have lived before. We live because they lived. If Albert Einstein could recognize that his "outer and inner" achievements were not entirely of his own making, perhaps we can do the same. Maybe giving back to the world as much as we have received is a good place to start on our road to healing after this loss.

Why not?

Death gets our attention like no other earthly experience. Death taps us on the shoulder and shouts into our ear ...this happens. What do you want to do with the rest of your life?

When my brother's ashes were being buried by the tired cemetery sexton, he stamped down hard on the unforgiving earth to make the urn fit into the too shallow hole he had dug. I could not help thinking, so this is what it all comes down to? Ever since that day I have thought about my own contributions to this world and what else I wanted to accomplish before I die. I believe this is worthwhile reflection.

My great sorrow makes me realize that I hope to give as much as I have received. I will continue working toward that goal.

❧ APRIL ❧

APRIL 1

*[My mother] died almost fifty years ago but I have
to admit she has never really left me. Even now
I can still remember her vividly. I remember her
voice; the things she told me. I can see every line and
characteristic of her face. And she has remained the
most important influence on my life. All that I am and
all that I have become is in some way a tribute to her.*

— Gary Player

How many stories will we tell about our beloved dead during the rest of our lifetime? Gary Player's description of his mother and her influence on his life are stirring as well as reassuring. If he remembers, so can I. So will I.

Love holds on forever.

I can still see my paternal grandmother dressed in her gingham floral print dress, the fabric thin at the shoulders, with a well-worn apron tied tightly behind her back. She is short, with the body of a woman who has given birth to seven children. Her eyes are sparkling with both mischief and strength. Her face is etched with the wisdom of her years, the "crow's feet" prominent from years of laughter. She is holding a wooden mixing spoon in her right hand, and judging from the aroma that permeates the room, has just finished taking a batch of cookies out of her oven. Her kitchen is heaven to this hungry boy.

"Ready for a treat?" she grins.

I have been afraid that I will forget the face(s) of my beloved dead. Now I know. I will not forget. Ever.

Like garlands woven from a heap of flowers,
fashion your life
as a garland of beautiful deeds.

– Buddha

My father was a barber in a small community in Kawkawlin, Michigan. "Cliff's Barbershop" drew in area farmers and businessmen alike. He had the traditional candy cane twirling pole and his seating area provided room enough for eight waiting customers. Endless stories were told and retold from those chair-thrones.

For more than sixty years, Dad wove a garland of beautiful deeds within those humble walls.

But Dad's heart did not close up for the day when he hung his "closed" sign on the door. On a regular basis, he packed up his cutting shears and headed to the local hospital to cut hair for patients too sick to get out for a trim. He refused to take any payment. "This is what we should do," he would say, "take care of those who cannot take care of themselves. That's what your grandmother did. Now it's my turn. Your turn will come soon enough." I never forgot his lesson.

Like garlands woven from a heap of flowers...

At Dad's funeral, several customers came forward and told stories of his kindness and his ability to tell non-partisan jokes. Many were surprised by their own tears as they spoke. They told stories of how they tried to lure Dad into taking sides during their endless arguments. Dad never took the bait.

My loss reminds me of what is important in this world... weaving garlands of beautiful deeds. It is my turn.

APRIL 3

April is the cruelest month.

– T. S. Elliot

For some of us, April is the cruelest month. If your loved one died this month, as did one of mine, you will always remember the details and the circumstances of the death. Love never forgets love.

And I have been reminded many times since my son's death: Life is not fair.

Most likely the arrival of spring will never be the first thing on our minds from now on. What were we doing that spring day? How often have we told our stories? How many times have we replayed the hours of that day to see if we can change the outcome? What craziness have we contemplated since the death? Suicide? Please, no. How many sleepless nights have we endured? How many daydreams? How many tears? How many times can a man's heart break? Endless questions. No answers.

Just silence.

And friends. Thank God for friends who have the courage to come into our lives and stay for the long haul. Thank God for friends who send flowers each year on the anniversary of the death. Thank God for friends who send cards each week for two years. Thank God for friends who throw life preservers when we are drowning in a sea of sorrow.

I thank God for friends. Perhaps for the first time I have learned the importance of being a real friend. When healing comes, and it will, I will remember and be a friend to others in need.

APRIL 4

One of the things that happens to people in grief is they secretly think they're crazy, because they realize they are thinking things that don't make sense.

– Joan Didion

Much of our thinking after the death of a loved one may indeed be crazy by definition. One thought may be... he's not really dead... he'll be back in an hour or so and laugh when he learns we were all worried... or another... this isn't really happening to me. This must be a movie I'm watching and it will end soon. Or even... I'm watching this happen to someone else...

We may think anything to make this unreal.

A totally irrational question I posed to my counselor after the death of my son was, "He's not coming back, is he?" She had the wisdom to respond truthfully, "No, he's not coming back." "I didn't think so," I said, "but I had to check." She looked at me with complete composure, as if I had asked her the day's weather report. No judgment. No criticism. Just love and compassion for my indescribable loss.

Crazy? No, just lost in a confused morass of psychological pain and heartache beyond all description.

I am not crazy. I am struggling to figure out what has happened to me.

APRIL 5

*Grief drives men into habits of serious reflection,
sharpens the understanding, and softens the heart.*

– John Adams

What is there about the death of a loved one that causes us to look back on our lives and reflect on our joys and sorrows? Is it the sense that time is indeed passing, this reminder we do not have forever after all, and that our time here is passing quickly? A common conversation might go like this:

"Time flies, doesn't it?
Sure does. Why it seems like it was just yesterday..."

The voice trails off into the past.

When we think of our childhood days, the neighborhoods we grew up in, and how slowly the days crawled by, we may have wondered if we would ever grow up. Old age and death were both so far down the road that for all practical purposes they did not exist. In a flash, it seems, here we are now. Today. Death has come knocking on our door.

Finally, we understand. We look on with gentle eyes. We touch softly. We whisper in hushed tones. Our arm slips around the waist of someone we love. We look without speaking. Our manner softens. We have become vulnerable and it feels right. Our hearts have softened. We are in love again. We may wonder why it took death for this to happen.

Dear _____, I am so sorry you died. I miss you so!

I'll always remember the good times we shared, our meaningful conversations, and how I loved you. I still do. I always will. Thank you for loving me.

The risk of love is loss, and the price of
    loss is grief –
But the pain of grief
is only a shadow
when compared with the pain
of never risking love.

– Hilary Stanton Zunin

William Shakespeare's words are so familiar they seem to roll off our tongue without us trying: 'Tis better to have loved and lost than to never have loved at all." But when grief is fresh and raw, this phrase may be poor consolation. We may even rage at the notion as well as the thoughtless person who expresses it. Or, so we think at the time.

But wait. The speaker means well. And soon enough we will know the words ring true.

When my son died, a friend of many years, searching for some sort of consolation to share, said, "At least you had him for twenty seven years. A lot of us have never had children at all." His attempt to offer comfort touched a grief-stricken nerve and I instantly snarled back, "I wanted him to live a full life!" Of course, my friend did too. They were friends. He was also heartbroken. My son's death was his loss as well.

I agree. Never to have risked loving you, _____,

would be more painful than the pain of losing you. Thank you for being such an important part of my life.

Ah, woe is me! Winter is come and gone,
but grief returns with the revolving year.

– Percy Bysshe Shelley

There are days when we think we have put enough distance between us and our loss that we can breathe a bit easier. But soon enough a milestone approaches. A birthday, the death day, a wedding anniversary, a holiday, or the passing of one season into another without our loved one.

The now-familiar ache returns.

Will this sadness cycle ever end? The wisdom of others who have suffered through the death of loved ones, say, yes, the sharpness of loss will eventually soften. The waves of grief will diminish. The anguish over the approach of these special days will dissolve into memories of good times shared, of laughter and love, of joy and sorrow existing side-by-side.

Before my beloved aunt's death, she wrote a poem in which she predicted she would die in summer. Her words brought great comfort to me. I was impressed by her confidence and descriptions of the day of her death. As it turned out, she died on a beautiful day in October, a day every bit as stunning as her original prediction. And I think of her now with great joy in my heart for having shared a part of her journey.

Seasons come. Seasons go. So do we. Grief comes. Grief goes. And so it will.

He that is thy friend indeed,
he will help thee in thy need...

– Richard Barnfield

Where would we be if a faithful friend did not step forward in our time of sorrow with open arms and a compassionate heart? Wisdom teaches that all guys need one friend to walk beside us through the valley of death. Today, we could use that man right about now.

And we hope he wants to hang out with us. Again. And again.

Did a fellow worker "just happen" to stop by today to see how you are doing? Has a neighbor dropped off a casserole for this evening's meal? Who made the chocolate cake that somehow ended up in your freezer? And where did the freshly baked loaf of bread descend from? Who may be waiting for a call from you, for an invitation to stop by for a beer and a barbeque? Who is watching you to make sure you do not stumble and fall?

The wonderful thing about a friend is that he doesn't have to say anything. I feel a flicker of hope when he is simply at my side.

APRIL 9

*Every man has his secret sorrows which the
world knows not; and often times we call a man
cold when he is only sad.*

– Henry Wadsworth Longfellow

And what of suicide, the great mystery? Perhaps most men consider suicide at one time or another during their lives. Who really knows? None of us like to admit it. But sometimes the pain and loneliness feels so overwhelming that leaving this world seems to be the only logical path to relief.

None of us should judge this choice.

A young unwed man, secretly a father to a beautiful son, has his deep sorrows and chooses to leave the world behind. A veteran of recent wars, deployed multiple times, comes home to great fanfare and adulation, but shortly afterwards, also leaves by his own hands. Similar stories abound.

Suicide is an exit from suffering that seems unbearable. What we do know is that suffering begins to ease over time. In fact, often those who commit suicide are on their way out of hopelessness. The rise out of the trough of depression is the start of getting better, but it sometimes gives just enough energy to turn ideation into action.

Enough said. For those of us left behind, well we wonder what part, if any, we had to play in our loved one's decision. Very little, if any at all, I would guess. For the most part, we are innocent bystanders. Our sorrow will always remain complex because we will wonder what we could have done to prevent this. Probably, nothing at all.

*Dear _____, my heart is broken that you took
your own life. I wish you were still here. I will always wonder
what I could have done to help you decide to stay.*

APRIL 10

Thus shall ye think of all this fleeting world:
A star at dawn, a bubble in a stream;
A flash of lightening in a summer cloud,
A flickering lamp, a phantom, and a dream.

– Buddha

Death reminds us of how fragile life is. "Here today and gone tomorrow" is still a common expression. Life is transitory, and we are called to make the most of it while we exist. One day we won't.

Look around.

What do you see? Is the world's beauty diminished because of our loss? Are the spring crocuses still pushing through the last remnants of winter's snow? Is the song of the cardinal altered in any fashion? Do we faithfully nod our greeting to a star at dawn, a bubble in a stream? Will we still notice a flash of lightening in a summer cloud, the red winged blackbird laying claim to its annual nesting ground, the white pine buds swelling in anticipation of new life, the warm breath of a gentle spring breeze on our cheek?

Death is a tap on the shoulder. Has it received our attention?

A flickering lamp, a phantom, and a dream...I see each of these when I close my eyes. And, when they are open as well.

*One cannot be deeply responsive to the world
without being saddened very often.*

– Erich Fromm

Being sensitive to the world's pain is both a blessing and a curse, especially when we are overwhelmed with sorrow. It is a blessing because we do not miss any detail about our loss. Every nuance is noticed and recorded on our heart, imprinted in our brain. But it is a curse for the same reasons: we do not miss anything. And sometimes we wish we did. Too many details may overwhelm us. Too much information may drag us down deeper into our grief.

We may wish we had an "off" switch.

But we do not. After my father's death, I sat on the edge of his hospital bed and held his hand. I looked around the room. The machines that kept us up to date on his dying were now silent. A lone nurse quietly and respectfully removed medication and drainage lines from his lifeless body. All of my family members were gone. I glanced at the windowsill where someone had placed his eyeglasses and false teeth. I wonder what in the world we will do with them now? I glanced at his beautiful hands, and noticed for the first time his wedding ring was missing. I gave his hand a gentle squeeze. Tears streamed down my face.

I am grateful for my responsiveness to the world and the pain that can accompany it. I am also grateful for the joy it brings.

The desire to know is natural to good men.

– Leonardo Da Vinci

When it comes to the death of our beloved one, we want to know more than anything else. Where is our loved one? Why can't we follow? We may want to go looking for them and bring them back home. They belong here. Not there.

Where? Where? Where?

The sad and universal truth is that none of us knows, but we all guess. Humankind has always wondered about the whereabouts of its dead. Most world religions teach that there is an afterlife somewhere "in the heavens." And we sometimes recognize the spirit of our loved one's presence in our everyday life. Can this spirit move back and forth between both worlds, the world of the living and the world of the dead? Does this spirit "help us out" from time to time? Intervene to keep us safe? Simply keep us company?

Since my son's death, I often speak to him and ask him to keep all family members safe on our travel adventures. I also "talk" with him during my work week, while walking to and from errands, and while taking lunch breaks. He is my constant companion, day and night. He is more present to me in death than he could have ever been in life. Is talking with him strange? I do not know. But I'm good with it.

I will always want to know where my beloved one has gone. The desire to know is natural to good men.

Death was a friend, and sleep was Death's brother.

– John Steinbeck

There are times when the death of a loved one is a blessed relief to us. Perhaps we have lost a parent, spouse, or child after a long and debilitating illness. We may have watched the vibrant and active person we knew shrink into an invalid with no hope of recovery. In this situation, death can be a gift.

Still, this is hard to watch.

Perhaps a friend died from cancer. Some cancer treatments often seem worse than the illness itself. Some drug and radiation therapies can age a person before our eyes. Patients appear to die from the treatment itself. Still, we fight for life regardless of the odds stacked against us. In the process, if life becomes a living hell, a blessed death can be the savior.

A long-time friend fought valiantly against leukemia. It quickly became clear that the struggle would last a long time with no assurance of a positive outcome. Near the end of his life, his sister donated bone marrow in a last ditch attempt to arrest the disease. The attempt failed to stop the illness's progression. His death ended a long and brave struggle.

I want to live my life well so I can enjoy a death without regrets. I will spend every day on earth as well as I am able.

APRIL 14

I mourn in grey, grey as the sleeted wind, the bled shades of twilight, gunmetal, battleships, industrial paint.

— Marge Piercy

What if we mourn in grey for the one who has died? What if we have feelings of relief co-joined in our hearts with feelings of sorrow? What then? Which way do we turn? Do we mourn or rejoice?

Perhaps both.

It is okay to feel relief and love and miss the one who has died. It is okay to be angry and sad at the same time. A friend's grandfather was the town drunk and a poor father. Her grandmother, who divorced him, was very special to my friend. After her grandmother died, my friend's aunt said the man had hurt her many times and the grandmother had known about the abuse and had done nothing. There was no way to confirm this. My friend's mother said, "I knew my dad was rotten, but if this is true he's a monster." Is it true? Her aunt is in and out of rehabilitation. It casts some grey on my friend's mourning her grandmother's death at times.

If I have mixed feelings about the death of my loved one, I will seek out a listening ear so I can share my story. Perhaps a rainbow dwells within every tear.

APRIL 15

We have to believe that even the briefest of human connections can heal. Otherwise, life is unbearable.

– Agate Nesaule

Humans are made to live in community with each other. We need each other. How else could we survive this death of a loved one? Not in isolation! When we suffer a grievous loss like this, we search for the eyes of those who understand and love without judgment. We need unconditional love.

We have no time for games.

On a recent visit to a high school play, I walked out of the men's room during intermission and came face-to-face with a friend I had not seen in years. We looked at each other with amazement, both surprised that we would encounter the other in such an unexpected place. The last I had heard from her was shortly after our son's death when she was living on the opposite coast. She had written an extraordinary letter expressing her sorrow at our loss. Now a mother of two beautiful children herself, she stared at me with a parent's understanding, a mother's grief. We embraced and cried together.

It is true. Even the briefest of human connections can heal. Otherwise, life is unbearable.

Do not surrender your grief so quickly. Let it cut more deeply. Let it ferment and season you as few human or divine ingredients can.

– Hafiz of Persia

We can usually see it in the eyes of well-wishers. Their words are predictable – "How are you doing?" – but their eyes have an awkward twinkle, their face a wary smile. They wonder if we are through grieving the death of our loved one. If we are ready to "move on" with our lives? They wonder if we are back to normal?

They do not yet understand.

If we have lost a child, there will never be a "normal" again. There will only be before and after. A parent's grief after the death of a child will ferment and season you as few human or divine ingredients can. So, do not surrender your grief so quickly. Let it cut more deeply. Let it cut so deep that your love spills out and into the arms of your beloved wife, your child's mother, your heartbroken partner, your best friend in this world. She grieves beyond the reach of all male understanding.

There is no timetable for healing. I will do what I can day-by-day to get by. I will stay in touch with my partner so we can walk and talk the healing road together.

APRIL 17

We can choose heaven or we can choose hell.
Right here. Right now.

– Clifford Denay, Jr.

Perhaps "hell on earth" simply means the life of someone we love is torn from our arms. What else of "hell" can we possibly care more about? We live. We love. We lose. How much more cruel can life be than to lose someone we love?

Today, we know something of the pain of hell.

What if having someone to love was heaven, and having no one to love was hell? Would we choose to live our lives differently? Would we be more interested in nourishing our relationships and less interested in living our lives focused on external measures of success?

Is there anything we would change about the time we shared with this loved one? Do we have any regrets about what we said or failed to say? If we had our life together to live over again, what would we do differently? What if we had a second chance? What if we had known our human time with a loved one was actually heaven? And that little time with a loved one was really hell? What if someone had warned us of the pain of parting? Would it have made any difference?

I want to be present for the relationships I have now and know that, even though they are imperfect, they are heaven.

Joy comes, grief goes, we know not how.

– James Russell Lowell

In the early days of grief, the eventual return of joy often seems impossible. How can we ever be happy again when our beloved one is dead? Our own life, too, it may seem, is over. Still the sun gently pushes through the curtains the following morning.

How can this be?

How is it that life goes on when our own is devastated? Everything we see looks normal. The traffic lights still work. Children are still swinging at the playground pushed by mothers who stand and talk. Teenagers pass by with cell phones clamped to their ears or texting as they walk. A train whistle sounds in the distance. Birds sing. Everything seems the same. Except us.

It is true. Joy will come, and grief will go, we know not how. But we can try to understand.

William Glasser, a psychiatrist, has written extensively about what he refers to as "choice theory psychology." One of his notions is our ability to change our feelings by choosing to change how we act. This does not mean grief disappears instantly. It does not. But if we act like we're starting to heal, perhaps we will feel like we are beginning to heal. And that is a start. There is no timetable. But if we give it a try when we are ready, it may help.

When I am ready, I will consider the effect of my actions on my feelings. I own my grief. I deserve to mourn this loss. But, I will not choose to mourn forever. My loved one would not want that for me.

Everybody goes through the pains of life. There's no shortcut. Life does not come with a menu – "I'll take a splinter and an earache. And that's it." Whatever comes to you in life, you have to deal with it.

– Sid Caesar

What would life be like if we could choose our heartaches? Would we be up to it? At first blush, our answer might be a resounding, yes!

If we could choose our heartaches, our temptation might be to ignore life's greatest sorrows. We might want those troubles we judge to be easy, like the splinter and an earache. But in taking the easy path, would we also miss out on life's greatest joys? How would we recognize joy without experiencing sorrow?

To be human is to suffer. But being a man does not mean we have to suffer in silence. Or alone. We can ask for companions to help guide us through the darkness. Being a man does not mean that we have to "deal with it" by ourselves. We can deal with it with the help of other men who have experienced the same before us. And being a man means we can gracefully accept our misfortunes and somehow grow from them.

I will take whatever comes to me and deal with it the best I can. I will not look for shortcuts. Everybody goes through the pains of life. Even me. But everybody also experiences the joys of life. Including me.

APRIL 20

I like not only to be loved, but to be told that I am loved; the realm of silence is large enough beyond the grave.

— George Eliot

The spoken words "I love you!" are sweet music to the ears of a bereaved man. They have healed many broken hearts.

And when we express sympathy to family members, "I love you" shows compassion if it is spoken from the heart. And why not? Wouldn't we hope to hear how much we are loved as well? When we are overwhelmed with grief, spoken love can relieve for a moment the cutting edge of our sorrow. Our pain is soothed by this healing balm of words.

And if speaking these words has never come easy, perhaps we can practice saying them in private during walks in the woods, talking with our pets, and eventually in front of a mirror. After all, the man in the glass loves you, too. Loving ourselves makes loving others second nature. By speaking your love to you, speaking your love to others will soon come naturally.

I like to be told that I am loved. I will practice telling others that I love them.

APRIL 21

Expect trouble as an inevitable part of life and repeat to yourself the most comforting words of all, this, too, shall pass.

— Ann Landers

Nothing is permanent in this world. Not even sorrow. Our grief, as strong as it is at this moment, will lighten up in time. This may be hard to believe, but the strongest winds eventually cease. Calm will return to our world.

Grief will melt into memories.

We may fight this notion. If we lose our grip on grief, will we also lose memories of our loved one? No. Our memories are here to stay. Always. And one day we will start to revive. We'll feel less troubled by our loved one's absence and more joyful over cherished times we spent together. And when that day arrives, we will know we are on the healing path. Truly, this too shall pass.

We have most likely heard the phrase, "Sometimes you win, sometimes you lose." Well, it is true. When joy comes our way, we usually do not wonder why it comes to us. We accept it for what it is. But, when sorrow lands at our doorstep, almost automatically we ask, "Why me?" Why have we been chosen for this particular tragedy? Well, we were not chosen. It just happened. Expect trouble as an inevitable part of life.

Sooner or later, everyone takes a turn being swallowed by sorrow. But, this, too, shall pass.

The more a diamond is cut the more it sparkles.

– Source Unknown

Grief can break us or help us grow. The choice is ours. This is not a choice we would ever invite into our lives. But here it is. Death comes and we have to deal with it somehow. How we handle it will determine our future happiness.

Our lives literally depend upon our choices from now on.

When my son died I spent a lot of time wandering around in our pole barn. We had divided the space so that he had room for his hobbies repairing cars, motorcycles, bicycles, street luges, and building amazing devices like a lounge chair mounted on a battery powered three-wheeled scooter. He spent countless hours and endless days in the barn with his friends and loved his work area. I called his name repeatedly in a vain and irrational attempt to find him. I could not believe he had died. But, he was dead. I could still be calling for him if I chose to do so.

Instead, I chose to seek professional counseling from a grief therapist, have read countless grief recovery books, have attended several sessions of a grief recovery group called The Compassionate Friends, have kept a journal where I have been chronicling thoughts and feelings since my son's death, have run a marathon that I dedicated to his memory, and have built a Little Free Library in memory of he and his friend who died with him. And more. You can do the same.

Who would have guessed? Each loss I have suffered is making me sparkle more.

APRIL 23

Following the light of the sun, we left the Old World.

– Christopher Columbus

This is what our loved one did too. Pushing off from the shore in search of a new world, our beloved one is now resting after a long journey. Could we ask for more for ourselves when we die?

Will we not push away from shore with the same gusto?

For much of our days on earth we are in constant search of "the light of the sun." We turn our faces to the sun when lounging on the beach. We sit in sun–filled places while resting, reading, or just playing with families and friends. We watch morning sunbeams stream through our bedroom windows. We search out the best locations to watch stunning sunsets. We face the sun to warm our faces on cold winter days. We carry sunshine in the form of firewood to heat our homes on blustery winter nights. Houseplants turn toward the sunlight while growing on our windowsills. The sun is our friend and our salvation. We could not exist without it.

Is it any wonder that Columbus followed the sunlight in search of the new world? Stories abound about the dying seeing a light at the end of a tunnel. Who are we, the living, to dispute their experiences? One day we will have a chance to see for ourselves. We, too, will leave the Old World for the New World. Then we will know.

I am spending my life in search of the New World. Surely I need only follow the sunlight to find it.

And this we owe to our beloved dead, whether young or old: to wipe from our memories all that was less than their best, and to carry them in our hearts at their wisest, most compassionate, most creative moments. Is that not what all of us hope from those who survive us...?

– Elizabeth Watson

If the death of our loved one is still fresh, our wounds raw and excruciating, Watson's suggestion may seem impossible. All our memories, good and bad, may be swirling around like a tornado, a bad movie without an end. Like a nightmare.

Classifying memories may be the last thing we want to do.

But if some time has passed since our loss, if we have even started to laugh a little again, then this message may be full of wisdom. Especially for men who may be inclined to dwell upon the faults of others.

Maybe we find ourselves telling stories about what we learned from the person who is now gone. Or, when faced with an unfamiliar task, we ask ourselves how he/she would have tackled the problem. Maybe we remember a story from the funeral visitation about an act of kindness that our loved one performed once, or even multiple times, for someone who is a stranger to us. Or perhaps we think about the grocery bag or box full of sympathy cards sent to us after the death, praising still other personal traits of our loved one and thanking us for the joy of having known him or her.

We remember the best of our loved ones because that is how we wish to be remembered.

I will make a conscious choice to remember _____ at his/her best, to recall his/her wisdom, compassion, creativity, and love for this world, and for me.

I would rather be ashes than dust! I would rather that my spark should burn out in a brilliant blaze than it should be stifled by dry-rot. I would rather be a superb meteor, every atom of me in magnificent glow, than a sleepy and permanent planet. The function of man is to live, not to exist. I shall not waste my days trying to prolong them. I shall use my time.

— Jack London's Credo

It is a delicate dance for us between playing it safe and being reckless in our behavior. We long for adventure, but our activities can quickly get us into trouble. We don't want to die, but we want thrills, chills, and a meteor-like life. We want to feel alive!

Two years after my son died in a boating accident on Lake Michigan, my wife had a dream in which he and the friend who died with him told her that all was well with them. In a conversation that Jane had with the boys, she urged them to be more careful the next time, to not take such chances again.

Dreams can bring comfort or dismay. Our son and his beloved friend were adventurous thrill-seekers. They thought they were prepared for a few hours on the water that day. They were wrong.

Will I listen to that still, small voice within me when I make decisions about the use of my time here on earth?

Tell me, what is it you plan to do
With your one wild and precious life?

– Mary Oliver

When we think of prayer, we may be remembering the formal prayers our mothers and fathers taught us as little boys. Some of us may no longer find those prayers helpful, while others find great comfort in remembering them. In these days of loss and sorrow, we may want to pray, but don't know how.

Prayer, however, can take on many forms. The monk Thomas Merton wrote, "I pray better by walking, than by talking..." So can we. As we think about God, we may turn to some of the formal prayers we grew up with. But we may also take a walk in the grassy field nearby, or feel the wind on our face, sense our loved one's presence and touch in that warmth. Perhaps a walk on the beach or in the woods is more healing. Or we can lie on our back in the tall grass on a warm summer night, looking at the moon and unspeakable number of stars that grace the glorious universe.

Prayer can be anything that heals. What prayer shall I choose today to help heal my one wild and precious life?

Whenever anyone discusses death, they talk about the inevitable loss, but no one ever mentions the inevitable gain. How when you lose a loved one, you suddenly have a spirit ally, an energy on the other side that is with you always, that is with you just by calling their name.

— Sandra Cisneros, Essay, *Los Angeles Times*, October 26, 1997.

In the early days and months following the death of our loved one, we can sometimes feel his or her physical presence even though no longer seen. We aren't losing our minds. This phenomena has often been reported through the ages.

Sensing the physical presence of a dead loved one troubles those of us who are used to using our reason and intellect to get us through each day. However, we must admit that there have been times in our lives when we simply did not understand an experience we had. There was no plausible explanation. We simply knew the experience was true.

Is it possible our loved one has now become our lifelong companion and confidante? A friend whose son died many years ago sets aside an appointment time each week to talk with his son. This regular discussion brings him great comfort and consolation.

Can I open myself to the possibility that my loved one is as near as the air I am breathing? That my loved one will always love me, regardless of death?

APRIL 28

Death is not extinguishing the light; it is putting out the lamp because dawn has come.

– Rabindranath Tagore

It's tough stuff, isn't it, thinking that we should rejoice in a new day, a new dawning, because our loved one has died? How can we rejoice about anything when someone we love has died? At first, we cannot. In the first few minutes, hours, days, weeks, our reaction is more like numbness, a haze, walking in slow-motion, doing what we are told to do by caretaking friends, grateful that we do not have to think or speak or make decisions. Simply staying alive is all that we can accomplish.

After my son's death, I told friends that I felt like I was walking through thickened Jell-O, trying to push my way forward but making no progress, caught like a fly in a spider's web. Struggling, struggling, struggling to absorb the reality of what had happened, but, thankfully, unable to do so. This cannot possibly be me! This cannot happen to my family. Things like this do not happen to good people.

But, of course, they do. Death happens. Everyone takes a turn.

But the death of our loved one also creates an opportunity for the new dawn about which Tagore writes. As the saying goes, when a door closes, a window opens. This is hard! We did not want the door to close. We did not want new opportunities for personal growth. We want our loved one back.

In spite of my loved one's death, can I name one reason to rejoice in today's sunrise? Just one?

APRIL 29

You can blow out a candle but you cannot blow out a fire. Once the flames begin to catch the wind will blow it higher.

– Peter Gabriel

If our loved one was full of energy and had an unquenchable appetite for life, a zest for the wondrous joy and excitement that this world can offer, then surely that great spirit lives on in the lives of those who knew and loved him or her. That kind of fire for living is contagious. We love to hang out with people who drink life in big gulps.

Whenever our son would walk through the door of our home, the whole house seemed to start thumping with energy. The walls seemed to want to dance with anticipation. He and his more sedate friends were often cooking up another adventure, usually something slightly against the grain, out of the ordinary. This tendency seems to be one of the differences between men and women. We men, once the flames begin to catch, tend to "push the envelope," with our activities, sometimes with dire consequences. Sometimes we die.

But, spirit begets spirit. Try stopping the wind.

My loved one's spirit is alive and well and living inside me. How can I best honor his or her life by an activity I choose today?

*Oh thou kind (Father)! Thank divine Providence
that I have been freed from a small gloomy cage
and, like the birds of the meadows, have soared
to the divine world – a world that is spacious,
illumined and ever gay and jubilant. Therefore,
lament not, Oh (Father), and be not grieved. I
am not of the lost, nor have I been obliterated and
destroyed. I have shaken off the mortal form and
raised my banner in the spiritual world. Following
this separation is everlasting companionship.
Thou shalt find me in heaven, immersed in an
ocean of light.*

– Abdul' Baha'

Most spiritual traditions teach of the existence of a heaven, a world just beyond this one that we know and love so well. Considering this belief can bring great comfort and consolation to those of us who think that this world and this life is the only one we will ever know. Our logical and rational thinking process has a hard time imagining a world that we cannot experience with our five senses. Feelings that such a world exists may be hard to come by.

And yet stories abound by folks who have had "near-death" experiences. Such stories tell of oceans of light, friends and family members waiting to receive them, beauty and peace beyond human comprehension, of love and acceptance like they have never known. And many of those who were "revived" and brought back to life tell of not wanting to return here because of the absolute joy waiting for them on the other side.

Can I ponder the possibility that some place exists on the other side? That my loved ones are waiting there for me?

∂ MAY ∂

Grief melts away
Like snow in May,
As if there were no such cold thing.

– George Herbert

Those of us who live north of the forty-fifth parallel long for spring after snowy winters. We have tired of winter activities and look forward to warmer days and the scent of freshly mowed lawns. Depression can run rampant if cold weather persists longer than expected.

And the death of someone we love adds to our bleak outlook.

Still, the crocus and daffodils insist on pushing through rude snowfall. Tree buds swell with anticipation of the coming warm days. The robins are back in full force, swarming in on front lawns and singing their distinctive songs as if they have not been absent all winter. Tulips stand ready to open, and the forsythia challenges our sorrow. The bright green tips of new growth on the cedar and pine branches indicate that nature is taking care of its own. It is Spring! And our spirits are rising almost against our will.

In the midst of every bitter winter, it is easy to think that warm weather will never return. And in the throes of early grief, it is also common to believe we will never be happy again. Just for today, though, let us embrace the hope that accompanies spring. Surely in the rebirth of this season we can be assured of the rebirth of our joy. We will laugh again.

I found myself laughing the other day. Is it possible my grief is starting to melt away?

MAY 2

Closed eyes cannot see the white roses...
So give them the flowers now!

– Lee M. Hodges

Closed eyes cannot see the white roses... Walk into any funeral home and what is the first thing that strikes us?

The smell of flowers.

Flowers matter. A lot. We know this instinctively when a loved one dies. Arranging for the flowers can take a lot of time. We want the perfect arrangement made of blossoms that our precious one loved most while alive. We say to each other, "He would have liked these," or "She used to pick these and put them in a vase on the kitchen table. She loved the way they smelled." And, at some funerals, we have seen coffins almost smothered by floral arrangements. Yet, wait. Who are the flowers for? "...Closed eyes cannot see the white roses... so give them the flowers now!"

The flowers are for us, the ones left behind. So why wait until it is too late to buy flowers for someone we love, male or female, adult or child, who would appreciate them while living?

Who can I buy flowers for today?

MAY 3

Keep me away from the wisdom which does not cry, the philosophy which does not laugh...

– Kahlil Gibran

Regardless of the wisdom talk we may hear while in the depths of this grief, we have a right to our tears. We have lost someone precious. We are wounded to our core and have a responsibility to push back against suggestions that we have mourned long enough.

We will heal in our own time.

And while we are waiting for brighter days, a part of us may long for the laughter we once shared with the one who is now missing forever. We may miss the pensive days of silence and sharing, of contentment and caring. We may miss the glance and the stance, the mischief and the malaise. We may miss the sound of our loved one breathing. Yet, if we listen carefully, perhaps we can still hear the familiar voice calling us from the kitchen table to a board game or a hand of cards. The accompanying laughter sounds just as real as always. And so are our tears.

Wisdom that has no room for tears does not speak to my heart. And philosophy without laughter leaves me empty and alone. In my own time, my laughing heart will return.

*Grief can awaken us to new values and new
and deeper appreciations. Grief can cause us
to reprioritize things in our lives, to recognize
what's really important and put it first. Grief
can heighten our gratitude as we cease taking
the gifts life bestows on us for granted. Grief
can give us the wisdom of being with death.
Grief can make death the companion on our left
who guides us and gives us advice. None of this
growth makes the loss good and worthwhile,
but it is the good that comes out of the bad.*

– Roger Bertschausen

None of us men asked for these "gifts" and "opportunities," wrapped in unspeakable sorrow, yet here they are. Likely, most of us were happy with the way things used to be.

There is something within us that does not like changes, especially those that death imposes.

So what can we learn from these sharp but true observations? That the death of a loved one encourages us to consider a closer and deeper intimacy with those we still have, those we love that we can still hold in our arms. That this open window of awareness may close more quickly than we think if we don't act upon it soon. That we have a chance to change the direction of our lives with the choices we make now, perhaps at this very moment. That this opportunity may be a "going away" gift from our beloved dead.

None of this growth makes the loss good and worthwhile. Absolutely none. But what good can I create out of this bad?

He who has felt the deepest grief is best able to experience supreme happiness. We must have felt what it is to die, that we may appreciate the enjoyments of life.

– Alexandre Dumas, *The Count of Monte Cristo*

The death of someone we love may shatter our lives like a wineglass shatters when dropped onto a soapstone countertop. Yet in our brokenness, we often awaken to a world we did not know existed. Our senses are sharper. Our new life feels unfamiliar. Happiness seems impossible. How could this be?

After all, we thought we were living with our eyes wide open.

This new world surprises us. Perhaps we built a wall around the distasteful realities of life, like death. The old phrase, "out of sight, out of mind" still rings true. But death respects no barriers. The loss of our loved one has possibly felt like a near-death experience. For the first time, we may understand what it might feel like to die. And, like a cracked eggshell being peeled away from the white, our old life has been stripped away and this awareness set free. Our priorities are now exquisitely clear. We are home.

Now I understand. Death has taught me that joy is a result of loving relationships. People are more important than things. And healing is a by-product of love.

Grief is itself a medicine.

– William Cowper

Absorbing the reality of our loss will take time. Like a filter, grief only allows as much pain to access our hearts as we can handle. Instead, the pain slowly seeps in like water from a leaky pipe, drip by drip. If we could instantly comprehend the extent of this loss, we would be overwhelmed. Perhaps permanently frozen in our tracks.

Grief gives us the opportunity to evaluate the extent of our loss. We realize we are wounded but aren't sure of the extent of our injuries. We look through an ever-present haze, evaluating the new world where we have landed. We rub our eyes in a vain attempt to clear the fog. Friends, old and new, appear. Many leave, but some stay. We cry, sleep, lock doors, and move slowly lest we fall, dress carelessly, ignore personal hygiene, and feel unconcerned about the affairs of the world. Let the world turn without me tonight. Grief is a shelter from the storm of death. Grief is a balm for the broken soul. But, thankfully, grief will step aside when we begin to heal in the land of the living.

To grieve is to practice living in a world we do not create. This takes time. I will sip my grief while I am healing.

...Blessed are those who carry
For they shall be lifted.

– Anna Kamienska

We who carry the coffins of our beloved dead will one day be lifted. Today, in our sorrow, we may bear other loads. The grief of a lost future. The regret of a past we cannot change. The loneliness of being left behind. A sense of being abandoned. The fear of living alone. The heaviness of our heart.

And we carry the weight of our what if's.

After my parents died fifty-eight days apart, it occurred to me that I had become an orphan. I would be the next to die if the "natural order" of death was to follow, the oldest first, the youngest last. That seemed frightening, but fair. Then, my son died. My earlier grief was transformed into the breathtaking sorrow of a father lamenting the untimely death of a child. The weight of such grief is almost beyond human capability. Almost, but not quite. We do not carry the load alone. Others who precede us know the pain and understand the sorrow. It is they we reach out to, other parents who have carried such grief in their hearts, too. They will lift us.

Being lifted is our hope.

MAY 8

There is no grief like the grief that does not speak.

– Henry Wadsworth Longfellow

Speaking our grief does not come easy to men. In fact, speaking our feelings at all can be challenging. Those we love often struggle to coax us into talking from our hearts. And when we are suffering from the death of a loved one, sharing feelings may be the last thing we want to do.

Still, putting our feelings into words might save our lives.

We have heard the phrase, "dying from a broken heart." Perhaps the wisdom found in these words implies that feelings bottled up inside may never escape. It would be similar to shaking a soda without taking off the cap. Try it and feel how tight the bottle becomes. The same thing happens to us. An author stops writing after the death of his child. Another father struggles to speak of his dead son. Yet, when he hears his boy's name, his eyes light up and he stands more erect.

I am slowly learning that there is no grief like the grief that does not speak. Perhaps I will practice whispering my loved one's name when I am alone. Maybe I'll feel better. What do I have to lose by trying?

MAY 9

The aim of life is to live, and to live means to be aware, joyously, drunkenly, serenely, divinely aware.

– Henry Miller

Perhaps it takes the death of someone we love to wake us up. I mean to really open our eyes to this amazing experience we call life. Being alive is nothing short of a miracle.

We take so much for granted.

The smell of coffee, every breath we take, this morning's sunrise, gentle rain that washes our world, the bickering of blue jays, the song of children's play, the wind dancing through white pine trees, the presence of our loved ones. One grieving friend said, "I thought I had a lot of time to talk about the important things with my son. What did he think about God? What were his hopes and dreams? What did he value the most about life? Now he is gone and I have lost my chance."

Those of us still living have another opportunity today to make a deeper connection with those we love, living or dead. If the one we wish to communicate with is deceased, we can write a letter with our questions and deliver it to wherever he or she waits for us. Crazy? Who knows? If, on the other hand, our loved one is living, we can call or text and make plans to share coffee or tea, and conversation. Share the joy of living. Who knows how much longer we will be here? Why wait?

I want to be aware, joyously, drunkenly, serenely, divinely aware. I want to live every second of my days as if life matters. And it does.

MAY 10

Every exit is an entry somewhere else.

– Tom Stoppard

Where do our beloved dead go? We search for them, but cannot find them. We sense their presence, but there is no answer when we call their name. We can no longer see them, hold them, touch them, feel them, listen to them breathe, or hear their voice call our name. We miss the familiar touch on our shoulders. We long for the beauty, love, and knowing looks in their eyes. We wonder who will comfort them when they cry. More than ever, we want to rock them to sleep while singing their favorite lullaby.

Where, in the name of God, are they?

While our son was living, our pole barn was divided into two work areas. My space was filled with a tractor that I used for mowing our lawn and snow blowing our driveway. We also stored bicycles, a toboggan, snow sleds. Shelves bulged with stuff not important enough to keep in the house. His side was stuffed with car and motorcycle parts, hand-built street luges, assorted bicycles, a frosty-freeze machine, old canvas jackets, and mystery items that I was never able to identify. I loved hearing he and his friends talk and laugh as they worked on projects through countless days and many sleepless nights. For several months after his death, I found myself calling his name from my side of the barn, hoping beyond hope he would stand, smile, and say, "Hey Pops."

I believe every exit is an entry somewhere else. I just wish I knew where the "somewhere else" is.

Death ends a life, not a relationship.

– Jack Lemmon

We men know this intuitively. A life is a physical thing, with a beginning and an end. A relationship is spiritual, an everlasting entity. Relationships cannot die.

Love always survives.

When we see the physical remains of our deceased loved ones, we know immediately that their body no longer functions. What has sustained their ability to live and laugh and love is no longer able to do so. And, because we are human beings, our profound grief overwhelms us because we can see our loss. It is profound. It is right before us. We can no longer hold our loved one in our arms. We are shaken to the core.

Yet, the relationship, the love remains. We also know this intuitively. When we are apart from those we love, we know that the distance does not separate us from their love. Death is a journey we can never understand across a distance that is immeasurable. But regardless of whatever the distance turns out to be, and one day we may know, the spiritual relationship remains alive and well. We will always feel the love. And that is proof enough.

Dear _____, regardless of your body's death, our love for each other remains alive and well.

MAY 12

Grief is the agony of an instant. The indulgence of grief the blunder of a life.

– Benjamin Disraeli

As we struggle through the agony of our grief, we wonder again and again how long, how long will we suffer? Will we ever experience joy again? Will we ever laugh and love and live again?

We may feel stunned, crippled by the death of the one we have loved.

How will we ever see past the day of our loss? Time seems to have stopped. We may not care for a future that does not include the one we grieve for. Yet, what would our loved one want for us now? Eternal sorrow? Endless tears? A hobbled existence for the rest of our days? Hardly. More than likely our beloved would want his or her life to be honored and then want us to get on with living our lives to their fullest. No endless moping. No deep depression. No missing out on the beauty of our existence. They would want us to turn our face to the sun.

Honoring the one I have lost, I will not indulge my grief until the end of my days. Instead, I will grieve, but when I am able, I will reach for joy once more.

Do you ever think
when the hearse goes by
that some day you
are going to die?
And the worms crawl in
and the worms crawl out
and the worms play pinochle
  on your snout.

– The Hearse Song

Until we lose someone close to us, death seems to stay at arm's length. We feel safe. Secure. Oh, we know people die. It's just that it is other people who do the dying. Not us, or people we love.

We may even feel immune.

When we were children, death stayed a playful distance away. Do you ever think when the hearse goes by that some day you are going to die? Back then, a hearse was something to gaze at, make jokes about, and imagine driving some day. Being sealed up in a casket and riding in the back of a hearse was most likely the last thing on our mind. Worms crawl in? We would have laughed at the thought.

My closest brush with death came in my senior year of high school. A friend who had too much to drink after a Saturday night party was found floating at the bottom of a swimming pool. Fortunately for him, his body had just settled into place when he was spotted by another reveler. He was rescued. Worms play pinochle? Then, Vietnam arrived, and in short order several good friends died there. Our laughter was stilled.

Now is this loss and what I have learned about death: to not suffer in silence, to not pretend to be "okay," to express gratitude to those who walk beside me, to give myself permission to grieve.

I am not alone with my grief. Others whose hearts have been broken before mine walk beside me. They will show me the way.

...like the laughter of the universe.

– Dante, *The Divine Comedy*

Dante describes his ascension from the gates of hell to the doors of heaven. As he nears heaven's entrance, he hears a sound like he has never heard before, "...like the laughter of the universe."

But Dante isn't talking about laughter in the face of death.

He goes on to suggest that God knows how it all turns out and that death has no power over the final outcome. Is it also possible for us that this is a hope worth reaching for? Is there comfort for us to consider that whoever or whatever is in charge knows more than we do and that laughter in spite of tears is not only possible, but perhaps even preferable? We might recall the familiar phrase, "he laughed until he cried." Maybe we can turn it around, "...he cried until he laughed."

Before our son's death, our kitchen table was the gathering place for him and his friends. Raucous laughter filled the air whenever they gathered. Food, friendship, and frolicking were the order of the day. And when the laughter finally subsided, a heart-calming peace would accompany me to bed for a sound night's rest.

In the voice of my loved one, I will always hear the laughter of the universe.

There are as many nights as days, and one is just as long as the other in the year's course. Even a happy life cannot be without a measure of darkness, and the word "happy" would lose its meaning if it were not balanced by sadness.

– Carl Jung

We certainly know the difference between "success" and "failure." Most likely we have had our share of each. But how would we recognize "success" if we had never experienced "failure?"

Happiness and sadness work the same way.

Yet, perhaps on some level we believe we could be perfectly content with infinite happiness. But, could we? When death arrives and pulls us into the black cave of sorrow, we may rebel at the unfairness of it all. We may believe we have already paid our dues at sorrow's front door, that this latest painful intrusion rightly belongs to someone else. Still, we cannot prevent death from multiple visits to our world. And if we could, would we? How would we recognize joy without an understanding of sorrow? From where would our comprehension of empathy, compassion, and sympathy come?

Ready or not, death happens to us all on the teeter-totter of life.

I understand the difference between joy and sorrow. Today it is my turn to grieve, but I believe that happiness will return. What is one thing I can do today to help me on my journey back to joy?

There is a time for everything,
And a season for every activity under heaven;
A time to be born and a time to die...

– Ecclesiastes 3:1 & 2 (NIV)

It is as much a part of human nature to rejoice in the safe birth of a child as it is to grieve the death of a loved one. We sorrowful men recognize that life eventually calls us to both occasions. Most of us would gladly skip the death invitation.

As Woody Allen once declared, "I don't mind dying. I just don't want to be there when it happens."

Still, there is a time for everything... And in our hearts we know this is true. We just don't want to think about it. We would rather keep our thoughts and hands busy doing fun things than consider our approaching own death. Death is like an underground spring that bubbles to the surface from time to time. We know it is there somewhere, but we don't search for it. We know deep down that death will find us in its own time.

The seasons of our lives come and go, ebb and flow, change colors like a kaleidoscope, and are sometimes stormy or calm. And if we expect to harvest the fruits of our labors, we have to plant in good times and bad. We cannot steal away in times of sorrow and expect to return to the joy we did not sow. I think of the losses suffered by families traveling to new lives in wagon trains. When loved ones died, they mourned their loss, buried them along the trail, and continued following their dreams.

There is a time to be born and a time to die. I embrace both.

Because I have loved life, I shall have no sorrow to die.
— Amelia Burr

Do any of us remember where we were or what we were doing before we became conscious of being alive? Do we recall details of our surroundings back then, sights, sounds, smells, smiles, foods, friendships, fears?

It is unlikely.

So what makes us fearful to return to this place that memory cannot recall? And why are we heartbroken that our loved one has journeyed before us? Whether we believe in an afterlife or not, it seems that we should have no fear. There will either be a realm where we will be reunited with our loved ones who have died, or we will return to the benign beginning we cannot recall. Either place, guys, we win.

In the meantime, our responsibility is to appreciate this magnificent existence. We have stories to share, memories to recall, tears to shed, laughter enough to go around the circle of love we dwell within. And, who knows? Perhaps our circle takes in all whom we have loved, dead or alive, from the start. One day, perhaps, we'll actually know. This is our hope.

Yes! Because I have loved life, I shall have no sorrow to die. None at all.

MAY 18

Of all the experiences we confront in life, the toughest to face is the sudden, unexpected loss of someone we love. Loss in itself is painful enough, but sudden loss is shocking. The shock doubles our pain and intensifies our grief.

– Judy Tatelbaum

The sudden death of our loved one can pierce our hearts and abscond with our very soul. How is it possible to have our loved one at our side one hour and in the very next find him or her gone? Forever absent.

How quickly we can die!

A friend's son awakes, washes, and walks into the woods to take his own life. Heartbroken over the death of his sister, he cannot fathom life without her. Now two children are suddenly gone. We contemplate the unimaginable, shake our heads in disbelief, wonder how and why good folks suffer. There are no answers. We plant a tree in their memories.

Our son and his friend decide on a quick romp on the bay on an unusually warm spring Sunday afternoon. Two young men in their prime, full of plans for their futures, hopes, dreams, and courage enough to carry them through the decades before them. An hour's frolic was the plan, but the wind and cold water took them away. We plant a tree in their memories too. We are forever heartbroken. Yet, we parents carry on. Somehow. Resilient.

A quick death is a gift for the one departing, but excruciatingly painful for those of us left behind. There is no time to say goodbye, no time for a final embrace, no time to say thank you, no time for tears, no time for anything but the breathtaking wonder of sudden absence. Then, eternal silence.

I will always be amazed at how quickly you went away. I wanted more time with you.

Faith consists in believing when it is beyond the power of reason to believe. It is not enough that a thing be possible for it to be believed.

– Voltaire

Many of us grieving men have trouble believing that anything of value exists beyond this life. Our loved one is gone, and that's that. No one knows exactly where. We know the burial site, but have no clue where our loved one's spirit has traveled. Unanswerable questions abound.

So reason rules. If we cannot see it, it's not there.

If something seems illogical, then it must not be true, we argue. Not real. Yet we find ourselves thinking that the essence of our loved one somehow remains. We cannot figure out this part of death. It's as though at times we can almost feel him or her with us in the same place. How can this be? Still, our inner doubting Thomas may overrule belief in an afterlife. Often we want to believe that something is there. Somewhere.

For now, why not consider the possibility that some incomprehensible love waits for us and our loved ones on the other side. Clearly love exists. And so might the other side.

Reason does not guide how or why we love and yet love can change lives and civilizations.

Today I will grieve the loss of my loved one without insisting that reason rules my heart. Who knows what I can set free within me as a result of this decision?

MAY 20

The best laid plans of mice and men
often go astray...
and leave us nothing but grief and pain
for promised joy.

– Robert Burns

Some of us who are grieving this day are young. We may have lost someone we planned our future around. Now, our broken dreams may be lying shattered in pieces on the floor. We may be numb, a sailing ship without a rudder.

We may wonder, why me?

And some of us are in the mid-years of our lives, nicely settled in, comfortable in our routines, until now. We may have lost a parent, or, inconceivably, a child. We may now be orphaned, or set adrift on the vast sea of sorrow that follows a child's death. Our compass may fail us. There may seem to be no chart to help guide us...nothing but grief and pain.

Still some of us are in our later years of life and our lost one may be our dearest of companions, the one with whom we have weathered many of life's storms. Suddenly we are sleeping in a cold bed and face an uncertain future. Fears may abound. Who will want us? Who will care for us? Who will love us?

What all of us may have in common is the loss of our "best laid plans." We had a lot of living to do yet, and now our chance has been stolen away... gone astray. Or has it? We can still listen to our loved one's guiding voice and carry on. We have hope. We still have work to do. And be assured, the one whose death we grieve still loves us, and always will.

Where is the joy that was promised? Perhaps here. Now. I am safe and secure in the memories I cherish and in my loved one's voice that always speaks to me.

*...if you can get through the twilight, you'll live
through the night.*
— Dorothy Parker

The "twilight" periods are the first minutes, hours, days, weeks, months, and sometimes years following the death of our loved one. These are the stun-gunned times when we are not sure what has hit us. We are conscious but struggling to figure out living through our nights of sorrow.

For men used to being in charge, this death is daunting. Possibly devastating.

Ironically, we can "hold on" by letting go of our need to control grief. Grief is under no man's control. It is what it is, and the harder we try to direct its course, the more likely we are to suffer. Grief will have its way. What we choose to do with our grief is what matters... if (we) can get through the twilight. If we surround ourselves with family members and friends who love and care for us, we will be holding on. If we respond to invitations for coffee or lunch, we will be holding on. If we answer unexpected calls from well-meaning neighbors, we will be holding on. If we express gratitude for flowers left at our front door, for meals delivered with love, for the hug that lasts longer than usual, for the warm smile from those who know, we will be holding on. Our job is to hold on by letting go.

As I hold on through this twilight, I know I'll live through the night.

*Is not the cup that holds your wine the very cup
that was burned in the potter's oven?*

– Kahlil Gibran

For most of us mourning men, hearing that sorrow brings us joy is not what we want to hear. Not now. Not ever. More happiness for us at the expense of the death of someone we love?

This is hardly a choice we would make.

Still, sages for centuries have declared similar messages. The final step in creating a piece of raku pottery involves the application of a glaze. The heat sears the "green" clay and bakes upon it the design of the potter, always beautiful, permanent. Perhaps our burning grief can glaze our lives into something more beautiful than before. Who knows? We would have never chosen this path to transformation. But what better parting gift can our loved one offer? To leave baskets of beauty along the trail they blazed during a lifetime?

I would never have chosen this path to transformation. Yet, here it is. The message is clear. The cup that holds my wine was once burned in the potter's oven.

If we could read the secret history of our enemies, we should find in each man's life sorrow and suffering enough to disarm all hostility.

– Henry Wadsworth Longfellow,
Driftwood, 1857

Even men we do not like or respect suffer. Friend or enemy, we are all in the same suffering boat when we lose someone we love. All men grieve. Perhaps this awareness can soften our hearts toward other men.

What do we have to lose by changing our attitude toward them?

A male colleague loses his wife and daughter in the same automobile accident. He is seriously injured. Our frequent disagreements over institutional politics fade quickly into the background in the face of his staggering loss. An unpopular corporate executive is diagnosed with melanoma cancer in an advanced stage. No treatment is possible. He has just weeks to live. What prior suffering has he endured? A local farmer sets out one summer evening to deliver hay in his old truck. His brakes fail as he approaches an intersection. He tries in vain to negotiate the ninety degree turn at a high speed. He is buried near my own son's grave. Old and poor die the same.

So do friends and enemies.

If I knew each man's story, how would that knowledge help shape my attitude toward him?

I would never trust a man who didn't cry; he wouldn't be human.

– Norman Schwarzkopf

Most men cry when a loved one dies – some of us cry on the inside and some on the outside. Norman Schwarzkopf was likely referring to visible tears. But invisible tears may be just as common when a man loses someone he loves.

Our culture is tough on a visibly tearful man.

Perhaps all families have men who were taught to be stoic in the face of loss. Some of this may be generational issues. Regardless, the old adage, "real men don't cry" is still alive and well in some family circles. We grieving men raised in this environment learned to be careful in expressing our emotions. "Be a man" meant not crying in front of anyone. Ever. Thank goodness times have changed.

It is tough to remain composed in the face of the death of someone we love. Now, though, we seem to have cultural permission to grieve more openly. Star athletes have helped pave the way. They often shed tears of joy or sorrow. Soldiers returning from a war zone sometimes kneel and kiss the ground of their hometown, weeping openly. My uncle wept like a child at the funeral of his father. And when my parents died, I could no longer hold back my own tears than stop breathing.

We men are human. Regardless of where or when our loved one dies, it is okay to cry.

Everyone is overridden by thoughts; that's why they have so much heartache and sorrow.

– Rumi

In the early days following our loss, turning our thoughts in other directions may prove impossible. The death of a loved one is a mighty blow, and we are not soon distracted by other earthy concerns.

Nothing much seems to matter anymore.

No wonder sorrow floods our every waking moment, washes over us again and again. It is like being trapped under a waterfall. We struggle to come up for air. What's a man to do? We may lie awake in the darkness night after night in a sleepless stupor. We toss and turn, hoping for peace enough to sleep. I sometimes whisper to my dead son asking him to help me rest. Often it works. But not always.

Fortunately, a few other suggestions have helped. My wife gets out of bed and heads for her favorite reading chair, her latest non-death related book in hand. She reads until she falls asleep. I have resisted her tactic, but lately have tip-toed down the stairs to the comfort of my writing chair. I stay until my pen falls from my hand. And when I am trapped by thoughts of sorrow during daylight hours, I turn to exercise. Walking, biking, hiking, anything that forces me to move. Movement temporarily releases me from the weight of loss.

So, what works for you?

If my sorrow feels relentless, I will choose to _____ in the hope that this activity will bring me some peace. If not, I will seek advice from a trusted friend or professional counselor.

Believe that life is worth living, and your belief will help create the fact.

– William James

When we are in the throes of grief, we tend to filter out the beauty of this world and hands reaching out to lift us up. This is not usually a conscious choice. It is a normal part of the grieving process. Simply put, it is tough to celebrate anything after the death of a loved one.

Happiness? Where?

Our work now is to integrate our loss into our lives. This will take time, perseverance, resilience, and courage. Struggling through grief is a painful process. Our mind can absorb only so much bad news at a time. After the death of our son, I quickly concluded that I would never be happy again. In time I learned I was wrong, but that is how I felt immediately after losing him. Our minds filter out information contrary to our loss. The healing information is temporarily trapped. In time, though, small bits of joy, like an unexpected ray of sunshine, begin to reappear. At first we are surprised. But then we think, ah, yes, I remember you!

I am a resilient man. I will be open to signs of happiness in my life. In time, I will celebrate their return.

*I bid you awake at dawn and discover I have gone
my way and left you free.*

– Sara Teasdale

This may be the most difficult truth for us to accept about the death of a loved one. Now, we are free. Free from the responsibilities that love requires. Free from everyday worries and concerns. Free from judgment and criticism. Free from endless work. Free from expectations.

Free to take our lives in new directions.

After our son died, my wife and I had a heart-to-heart talk about what we wanted for each other after our own deaths. We both wanted the other to be free. Free to choose how and with whom, if anyone, to spend the rest of our lives. We gave each other permission to marry again, or not. We gave one another a blessing to choose a lifestyle that would work for the next stage of life. We both agreed that neither of us should have our hands tied by pre-death promises. In a capsule, we gave each other what may be love's greatest gift, the freedom to choose one's own way.

*I bid you awake at dawn and discover I have gone my way
and left you free. Thank you!*

Do not be daunted by the enormity of the world's grief. Do justly, now. Love mercy, now. Walk humbly, now. You are not obligated to complete the work, but neither are you free to abandon it.

– Rabbi Tarfon

This death may have shaken us to our core. Our life may be in a free-fall. Suddenly we may feel abandoned, living in a world we no longer recognize. Everything may appear sinister. Where will the next shoe drop?

On us?

Just for a moment, let us leave our fears and the world's problems on the kitchen table and walk into a sun-filled room. Too much anguish is too much. We can only handle our own burdens for now. The world's sorrows will have to wait. For today, let us... do justly... love mercy... and walk humbly. Perhaps there is a community issue this day to which our perspective may add an element of fairness. Or do we have smoldering anger toward someone we can choose to release today? Or can we swallow our pride and give in to a disagreement with a family member? Is there an unfinished project begging for our attention?

I will not be daunted by the world's grief, or my own for that matter. When I am ready, the world is waiting for my return.

*The excursion is the same when you go looking for
your sorrow as when you go looking for your joy.*

– Eudora Welty, *The Wide Net*

When we are suffering from the death of a loved one, many
of us would have a hard time admitting that the excursion
involved in grieving is the same as the journey to joy. We feel
entitled to our grief. After all, someone we love is dead.

How can both journeys be the same?

Well, we choose to grieve. And we also choose to search for joy.
The effort in either case is the same. Many people die every
day. From how many of those deaths do we suffer? We grieve
for those we know, the persons whom we love and with whom
we share a history. We cry over lost intimate moments. The
death of a stranger means little to us.

After we tire of grieving, perhaps we can turn our energies
back in the direction of joy. This will take no more effort than
what we have been spending in our sorrow. However, it will
require a conscious decision. Our loved one will understand.
In fact, this is what they desire: For us to grieve them and then
return to the land of the living. There will be time enough for
reunions when our own deaths occur. Until then, this is where
we belong.

*As soon as I am able, I will dip my toes back into my circle of
friendships. If I don't have any friends, I will look for one. The
land of the living is where I still belong.*

I like living. I have sometimes been wildly, despairingly, acutely, miserably, racked with sorrow, but through it all I still know quite certainly that just to be alive is a grand thing.

– Agatha Christie

Regardless of this painful death, we know with perfect clarity that we are still alive. This is a good thing. We still stand, breathe, eat, sleep, drink, make love, laugh, cry, work, enjoy friendships, appreciate the beauty of nature and of our pet asleep in our lap.

In spite of our loss, we still exist... just to be alive is a grand thing.

Yet, we may struggle with feelings of guilt for having outlived the one who is now gone. Perhaps we even feel that it is we who should be dead. How would our loved one view this? Isn't it possible he or she would rejoice in the fact that we still live and strive for the happiness we most likely share with them? Is it possible he or she would judge our guilty feelings as wasted time that could be better spent on laughter? And if the tables were reversed, what might our loved one be doing with his or her time in our absence?

I like living. Just to be alive is a grand thing. When I finish grieving, I will enjoy the time I have remaining. Who knows how long that will be?

Grief is like the ocean; it comes on waves ebbing and flowing. Sometimes the water is calm, and sometimes it is overwhelming. All we can do is learn to swim.

– Vicki Harrison

It may be hard for us to think about future anniversaries of the death of our loved one. Especially now, when our grief is so fresh and raw. Still, time waits for no man. In the years to come, if we are still alive, we will remember the day our loved one died. How could we forget?

Grief ebbs and flows. Sometimes it overwhelms.

In the cemetery where our son is buried, my wife and I have planted a Weeping Larch and a flower garden next to his headstone as a memorial. We visit often to care for the flowers, pick out weeds and dead leaves, and leave small reminders of our time together with him. Many of our visits are calm and relaxed; we laugh a lot and tell stories about his life. But some visits are difficult and brooding. Heavy. At times like these we tend to be quiet, do our work quickly, and leave without having said much at all. And we never know until we arrive how we will feel during the visit. Grief is like the ocean; it comes on waves ebbing and flowing. Who would have guessed grief could be like this?

Sometimes the water is calm, and sometimes it is overwhelming. All we can do is learn how to swim.

❧ JUNE ❧

JUNE 1

The body is only a garment. How many times have you changed your clothing in this life, yet because of this you would not say that you have changed. Similarly, when you give up this bodily dress at death you do not change. You are just the same, an immortal soul, a child of God.

– Paramahansa Yogananda

Many of us take great comfort in the words above. When a loved one dies, one of our great longings is that we will see our loved one again. Some of us even start the search right away. We look for the one we have lost in all the familiar places.

We call his or her name and hope beyond hope for a recognizable reply.

When our adopted son's father died, they made a father-son pact. His dad promised to get in touch with him after his death. He promised the contact would be familiar enough that his son would know it was him. His dad died several years ago, and I still ask him from time to time if he has heard anything from his dad. So far, his answer has always been "no." Then he smiles. Is this hope for life beyond death futile? Or are we humans incapable of understanding the communication of an immortal soul? The body is only a garment...when you give up this bodily dress at death you do not change.

I do not know if I will change after I die. I hope to be the same, an immortal soul, and a child of God. I also hope this for the one I have lost. This hope brings me great comfort.

JUNE 2

Though lovers be lost, love shall not. And death shall have no dominion.

– Dylan Thomas

Here is the most important thing that we can be sure of: the death of this loved one shall never diminish the love we still share. Throughout eternity, our love will prevail.

Out of sight will never be out of mind.

If this were not so, why do we feel the continuous presence of our loved one? From where does his or her voice come to us, spoken with the familiar clarity and forcefulness, with the certainty we were used to hearing? How do we hear the laughter and everyday gaiety? Why are we able to sense the sorrow? The excitement? The calm reassurance? How is it that from time to time we can feel the familiar touch? And, is it the wind that tosses our hair asunder when no branches in our sight are otherwise moving? Though lovers be lost, love shall not.

Of this I am certain: death has no dominion. If it were not so, someone would have told us.

JUNE 3

Goodbyes are not forever.
Goodbyes are not the end.
They simply mean I'll miss you
Until we meet again!

– Source Unknown

Death may feel like a permanent goodbye to most of us. Our hearts ache at the thought of no further communication with the one we love. And when we speak to our missing one, our voice falls onto the silence.

Goodbyes are not the end?

On the day our son died, he hugged and kissed my wife and me and told us he loved us. This had been a part of our "good-bye routine" since the days he became independent enough to leave our home without us. Always a hug. Always a kiss. Always an "I love you!" And always encouragement to drive carefully and stay safe in whatever activity was on the day's horizon. His promise to do so always followed. And, as he grew and learned to speak Spanish, I usually added, "Vaya con Dios, mi hijo." Go with God, my son. He always promised to do so.

And I believe that on that afternoon he did just that.

Goodbyes are not the end. I'll always remember the look on my son's face as he ran from the house that afternoon. His smile was full of excitement and adventure. Anticipation. A permanent goodbye for him was simply unimaginable. He drank life like a cold soda on a hot July afternoon. Reunion "later on" was a given. Perhaps his certainty can provide hope for those of us who wonder.

Dear _____, I'll miss you until we meet again. I am hopeful we will.

JUNE 4

If there are no dogs in Heaven, then when I die, I want to go where they went.

– Will Rogers

And why shouldn't dogs be in heaven? Who among us wants to leave this world thinking we may never see our friend and companion again? Many of us have loved and cared for a beloved dog (or cat) since we were boys. And perhaps the one we mourn this day has also left behind one or the other. We understand.

Unconditional love. This is what pets provide.

Most of us have heard stories about faithful dogs and cats. The chocolate Labrador retriever who sleeps for days next to his dead master's bedroom slippers. The calico cat that cries relentlessly and paces the floor waiting in vain for his missing master's return. Our fourteen year old Chihuahua, during visits to the cemetery where our son is buried, often walks back and forth over his grave, seemingly looking for her missing playmate. He loved to take the dog in his messenger bag on short motorcycle excursions. He positioned her deep in the bag so that only her head stuck out. Why shouldn't they be together again?

If there are no dogs (or cats) in heaven, then when I die, I too want to go where they went.

JUNE 5

The winter it is past, and the summer comes at last
And the small birds sing on ev'ry tree;
The hearts of these are glad, but mine is very sad,
For my love is parted from me.

– Robert Burns

Signs of summer surround us. Birds sing. Warm rain brings out the worms. Lilacs are in full bloom. Daffodils and tulips bow down to early June roses. The clean birdbath is ready for visitors. The sun warms our face. The car is washed and waxed.

But our hearts are still broken.

It is hard to greet the summer months with gusto when our thoughts are consumed by the death of our loved one. We may not even notice or care about the weather. We may still be numb, our vision focused only on our missing one. We may be examining our loss from a variety of angles in the vain hope that new insights may somehow change the past. They won't.

At a ceremony honoring loved ones who had died, I asked a bereaved father if the candle-lighting event and the reading of names got any easier with the passage of time. He shook his head no then, turned away. I had been hoping for a less painful answer. What I am learning, though, is that the sharp edges of the pain eventually begin to soften. We learn to live with the sorrow without it repeatedly bringing us to our knees. We learn to let go so we can live.

Dear _____, I'll always love you, but today I am letting you go. I smell the fresh-cut grass and have work to do in the yard. Thank you for understanding.

JUNE 6

I keep six honest serving men
(They taught me all I knew);
Their names are What and Why and When
And How and Where and Who.

– Rudyard Kipling

Even in the midst of our sorrow, one recurring thought may keep pushing into our consciousness, tapping us on the shoulder. What did I learn from the one I have lost?

The answer to this question will keep us company the rest of our days.

I'll always remember learning how to shave from my father, a barber most of his adult life. He taught me how to hold the razor, to never shave "against the grain" of my growing beard, and the best approach to each portion of my face. I hear his voice each morning as I lather up once again.

My mother taught me patience and perseverance. She taught me the value of an education and how to iron clothes. I learned how to make bread, can fruits and vegetables, and to stay up late if necessary to finish my homework. She made sure I always knew how much she loved me.

My son taught me to live a frugal existence, to not buy "things" that had already been made and could be purchased second-hand, to make tools from unexpected everyday objects, and to trust as many folks as possible. Usually his trust was returned and so has mine. He taught me how to laugh and to celebrate every moment of our holy existence.

Dear _____, one thing you taught me
that I will never forget is_____. Thank
you for being such an amazing teacher.

Prophets, apostles, preachers, martyrs, pioneers of knowledge, inspired artists in every art, ordinary men and the Man – God, all pay tribute to loneliness, to the life of silence, to the night.

– A. G. Sertillanges

The death of a loved one delivers us to the sounds of silence, the land of loneliness, and the numbness of night. Many of us would never come here willingly. But death respects no intentions. Here we are, ready or not.

And few of us are ever ready.

Upon reflection, though, we slowly come to realize that it is in these lands of solitude – loneliness, silence, and the darkness of night – that our growth is most possible. The stark loneliness that follows the death of our family member nudges many of us to reach out of our comfort zone for the support and love of others. New friendships may result.

And a story is told of a young man who slept for many years in a forest beside a bubbling brook. The townspeople thought he was crazy. One morning he awoke and began gathering stones that he proceeded to use for building the village a magnificent cathedral. Loneliness can be a springboard for creating community.

And how could we appreciate the glory of a sunrise if we had never experienced the silence of the night?... inspired artists in every art... pay tribute to... the night. The darkness that this death has brought on will one day be transformed into the light of a new day.

This death is my opportunity for transformation. I would never have chosen this to happen. Yet, here it is. This is my silence, my life. I will make the best of it.

JUNE 8

That's how we absorb the weight of each other's pain, through story. And once we do that, we each carry some of each other's burdens.

– Jonathan Olinger

When we gather at the funeral home for the service of our loved one, the first thing we do is tell stories about his or her life. And the stories abound. Stories from the beginning of life to this end. Stories of happiness and of sorrow. Mostly, though, stories of adventure, accomplishments, and joy. Stories define us.

Stories matter.

Stories prove our existence. That we lived and loved. That we had an impact on the world. And when we share those stories after a death, our grief is somehow lighter and easier to carry. It is proof that we share a common humanity.

A popular tradition at recent funerals is for the presiding minister to ask family and friends to share stories about the person who has died. Spouses, parents, children, grandchildren – all are welcome – and the stories they share are often poignant as well as humorous. Participants have the opportunity to laugh, cry, and sometimes howl with amazement at the life of the one they love, the life they have come to celebrate. The stories bring folks together into a common human bond. Here stories begin to heal our broken hearts.

When men come to funerals, we come to tell our stories. This tradition is not simply a diversion. It is a part of what defines us as human beings.

For nothing can be sole or whole that has not been rent.

— W. B. Yeats

At first the words of Yeats can be troubling. How can it be that a man cannot be "sole or whole" without being "rent?" The Oxford Dictionary defines the word "rent" as "...a large tear in a garment." That is what the death of someone we love does to us.

It tears us apart.

Suffering pries our hearts wide open so that we have more room for greater love and compassion. Not that we would have chosen this path to wisdom. Not at all. We may have even have thought we had the compassion thing down quite nicely, thank you. We were wrong. Suffering encourages us to pay better attention to the suffering of others.

At the funeral for the father of a young friend of mine, she pressed her head against me, hugged me tight, and sobbed. To this day, when I see her, we share hugs and hold on for an extra moment. We both understand. Nothing can be sole or whole that has not been rent. In each other we recognize a fellow suffering companion.

Though my heart may be torn in two, I will one day be made whole again.

JUNE 10

The work will teach you how to do it.

– Estonian proverb

We men may be surprised to learn how much work grief can be. And the work of grief is "on the job" training. We read stories about how other men have survived death, but each survivor had to find his own way. And we quickly learn grief itself can be our teacher.

There are signs to guide us.

Grief quickly teaches us that we need each other. Other grieving men and women surround us in a circle of love. Most are willing to share thoughts and ideas that helped them find their way. Grief drags us to the side of the road and points to the splendor of nature, to our pets that comfort us, to the scent of flowers, to the poetry of birds in flight, to the sound of the surf washing ashore, to the warm breeze that caresses our face, to the smell of a newborn baby, to our amazement that we still exist.

Grief teaches us that we will one day die. We may be surprised at this realization. Grief stirs up questions about what comes next. We search for rational answers that only have spiritual dimensions. We feel certain, then doubtful, and finally hopeful about where this existence leads. Grief teaches us to trust in the unknown destination. Grief teaches us to let go of the need to know.

I will let go and allow my grief to teach me how to survive this loss. I am not alone with my sorrow. I will allow other grievers to help me along my journey.

She thought of the other women at Chicken Little's funeral...What she had regarded since as unbecoming behavior seemed fitting to her now; they were screaming at the neck of God, his giant nape, the vast back-of-the-head that he had turned on them in death. But it seemed to her now it was not a fist shaking-grief they were keening but rather a simple obligation to say something, do something, feel something about the dead. They could not let that heart-smashing event pass unrecorded, unidentified.

– Toni Morrison, *Sula*

How do we let loose with our anger toward God, The Universe, or The Power into which we have placed our faith, after the death of a loved one? We may be filled with a rage that burns and sears our souls. Especially if the death was sudden, or if the one who is dead was young.

We may rightly feel cheated out of what we thought life had promised us.

But many men hold in their rage and present to the world a calm exterior. Perhaps we have even been complimented at how well we are grieving. Such feedback reinforces our decision to keep grief to ourselves. But let us remember why a "full life" for men is several years shorter than for women. We may be smiling on the outside and dying on the inside. Women let loose with their tears and rage. We guys hold them in to our detriment. "...they were screaming at the neck of God, his giant nape, the vast back-of-the-head that he had turned on them in death."

It is okay for men to scream at God, too. We do not have to let this heart-smashing event pass unrecorded, unidentified.

JUNE 12

If you want to understand the Creator, seek to understand created things.

— Columbanus

We want to know: Where has our loved one gone? And what kind of Creator would steal him or her away? We have heard some of the platitudes about God needing our beloved more than us. Many of us are outraged at the thought. Some are comforted. All may be perplexed.

God has gathered billions in the afterlife. Why would this Creator need my loved one?

Yet, this death may have brought relief to both sufferer and caretaker. If the suffering has been long and lingering, this death may be a gift. We may believe the hand of God has reached out to ease our pain. Sudden death, though, catches us off-guard, off-balance. So we wonder, who is this supreme being?

We do not know.

But we can look for hints in the wonder of creation. Consider the intricacies of our bodies, the form and functions of our anatomy and physiology. Look at your hands and feet. Peek into your eyes. Think of your heart and how it perfectly performs without attention from us. Consider the source of laughter and tears. The mystery of our souls. Watch a bird in flight, a puppy, a kitten, a worm traveling across the sidewalk. Look at seedpods falling from trees every spring without fail, clouds that quietly pass, lightening, warm wind, refreshing rain, ice, and sparkling snow. Trees! Consider the source of ideas, our desire to endlessly drink in the wonders of life. Think about our never ending quest for understanding.

If I want to understand the Creator, I must first seek to understand created things, especially the one I have lost.

JUNE 13

Love is the only thing we can carry with us when we go, and it makes the end so easy.

– Louisa May Alcott, *Little Women*
(Book Two: *Good Wives*)

We may be surprised at how easy it is to die. Here one minute, gone the next. Granted, many deaths are not easy at all. But sudden deaths are quick, suffering limited. "At least he didn't suffer long," we say.

It makes the end so easy... we hope.

Four male friends recently reflected on death and dying. One said, "Do you realize we are all one heartbeat away from everything we own belonging to someone else?" Two heads turned quickly in the direction of the speaker. "What do you mean?" one said. "I mean we come into the world naked and we will leave the world naked, except for a few pieces of going-away clothing. All of our money, toys, and every belonging will end up in someone else's hands. Everything gone, except, of course, the love you leave behind. What do you think about that?" A hush came over the four while the thought sank in. "That sucks, doesn't it," another said. Then, someone changed the topic to sports.

Love is the only thing we can carry with us (and leave behind) when we go, and it makes the end so easy. Clean. Simple. Uncomplicated.

I believe that in our constant search for security we can never gain any peace of mind until we secure our own soul.

— Margaret Chase Smith

There is nothing like the death of a loved one to shake our secure foundations and turn our thoughts inward. We thought we had life figured out. We had a plan and were sticking to it. We did not count on death stepping in to toss our plans aside like so much debris.

Everything is different now.

On our last hospital visit to see my dying uncle, he looked up at my father, his brother, and whispered, "You're in charge now." The two of them had been talking of financial matters, but my uncle's tone of voice made it clear that he was also speaking of the big picture. His impending death. Soul stuff. Peace of mind.

This death gives us an opportunity to examine our own lives to see if we are living with integrity. Not as judged by anyone else or a faith system but as judged by ourselves. We are our ultimate judge. Are we living according to our professed principles or are we shaving corners and justifying the means for the end? These are tough questions. But this is our one, precious existence. It will never be repeated.

This is my precious life. From this day forward, I will work on my own peace of mind.

JUNE 15

I postpone death by living, by suffering, by error, by risking, by giving, by loving.

– Anais Nin

Some of us may be dead on our feet. And the death of our loved one is a wake-up call. This death may be an once-in-a-lifetime chance for our own resurrection. A second chance at life.

An unexpected gift.

So today we may want to consider breaking out into a new world of joyful living, fearless suffering, embraced errors, real risk-taking, generous giving, and long-lasting loving. Why not? How much time do we think we have left to live? Are there any guarantees we will live that long? Perhaps we have existed in life's shadows, living on the fringe, safe and secure, every detail planned, no deviations, with spontaneity long gone. Bored to almost-death. We may be able to postpone our death by living our lives to their utmost. What do we have to lose by trying?

We may all know men who started over after a major life crisis. They changed the way they dressed, took dancing lessons, bought a new car, started traveling, and did not wait for someone else to invite them over. Instead, they offered the invitations. And some even fell in love again. Why not?

The old saying, "If the shoe fits, wear it," may apply to me. If so, today I will step out from one of my old habits and into the waiting world. Who knows what pleasant surprises I may encounter?

JUNE 16

For loneliness is but cutting adrift from our moorings and floating out to the open sea; an opportunity for finding ourselves, our real selves, what we are about, where we are heading during our little time on this beautiful earth.

– Anne Shannon Monroe

Perhaps loneliness is our biggest enemy when we are suffering the loss of a loved one. We look for the one who is dead and find we are alone. The telephone is silent on the usual day for calls. Our hearts may ache for the comfortable sound of the missing voice. We miss the latest reports, the updates on life adventures.

We feel adrift on the open sea.

We miss having someone to tell our stories to, as well. We long to talk of the flowers blooming in the garden, the song of the red-breasted grosbeak in the sugar maple tree, the smell of the bread baking in the oven, the laughter of people passing by on the street, the latest news of the pregnancy, the plans for travel, the weather, the first steps of our friend's grandson, how fast time flies.

Yet, loneliness is... an opportunity for finding ourselves, our real selves, what we are about, where we are heading during our little time on this beautiful earth. Shall we seize this moment and reach out to someone who has reached for us?

This is my life. I will not live it again. What else would I like to do before I die? When will I begin?

*It is a curious thing, the death of a loved one. We
all know that our time in this world is limited, and
that eventually all of us will end up underneath
some sheet, never to wake up. And yet it is always
a surprise when it happens to someone we know. It
is like walking up the stairs to your bedroom in the
dark, and thinking there is one more stair than there
is. Your foot falls down, through the air, and there
is a sickly moment of dark surprise as you try and
readjust the way you thought of things.*

– Lemony Snicket, *Horseradish:
Bitter Truths You Can't Avoid*

Curious is most likely not the word we would use to describe
the death of a loved one. Horrible. Terrible. Unimaginable.
Devastating. Rotten. Tragic. These and many more. Some are
not pretty at all.

Yet, curious may be the best descriptive word.

After all, we are taken by surprise... when it happens to someone we know, even if the death follows a long sickness. Or we
are taken off-guard because he is a friend. One friend in his
mid-sixties, an avid runner in our small community and one
of the top ten in his age group in the nation, dies after running
sprints to celebrate his latest birthday. No one could have predicted that a man in such fine physical condition would col-
lapse and die. It is like walking up the stairs to your bedroom
in the dark, and thinking there is one more stair than there is.

I have to readjust the way I thought of things. Everything.

Every morning has two handles. We can take hold of it with the handle of anxiety or the handle of faith.

— Henry Ward Beecher

The death of a loved one rattles our faith in a world we thought was predictable. We did not plan for this. Death is almost always over the horizon, somewhere in the distant future. Certainly not now. Especially if this death was sudden.

God should have given us a warning.

Yet some of us live our lives looking for sorrow, pain, and heartache. We're not happy without it. And we are seldom disappointed. Our world is full of trouble and despair. But we have learned to filter out good news and only allow the bad stuff to get inside us. No wonder we suffer. Perhaps we are men who tend to see life this way and this death is really hard on us. We may see it as a realization of our view of the world, but take heart. Our view can change! There is a story about a man who always greeted each new day by looking out on the world through the same front window of his house. He never varied his routine. One day his wife called him to the window next to her chair instead to watch a blue bird preening itself on the feeder. He was surprised to see such beauty through her window rather than his accustomed morning view of the street.

This death gives us a chance to look at life from a new angle. Will I take advantage of this opportunity?

I can take hold of each day with the handle of anxiety or the handle of faith. Today, I hope to choose the handle of faith.

Participate joyfully in the sorrows of the world. We cannot cure the world of sorrows, but we can choose to live in joy.

– Joseph Campbell, *The Hero's Journey (On Living in the World)*

Participate joyfully? Well, not yet. Not today at least. But, perhaps down the road, when our crushing anguish over the loss of our loved one has eased up a bit, maybe then. Campbell suggests that we fully embrace our sorrow and walk as gracefully as possible, with the help of family and friends, through the valley of tears. But when healing eventually comes, and it will, we can choose to live the rest of our days in joy.

Isn't this what our loved one would want?

On a recent visit to a local furniture store, one of the sales people said to me, "Cliff, we think about you and Jane every day. There isn't a day that goes by without both of you being on our minds." Her smile melts hearts. You have to love small town America. Many folks know us and knew our son. They are seldom afraid to mention his name and our loss. We love them for that. Yet, it was the look in her eyes that spoke to my heart. You see, when we walk into local establishments, we greet the owners with a joyful countenance. Yes, our son is dead. No, we are not. We are choosing to live our lives in joy despite his death. We have no doubt he would want us to live this way.

Dear _____, thank you for showing me how to live in joy.

JUNE 20

Losing people you love affects you. It is buried inside of you and becomes this big, deep hole of ache. It doesn't magically go away, even when you stop officially mourning.

– Carrie Jones, *Captivate*

In the early days of our loss we may feel like we are living in a big, deep hole of ache. It may seem there is no way out. We may yell and throw things and say we don't care. But, of course, we do. We care so much we sometimes want to die.

That is the devastation wrought by the death of our loved one.

We wander in the maze of grief, wondering if we are grieving correctly, as if that is something someone can measure. It cannot. We try to keep our old composure, the before us, even though we are the after us. Nothing looks familiar. We have no compass to guide us in this new land. We look for help. Thank goodness there are those who adopt us into the family of grievers. For a while, they take over day-to-day work so we can rest, sleep, or simply wander. They know. They understand. We are amazed we didn't recognize them before.

I have lost someone I love. At first I wanted to die. Now I want to live. Eventually I hope to heal.

JUNE 21

When he shall die,
Take him and cut him out in little stars,
And he will make the face of heaven so fine
That all the world will be in love with night
And pay no worship to the garish sun.

– William Shakespeare,
Romeo and Juliet

We pay homage to our dead by imagining where they are or what they have turned into. Are they now in the heavens and have they turned into stars? Is our mind playing tricks on us? Is this imaging a normal part of the grieving process? Most likely. If Shakespeare did it, we can do it.

And what harm is there to think this way? None at all.

This short excerpt from Romeo and Juliet beautifully captures eternal love... he (or she)will make the face of heaven so fine that all the world will be in love with night and pay no homage to the garish sun. How we struggle for words to express our love for a departed family member or friend. We wish them well and want to praise their lives, that they lived and loved and laughed. To imagine a loved one... cut out in little stars... so that he or she will add so much beauty to the night sky that the sun becomes inconsequential, well, that's love enough for the ages.

What more can we say in gratitude for a life well loved? He or she will make the face of heaven fine. Indeed!

Each night, when I go to sleep, I die. And the next morning, when I wake up, I am reborn.

– Mohandas K. Gandhi

Gandhi's thoughts on death and rebirth are not the way we usually think. Perhaps we have never given much thought to where we go when we fall asleep. Maybe we do "die" in some sense of the word, especially if dying simply means becoming unconscious. Do we also temporarily "die" when we are sedated for surgery? Perhaps.

Yet Gandhi's observation was intended to ease fears of death and to celebrate life. Being reborn in this context means we have another chance to participate in the land of the living. If we do not fear sleep, why should we fear death? Both take us to a new world. A world, apparently, that tenderly holds us in its infinite arms. Sounds cozy to me and certainly nothing to be afraid of.

I am afraid of the unknown, but I am not afraid to fall asleep each night. Perhaps I can think about sleep as a kind of death. If so, my fear of dying may possibly diminish. I would like that.

To live in hearts we leave behind is not to die.

– Thomas Campbell

Many of us men do not usually think the way Campbell suggests. When we think of dying and leaving a legacy, we think in terms of something physical or monetary, not something stored in hearts. Yet, which is more important?

Only we can decide.

A neighborhood friend, before his own death, often reminisced about his deceased father. He liked to start his stories by saying, "Pops used to say...." Then he would launch into words of wisdom he had picked up from his dad earlier in his life. He loved his father. Clearly his father lived in his heart.

And often when I think of my own dead father, I picture myself sitting in the barbershop chair that he set up in the basement of our family home after his final retirement from cutting hair for more than sixty years. (He cut my hair until just a few days before his death.) I hear him asking me questions, taking an active interest in the lives of my wife and children: "How's the family? The children okay? Do they like school? Is Jane happy with her job? Does she like being a mother? Being a parent is a lot of work, huh?" And, then, "What about your job? Is your work fulfilling? Do they treat you right? Are you being fairly paid?"

Maybe everyone we love, living and dead, lives in our heart.

I am grateful to learn that I will live in hearts I leave behind. I will not die.

JUNE 24

Our sweetest songs are those that tell of saddest thought.

— Percy Bysshe Shelley

What is there about sorrow that calls us broken-hearted men to music? Why do sweet melodies soothe troubled spirits? What is the healing magic in a soul-soothing song? And why will we listen to a particularly poignant song over and over again?

Doing so may bring us comfort.

Another possibility is that music gives us hope in the midst of despair. At times we drink in lyrics. At other times it is the music itself, the instrumentation, that we seek. The melody pulls out our sorrow so we can examine it safely, without prying eyes watching us grieve. Our sweetest songs are those that tell of saddest thought.

There are sad moments when I purposely play a song I know may bring tears to my eyes. It is almost like I need confirmation of my sorrow. In the first few days following my son's death, his brother-in-law gave us music recorded by Mumford and Sons. The lead song, *Cry No More*, has brought me unimaginable peace. I have listened to it countless times. In contrast, my spouse finds it painful to listen to the song at all. All of us mourn in our own fashion. There is no formula, no right or wrong. There is only each of us men and what brings us relief... our sweetest songs.

What music brings me sweet relief?

Clouds come flooding into my life, no longer to carry pain or usher storm, but to add color to my sunset sky.
                                    – Rabindranath Tagore

Not now, perhaps, but in time Tagore's words may comfort our despairing souls. Now we may be huddled in the heart of darkness. Then, we may be ready again to lift our eyes toward the light.

It is good to remember there is still light.

Now, we may see no passageway through this tunnel of trouble. Then, the road ahead may be illuminated. Now, we may see no reason for living. Then, we may see no reason for dying. Now, clouds bring storms, crashing and smashing down upon us. Then, clouds will come flooding into our lives, no longer to carry pain or usher storm, but to add color to our sunset sky.

In the early stages of building the house our son designed for us just before his death, dark clouds appeared over the northwestern sky. We had stacked above the ground large Styrofoam blocks for our poured concrete basement walls. They were ready to be installed in the hole that would become our basement. Our son did not like concrete. In short order, heavy gusts of wind and rain sent our blocks end over end, spreading them across three vacant lots and into the street. I tried in vain to run and catch the flying pieces to minimize damage. My friends took cover. Later we laughed at the incident and proclaimed that our son had sent the storm as retribution for not following his plans exactly.

Clouds carry both darkness and light. I am looking forward to eventually adding color to my sunset sky.

JUNE 26

*Who will tell whether one happy moment of love
or the joy of breathing or walking on a bright
morning and smelling the fresh air, is not worth
all the suffering and effort which life implies...*

– Erich Fromm

How much joy do we need to say that life has been worthwhile?
We joke about reading the obituaries. We want to see if our
name is there, we say. We look for each dead person's age to
compare it to our own. How much time do we have left, we
wonder? We may seldom ask ourselves, "What do I want to do
with the time I have left?"

There is no need to worry, guys. One day all our names will
appear in the obituaries. Guaranteed. Just not yet, we hope.
Today's heartache is enough.

Do we judge life worthwhile based upon the number of years
we live? Does quantity of years trump quality of years? Who
will tell whether one happy moment of love is enough? For ten
years a high school friend has sat motionless in a wheelchair in
the living room of his home. He is breathing but cannot per-
form the most basic of human self-care functions. Recently, he
has been hospitalized in the intensive care unit of his local hospital and has had a tracheotomy to allow the continuation of
his breathing. He will likely die in the near future. His wife has
been his caregiver. She thanks my brother, her neighbor, for
years of conversation and stories that often made them laugh.
"Not many people visit us," she said.

*Is the joy of breathing or walking on a bright morning and
smelling the fresh air worth all the suffering and effort life
implies? We each have the power to decide.*

*Friendship improves happiness and abates
misery, by the doubling of our joy and the
dividing of our sorrow.*

– Marcus Tullius Cicero

Sharing sorrow may seem strange to us. We have been taught to be brave and strong, to stand on our own two feet. Yet the women we love have much to teach us if we let them. Creating a community of grievers is a feminine skill men can learn. Why not? This skill may save our lives.

Perhaps simple friendship is the answer. Friendship improves happiness and abates misery.

Our male intuition has always told us this, but we may be guilty of not paying attention. But today is a new day. The death of our loved one provides an opportunity to grow closer to male friends, men who show up, men who have walked beside us through joy and sorrow, men who do not judge or criticize us. Men who care about us.

Cicero wrote the above words nearly two thousand years ago. They have stood the test of time. So, perhaps this wisdom is for us as well. Today. Half as much sorrow? Twice the joy? Where do we sign up? With our closest friend.

I will reach out to one friend today. Perhaps he has been waiting for a sign of friendship from me.

JUNE 28

The richness of life cannot be found in the deep recesses of the hillside. We have to find a way to emerge from the cave, perhaps with the thick skins that only scars can provide.

— Kim Johancen-Walt

Hiding somewhere may be our first inclination after the death of someone we love. Running away seems logical.

Many of us do.

Alcohol, drugs, sex, food, toys, travel, you name it. We do it. But when we try to stuff our pain deep down inside, we end up hiking in circles and carrying a backpack full of grief. If we choose to not face our sorrow head on, we will return from our wandering ways to the trail head. And, our broken hearts will be waiting there for us.

My brother chose to wait in the visitor's room while our father was dying. He could not face the pain of his dad's death. Is it possible that his death years later came early, partially as a result of unresolved grief? And stories of spouses dying close together, sometimes on the same day, are often in the news. Coincidental? Death may be the ultimate hiding place from grief. Yet, family, friends, professional counselors, social workers, pets, and lifestyle changes have also helped grief-stricken men. They can help us, too.

We will find a way to emerge from the cave, perhaps with the thick skins that only scars can provide. Our healed wounds may eventually help us heal others' wounds, too.

So whatever you do, don't shut off your pain;
accept your pain and remain vulnerable. However
desperate you become, accept your pain as it is,
because it is in fact trying to hand you a priceless
gift: the chance of discovering, through spiritual
practice, what lies behind sorrow...If you keep
your heart open through everything, your pain can
become your greatest ally in your life's search for
love and wisdom.

– Sogyal Rinpoche

Pain as an ally? In the face of the death of someone we love? Well, possibly. Perhaps not now. Not tomorrow. But, down the road a distance?

Life is full of mystery.

One of the things I have learned since my son's death is to walk into others sorrow without hesitation. I have suffered the ultimate loss, the death of a child. There is no greater loss for me to endure. I now have no fear of wading into the morass of grief that death brings to all. So don't shut off your pain. It is in fact trying to hand you a priceless gift: the chance of discovering, through spiritual practice, what lies behind sorrow. Our loss somehow gives us strength. And our strength can be a guiding light to others.

Regardless of our spiritual practice, accepting the mystery of the great unknown, with our countless questions, may be our ultimate human challenge. A renewed or new spiritual practice may help us through our tears. We are searching for love and wisdom in the midst of our grief. Our search may provide both. Perhaps the journey itself is our spiritual practice, our ultimate destination.

I will not shut off my pain. I will accept it and remain vulnerable because I want to learn what lies behind my sorrow. I want a spiritual life that makes sense to me, one full of love and wisdom.

JUNE 30

I think of death as some delightful journey that I shall take when all my tasks are done.

– Ella Wheeler Wilcox

Can we think of this death in such a fashion? A delightful journey at the end of a lot of work? Perhaps. If our loved one lived a long life, it is easy to imagine such an ending. But if our lost one was young with a full life ahead, such a thought can be disturbing. We may rightly feel that the death was "out of order." A horrendous horror.

Still, all life is a journey with an end.

My wife's eighty-seven year old grandmother was cleaning freshly picked strawberries from her garden at the kitchen sink when she collapsed and died. Perhaps we can only hope for such an end to our days. And my uncle was sweeping a fresh supply of light snowfall from the front walk when he had a heart attack. When my older brother found him, his eyes were open in surprise, and he still held the broom in his cold hands. But when another brother's granddaughter died at the age of seven from a stomach tumor that refused treatment, well, her death shattered all hopes and dreams for a delightful journey for her.

We have hopes for how each person's story should go, but we have to see the story as it is. A seven year old girl dies, and that does not fit our narrative of lives, but has it another wisdom? Are there as many life paths as stars in the sky?

Dear _____, I hope you felt that your death was ending a delightful journey and that your tasks were done. If this was not possible, I hope your death was as gentle, swift, and pain-free as possible.

❧ JULY ❧

Grace strikes us when we are in great pain and restlessness. It strikes us when we walk through the dark valley of a meaningless and empty life.

– Paul Tillich

Men usually do not think much about grace. Until a loved one dies. After someone we love dies, a window into our soul opens temporarily and we may see some part of our life that feels meaningless and empty. Grace is a life-preserver thrown to us just when we feel that we cannot swim alone any further through the waves of pain.

Grace is not something we earn. Grace is a gift freely given. Freely offered.

Two organizations that are full of grace for us grieving men include the National Widowers' Organization if we have lost a spouse or partner and The Compassionate Friends if our child has died. There is something miraculous and healing about walking into a room full of grieving men who know how you feel without you having to speak one word. Where else can we find unconditional acceptance, love, and friendship in the midst of our tears?

Grace is a gift we do not have to give back. No one in these organizations needs or wants anything from us. Simply put, they understand our pain when we think no one else possibly could. That is the gift. That is the grace. Understanding. Our hunger for grace is a hunger for a free gift at a moment when we feel we have nothing left to give.

Has grace knocked at my door without me recognizing him or her? Who brought that last bowl of salad, the blueberry crisp, the platter of fried chicken? Who asked me to go to the children's play at the middle school? Who offered to help wash windows? Cut the grass? Come over for a barbecue?

JULY 2

To you, wherever you are and in whatever condition, I send thanks for all your faith and courage, for all your help and encouragement, for all that strength of character that conquered your fears and that clearness of mind that could tell a cruel deed in spite of all its wrapping in noble words.

– Alan Patton

Saying "thank you" to our departed loved one takes a lot of courage. But when we consider the gifts this person left behind to help us live the rest of our lives, don't we have much to be grateful for?

What can we thank our beloved departed spouse for? Clean laundry, countless meals, apple pies, raspberry jam, yeasted waffles, baked chicken with mashed potatoes and gravy, a listening ear, endless hugs, sensitive sex, children, faithful friendship, encouragement, shared laughter and tears?

What shall we thank a lost child for? Teaching us how to be brave, nudging us out of our comfort zone, challenging our values and encouraging us to live by them, expressing love for us in countless ways, weekly calls, birthday cards, backrubs, cuddling, holding our hands, hugs and kisses?

And what shall we thank a special relative or friend for? Unconditional love?

Each one of us will have a unique list. It is important that we write it down. Some of us may want to deliver it to the cemetery, crypt, or mausoleum. There is no "right" or "wrong" way to do this. Just our way.

How can I say "thank you" to my departed loved one today?

JULY 3

I believe that imagination is stronger than knowledge. That myth is more potent than history. That dreams are more powerful than facts. That hope always triumphs over experience. That laughter is the only cure for grief. And I believe that love is stronger than death.

— Robert Fulghum

Fulghum's words paint a tricky picture for we who have lost a loved one, especially a child. Do we describe the loss using the present tense "I have a son who died." Or do we use the past tense "I had a son who died." Which is correct?

Perhaps both.

What means more to us now, after the death of the one we love, imagination or knowledge? Does myth influence the story of our loss more than history? Do dreams rule our days and facts rule our nights? And how do we hope in the face of this immeasurable loss? Will we laugh again? Is love everlasting or does death snuff it out? How we answer these and endless more questions will influence our choice of verb tense. Ultimately, it is our call. This is our life. This is our loss.

I believe that love is stronger than death.

JULY 4

Whether we are born high or low...the same things come to us all.
— Valiska Gregory

It doesn't matter if the casket is a simple pine box or a jewel-encrusted work of art; we all end up in the same place. A walk through any cemetery will remind us that we differ in the style in which we leave the world, but the substance of our departure is identical. Remember, man, thou art dust.

We all eventually die. There are no exceptions.

What we can choose is how we wish to live. Yes, we have choices. Are we living lives in line with our values? Our beloved one has departed. His or her opportunities to choose are over. However, even through our tears, we can see that we still have time to make adjustments.

Death awaits all of us, men and women, rich and poor. The same things come to us all. None are immune. But choices about how to live? Ah, yes, I still have time to choose.

JULY 5

Speak, move, act in peace, as if you were in prayer. In truth, this is prayer.

– Francois Fenelon

Spoken prayer may be our last resort after suffering the death of a loved one. When we can think of nothing else to do, we might turn to prayers we learned as little boys. We may have already discovered that some bring us relief from suffering.

I remember the opening verse of this prayer from my childhood, "Now I lay me down to sleep, I pray the Lord my soul to keep..."

Perhaps we were taught that prayer must be spoken. In fact, prayer can be any human activity that is directed toward the divine. This news may bring relief to our troubled soul. Many of us may have been praying all along and did not know it. That still, small voice we hear within us may be a voice of action prayer, doing rather than speaking. This is good news. A beloved hobby, well attended, can be a form of prayer. Think of woodworking, gardening, camping, hunting, fishing, running, walking, biking, kayaking, writing, or any other activity that stirs our hearts into action.

When I was a child, my Catholic priest uncle would leave the dinner table after the meal to say "compline," evening prayers for members of the clergy. He always walked when he said his prayers. He was into action prayer a long time ago. And the daily practice brought him peace. He was a man who brought joy and laughter into our home with every visit. I loved that man.

I may or may not know much about prayer. But this I do know: I know how to walk and talk and think about the divine. I am pleased to know this is also prayer.

JULY 6

Every man casts a shadow; not his body only, but his mingled spirit. This is his grief. Let him turn which way he will, it falls opposite to the sun; short at noon, long at eve. Did you never see it?

– Henry David Thoreau

Perhaps we can work our way through the days better than through the nights. The daylight hours bring us routines. We know where we need to be, what we will be doing, and how to function as competent men. The black nights are different.

"I'm okay at work," a sorrowful father and husband declares, "It's when I go home that I struggle."

And so it goes. Let him turn which way he will, (shadows) fall opposite to the sun. Grievers may be surprised to learn they often need to comfort those who struggle to comfort them. Who would have guessed? After all, it is we who suffer. Yet words often fail our would-be supporters, so they error by saying nothing. Perhaps we have all done this in the past. So to ease an awkward situation, we offer words of comfort to them.

But waking in the night we are alone to ruminate and suffer anew. This may be the time to slip out of the bedroom and put pen to paper. Or call a friend who understands. Or turn on soft music. Or pick up a helpful book. Do something to soothe our mingled spirit. Step out of our grief and into the sun. Just for a moment or two. The sun is shining when we look for it. Even at night.

In spite of my shadow, I will still choose to face the sun.

...growing up means to live with unsatisfying and incomplete endings, with people whose lives are cut off before they should be, or spin out in unexpected directions and sometimes crash in flames. No matter how ordinary they are, all our lives end with a kind of question mark as we reach the threshold of the final mystery.

– Harvey Cox

Certainly woven into the fabric of our grief are unsatisfying and incomplete endings. This may surprise us men who are used to tidy conclusions. Death is seldom tidy. Death often forces us to contemplate a future full of many questions and few answers.

Suicide survivors are painfully aware of this searing sorrow. When a loved one chooses to end his or her earthly existence, unfinished business abounds. Those of us left behind, however, might never describe their "survivor" status as being a part of growing up. And yet growing up is what we all do when a loved one takes his or her life. We grow in our willingness to embrace the questions. We grow in our ability and willingness to accept inexplicable happenings. We grow in our realization that our lives are time limited. None of us live forever. We grow in our acceptance that life is not, never has been, and never will be, fair. And we celebrate that in spite of this death, we still live, love, and laugh. This death was not our choice. We choose life.

I choose to live even if my loved one chose to die. And my love for _____ is eternal regardless of the circumstances of his or her death.

JULY 8

Dye mon, gen mon (Beyond the mountain is another mountain).

– Haitian Proverb

Death is a mountain we all have to climb. Sooner or later, while we camp in the foothills, we know full well that our final morning trek will come with a future sunrise. Who knows when? In the meantime, our "practice hikes" are grieving the deaths of those who travel before us. Many of us have had a lot of practice. Others may be newly initiated into this band of grievers.

We all climb together.

There will be other mountains to cross before we return to some semblance of happiness. Sorrow, loneliness, anger, depression, a sense of abandonment, fear, and frustration are some of our obstacles. We can climb only one at a time. Perhaps we may come to see that the journey out of grief is more important than the destination we have in mind. The journey is all we have to handle. The destination will reveal itself in time.

We do the work of grief one step after another, accepting help from family, friends, and fellow travelers along the way. We accept life's consequences, but do not forget to look for flowers along the trail.

I know this death will not be my last mountain, but I refuse to turn around on life's trail. I have learned much about grief, and have much to learn. Perhaps I will be the teacher one day.

JULY 9

The balloon looked happy,
Waving
Goodbye.
> – Laurel Blossom

After the death of a loved one, we look for him or her everywhere. Like looking for a runaway balloon, we look for our missing beloved. Maybe we'll look forever.

Does hope ever die?

A friend out for a bicycle ride sees me working in the yard and stops to chat. "How are you?" he asks. I am used to this question since my son's death. I try to determine if he really wants to know. He does. "No," he says, "How are you, really?" "Well," I say, "I wake up every morning searching for my missing son. It makes no sense, but I still do it." "Of course you do. Of course you do," he whispers back. His eyes fill with tears.

This is my hope. That my loved one was happy waving goodbye.

JULY 10

Time is too slow for those who wait,
too swift for those who fear,
too long for those who grieve,
too short for those who rejoice.
But for those who love,
time is eternity.

– Henry VanDyke

Perhaps we have secretly sensed that love is the only thing that outlasts eternity. Today we may know this truth completely. There is no need anymore to hide thoughts about what comes next or when. None of us knows.

Just in time, huh? Time is... too swift for those who fear...

The things of this world may encumber us until we admit to ourselves that we will die and have to leave them all behind. Then we begin to hold them more loosely, knowing that one day we will release our grip completely. It is hard work to say goodbye to people and possessions that have brought us pleasure or peace. But death, the great teacher, helps us recognize that time is our most valuable possession, and... too short for those who rejoice. This may be where the phrase, "Time flies!" comes from. We want the good times to last indefinitely. Who wouldn't?

And we would take a pass on the sorrowful times. A loved one suffers from cancer or a parent has succumbed to Alzheimer's, both struggling with no end in sight. Because of their suffering we may pray for a quick death. Still, time marches on. Time is too slow for those who wait... too long for those who grieve.

Still, "letting go" of time never stops love. Ever.

...for those who love, time is eternity. What time is it? Time to love.

Flowers grow out of dark moments.

– Corita Kent

Sometimes we fixate on a particular moment of our loss. We choose one horrific detail and paste that picture in our mind so we can look at it repeatedly. This is not helpful in the grieving process. We can get stuck back there.

Talking with a mental health professional may be beneficial.

In the counseling process I learned how to replace a troubling image with one of serenity and peace. Now whenever the agonizing image reappears, I "turn the page" to the picture of my dead son as a little boy curled up with a sleeping white-tailed fawn. Both are napping in the shade of a sugar maple tree growing along the banks of a river near our home where he played as a child and later as an adult. He loved the out-of-doors and often slept under the stars. The two of them are nestled together, a perfect pair, without a care in the world.

Flowers can grow out of dark moments. My loved one wants to be joyfully remembered.

I drink not from mere joy in wine nor to scoff at faith – no, only to forget myself for a moment, that only do I want of intoxication.

– Omar Khayyam

Losing ourselves in drink is a danger for us. To drink to forget ourselves for a moment, to forget our loss. We know drinking can lead to more misery. One drink can easily turn into two, then three, or more. Then, we slip into oblivion.

Drinking to intoxication is not helpful in the grieving process. It is a detour that can take us back to the beginning. Repeatedly.

And who wants to start over? One loss is more than enough for now. We may need family and friends to help keep an eye on our behavior if it seems to be turning self-destructive. My temptation is to drink to a level of numbness. Still, the psychic pain, the overwhelming sense of loss, remains even while I dwell in the fog of alcohol. Self-medication changes nothing. Calling a friend to talk is more helpful.

To lose our ability to think clearly is also to lose our ability to grieve completely. This is a temptation we cannot afford if we want to live the rest of our days honoring the one we have lost.

I drink not from mere joy in wine nor to scoff at faith – no, only to forget myself for a moment... and only a moment.

*It is unwise, because it is untrue, to idealize the
dead... we will spend a lot of needed energy
keeping that illusion in place and we will not
honor the vigor and truth of the [one] who has
died... the myth of perfection is hard to maintain.
We do not need it. We can give it over – to God, if
you will. Leave it there. The [person] as he or she
was, was God's child, acceptable, loved, all right.
And so are we.*

– Martha Whitmore Hickman

In the early days following our loss, we men may be inclined
to go to one extreme or another in describing our lost love. In
truth, and we have no time for falsehoods, we are all divine and
human.

Let he who is without sin cast the first stone.

At the funeral service for my son, I tried my best to describe
him as I would want to be remembered, as a real man, warts
and all. Perhaps this is the way all of us want to be remembered. I described him as an adventurer in love with life. I told
how he did his best to create community wherever he roamed,
how young and old enjoyed his companionship. I said he was
intolerant of falsehood, a naturalist in every sense of the word,
and that he loved his wife and they looked forward to teaching
their children to love.

Perfection is an illusion. Our energy is better spent by embracing our loss and seeking the wisdom that is sorrow's gift.
Everything else... we can give it over – to God, if you will...
leave it there.

*The one I mourn was God's child, acceptable, loved, all right.
And so am I.*

JULY 14

When you pass through the waters I will
*   be with you;*
And through the rivers, they shall not
*   overwhelm you;*
When you walk through fire you shall not
*   be burned,*
And the flame shall not consume you.

– Isaiah 43:2 (NIV)

These comforting words may encourage us to believe we have special protection from the world's dangers. We know this is not true. Bad things happen to good people. Including us.

Even good folks suffer and die.

When we lose those we love, we may push away from our childhood vision of who and what God is. The Wizard of Oz God, pulling the ropes and rattling the sheet metal thunder behind the screen, is hard to believe. If we accept Isaiah's words literally, then no harm would befall anyone, ever. But we know everyone eventually suffers. This is the way of life. The law of the universe.

So we accept Isaiah's words as a comfort not a cure for our grief. We drink these words as balm for our aching hearts. We believe them for what they are. Soul food.

I am walking through the waters, rivers, and fires of hell, but know I shall not be consumed. For God is with me.

He did not say you will not be troubled, you will not be belabored, you will not be disquieted; but he said: You will not be overcome.

– Julian of Norwich

Being overcome in the face of the death of a loved one may be our biggest fear. After all, we are used to being in charge, being in control. But grief is hard to grasp, almost impossible to manage alone. We feel it, but cannot direct its path.

We are often disquieted, whether we admit it or not.

When another loved one dies, memories of earlier losses swirl through our thoughts, bringing back images of old pains and sorrows. For the same reason we sometimes cry at weddings, we often cry at funerals. Both take us back there to see and touch tender spots that have been in hiding for years. Our tears are for the present moment and also for the fact that we have been discovered. Sometimes we are embarrassed. But remember, a crying man is also a strong man.

What does it mean to not be overcome? It means we summon the strength and courage to ask for help working through our grief. It means when we feel the least capable of making it down this tough road, we accept the hands reaching out to us. It means we reach back to those trying to figure out how to help us. Not being overcome means we accept our new status as healers for others. It means our role as grievers is temporary, and life awaits our return.

I will not be overcome.

*For now we see in a mirror dimly, but then we shall
see face to face. Now, I only know in part; then I
will know fully, even as I have been fully known.
And now faith, hope, and love abide, these three:
and the greatest of these is love.*

— 1 Corinthians 13: 12-13 (NIV)

Death is the great mystery destination. How little we men
know of it! It is no wonder we grieve when a loved one dies.
Much has been written about death, but only by those who are
living. And what are we to make of those who claim to have
crossed through death's door and returned?

What are we to make of their declarations?

Most faith traditions argue in favor of the existence of an afterlife. Before my aunt died, she told of her anticipation of meeting God face-to-face and living happily ever after in paradise.
Her face often glowed as she spoke. She claimed to know with
certainty that an afterlife awaited her.

Still many are not convinced. This life is it, they say; there is
nothing after we are gone. These folks are busy packing as
much living as possible into the here and now. They seem
unconcerned with arguments either way.

Regardless of which belief we embrace, living and loving in the
here and now following our loss is all we can do. We have no
power to undo the past and the future is yet to come. If faith in
an afterlife is part of our spiritual tradition, we can embrace it.
If not, we can hope the love of others will see us through our
sorrow. And we can love them in return.

The greatest gift I can offer the world is love.

What saves a man is to take a step. Then another step.
It is always the same step, but you have to take it.

– Antoine De Saint Exupery

When a former colleague lost both his wife and daughter in a car accident, he said his most important task now in life was to keep moving, to not let their deaths stop him in his tracks. He knew he would die too if he allowed their absence to control the rest of his life.

He knew he had to decide to live.

Men are used to taking action. We want to do something to make things better when our lives seem to be falling apart. Perhaps this tendency can help us heal following the death of a loved one. Staying faithful to a morning routine can be a choice we make. Of course, we may need to make changes to allow for the absence of our loved one. But that familiar routine, our early morning walk, run, or bicycle ride, can be salve for our broken hearts. Take a step. Then another step. Even if we don't feel like it. Especially if we don't feel like it. Our feelings change when we act.

Or, perhaps we love to read. Any reading material will do as long as it provides comfort: poetry, a favorite author, something spiritual. Or, maybe it's time to finish that woodworking project or start one. Busy hands can help mend broken hearts.

What will I do today to help me keep moving? What activity do I find most comforting?

JULY 18

The shell must be broken
before the birdling hatches.

– Harold E. Kohn

Since the death of our loved one, we have all heard well-meaning observations about death from family and friends alike. Some of these words have brought great comfort; others have brought great pain. The speakers have tried to say something meaningful, something to ease our pain, and also, of course, to calm their own fears. This is human.

And, in a strange twist, we mourners may have become the comforters.

"God needed another voice in His choir," we may have heard, or "your loved one is in a better place." "God has a plan we do not understand" is another proclamation. Depending upon which of your loved ones has died, these words may or may not bring comfort. If your child has died, these words may cause great pain, even rage. "What kind of God would take my child?"

Those who suggest that the death of our loved one is a necessary step into a better world may not understand the depth of our grief and loss. We are suffering. We are not interested in "broken shells and hatched birdlings." We want our loved one back.

I will take the comments of others in the spirit of their best intentions. Most folks simply do not know what to say.

When we think about death, we often think about what will happen to us after we have died. But it is more important to think about what will happen to those we leave behind... The greatest gift we can offer our families and friends is the gift of gratitude. Gratitude sets them free to continue living without bitterness or self-recrimination.

— Henri J.M. Nouwen

And also thanking our departed loved one? Is it possible that we owe a debt of gratitude to the one who has died? Can we think of reasons to be grateful? A special favor done on our behalf without us having to ask, some job that required four hands instead of two, something so heavy that we could not move alone? Packing the moving van? Painting the living room? Holding our ladder? Preparing a meal? Mowing the grass? Shoveling the snow?

Listening to our stories?

Or, if death came quickly, perhaps we have silent thanks that our loved one didn't suffer long. And if the illness that ended our loved one's life was stretched over a long period of time, we may be grateful that the struggle is over. Perhaps our gratitude is simply that we had time to say goodbye, to talk about our life together, our adventures, the good times. We had time to express our sorrow that it was all coming to an end. Time to apologize, if necessary. Time to cry. Time to say a final good-bye.

Thank you for sharing your life with me. Thank you for loving me. I'll always love you.

I come into the peace of wild things
who do not tax their lives with forethought
of grief...
— Wendell Berry

When a loved one dies, perhaps especially a child, it is easy to fall into despair. Particularly for men. We tend to be loners in the first place. Our culture has taught us to "be a man," and that "big boys don't cry." Oh, but we do.

Our tears may be visible to others, or we may keep them tucked away inside, secret teardrops, drip, drip, dripping from our broken hearts, our wounded souls. We may be "crying on the inside while we're laughing on the outside." But we need an outlet.

A walk in the woods or alongside a river where we surround ourselves with endless varieties of birds, deer, squirrels, chipmunks, raccoons, beaver, otter, muskrats, and the occasional fox... the peace of wild things... can help begin to mend our broken hearts.

Grief recovery groups are found most everywhere. Compassionate Friends, a nation-wide organization for parents whose children have died, can be a life-preserver tossed to grief-struck parents trying to keep their heads above water. You do not have to speak if you choose to attend. You can simply listen.

There is something healing about looking into the eyes of another man who knows exactly how you feel. It is a moment of grace.

All journeys have a secret destination of which the traveler is unaware.

– Martin Buber

Grief is a journey, but we do not know where we are going. Some of us refuse to use maps in the best of circumstances. This is, however, the worst of circumstances. And we have never been down this particular road before. The needle of our hunting compass keeps spinning. Like our thoughts, it does not know which direction to point. We are lost. Alone. Afraid.

A loved one has died. We are struggling. None of the life rules we have learned up to now seem to apply to this situation. We do not know what to do, where to turn, how to handle our feelings. If a child has died, some of us may be thinking about suicide as a remedy. Perhaps we can find our child "on the other side" if we are dead too. These thoughts are normal but not helpful.

When our son died in a boating accident in 2010, my wife Jane and I made a "no suicide, no divorce" pact. We promised each other that we would not kill ourselves and that we would not run away from our pain by divorcing each other. Suicide and divorce are painfully common "solutions" for bereaved parents. We decided that neither of these options would become our destination. This has not been easy. Still, we persist in our commitment.

We men are not as comfortable with secret destinations as women. But, can I trust that my personal grief journey will take me to where I need to go? Is it possible that the journey itself is the destination?

The abyss of God's love is deeper than the abyss of death.

— Dan Garnaas

When death stares us in the face, we tend to fall back onto the religion of our youth. Prayers we learned as children years ago may come to mind. A favorite Sunday school teacher's face may appear, that familiar smile, those kind eyes, the gentle demeanor, the encouraging voice.

The black hole of death feels like it has no bottom. Our hearts have been tossed into it, and we keep falling. And yet, somehow, somewhere, we may begin to feel a glimmer of hope in the black space surrounding our broken dreams. It's not that we see a way out exactly. But we are beginning to feel that a way out may actually exist. This is a new feeling and a surprise given the death of our loved one and the depth of our despair.

Can we have faith that whoever is in charge of the universe knows of our pain and sorrow? That we are not alone in our grief, that there is a presence who walks beside us, holding our hand, watching over us, protecting us from further harm, especially if our grief is fresh and raw?

In spite of my doubts, I will stay open to the possibility that a healing presence may help me on this grief journey.

A drowsy, half-wakeful menace waits for us in the quietness of this world. I have felt it near me while kneeling in the snow, minding a trap on the ridge many miles from home. There, in the cold that gripped my face, in the low, blue light failing around me, and the short day ending, in those familiar and friendly shadows, I was suddenly aware of something that did not care if I lived. Or, as it may be, running the river ice in mid-winter: under the sled runners a sudden cracking and buckling that scared the dogs and sent my heart racing. How swiftly the solid bottom of one's life can go.

– John Haines

How fast death can find us! We are living our lives with what appears to be predictable certainty. We have plans in place. We tease each other about daily details and often talk like we have forever to fine tune our journey, make life just right for our personal needs. Suddenly, death finds us.

Some of us are in our teens. Life is spread out before us on what appears to be an endless horizon. Or we may be in our busy middle years with jobs, family demands, and personal fulfillment on our plate. Or, for some of us, retirement, with its hopes, dreams, and fears, looms on the horizon. Then, unexpectedly, death, the ultimate game-changer, arrives. How swiftly the solid bottom on one's life can go. How quickly our plans evaporate.

Still, we live. We hope. We pick ourselves up. Our former plans were before. Today's plans are after. We will start again.

Who will I call today to help me talk through my grief about this death of my loved one and about making new plans, now that my old plans have evaporated into thin air?

Everyone once. Once only. Just once and no more.
And we also once. Never again. But this having
been once, although only once, to have been of the
earth, seems irrevocable.

– Rainer Maria Rilke

For men, the frightening finality of death, sooner or later, gets our attention. We thought we had forever. We were wrong. Our loved one's death is a tap on the shoulder, a reminder that this world, as beautiful as it is, is temporary. We are just passing through. We are visitors. Irrevocable visitors, but visitors nonetheless.

Our retired friends may know this with greater certainty. Those of us who are closer to death, age-wise, usually stop teasing ourselves and others about how much time we have left. We ask each other our ages and reflect on the answers, trying to calculate how many days remain in our friend's life. Truthfully though, we simply do not know. We have today, this moment. This is it. We are breathing now. There is no guarantee that we will be breathing later today, or tomorrow, or next week, month, year.

Just this moment. Our chance for life. Everyone once.

This day will never return. What will I choose to do with this most precious gift of time, this now, this moment, this once?

Bit by bit, nevertheless, it comes over us that we shall never again hear the laughter of our friend, that this one garden is forever locked against us. And at that moment begins our true mourning... nothing can match the treasure of common memories, of trials endured together, of quarrels and reconciliations and generous emotions...one by one our [loved ones] slip away, deprive us of their shade.

– Antoine De Saint Exupery

Our inclination to be loners makes men even more susceptible to long-term grief. We grieve differently than women.

Women join hands and share their losses with other women. We men fold our hands and withdraw into ourselves even further than normal. We look for places to hide. We try to suck it up and handle grief on our own terms, usually without a lot of success. Some of our self-destructive habits may come roaring back: smoking, alcohol, excessive eating, reckless sex, drug abuse. Anything to get away.

But true mourning requires something we do not want, openness to the excruciatingly painful reality of our loss: my loved one is dead.

What can I do? I need to talk about my loss. I can step out of my comfort zone and ask for help. If I have ever needed help, it is today, now, at this very moment. I can call a friend or my doctor. I can call a trusted family member. I can join a support group at my local hospice, church, synagogue, or temple. I can take better care of myself.

How can I reach out for help at this very moment? Now?

The heart has its reasons which reason knows nothing of... We know truth not only by the reason, but by the heart.

– Blaise Pascal

Mourning men have an intuitive sense just as strong as women, but perhaps we seldom pay attention to it. Now may be the time to listen to our hearts. When a loved one dies, reason alone cannot guide us.

Our heart will direct our mourning if we give it a chance.

The truth of mourning is that we must work through it or possibly suffer the rest of our days. Working through grief means showing up to mourn, be comforted, encouraged, and loved by friends and family. To be sure, not every consolation offered will help. But many will. And participating in the process will allow us to receive the help that may matter the most. Our heart knows the importance of being there. We cannot allow our reason, our logic, to keep us away.

When my father was dying, my oldest brother came to the hospital but could not force himself to go into dad's room. Instead, he sat in the visitor's lounge while the rest of us family members gathered in time for my father's last breath. His absence may have added an extra layer to his own grieving.

My heart has its reasons, which I do not always understand. Nonetheless, I will give it its due.

Within the circularity of it all –
The cosmic riddle of
life – and death –
and life – again –

– Gwen Frostic

When we lose a loved one, it is often hard, if not impossible, to consider our place in the universe and the circle of life. All things have a beginning and all things have an ending. None escape this universal truth. Not even us. Our loved one is gone. Yet, for a time, we still live.

Are we surprised?

I recall glancing at my son while he was filling out the Organ Donor Information Form on the back of his Michigan driver's license. He checked the box that indicated a recipient could use all possible organs in the event of his death. I told him I hoped nothing life-threatening ever happened to him. He laughed and agreed.

I have checked the same box throughout my life whenever I renew my license. It always seemed like an academic exercise until the day my son died shortly afterwards. The unthinkable happened. But, others are alive and well because of his remarkable generosity. This is what he intended and what I also still intend. The circle of life continues because of the organ donation program. The organs we no longer need after death can be life-saving for someone suffering or on the brink of dying. This act is the ultimate re-cycling program...within the circularity of it all.

Life precedes death, then death follows life, and the circle of life continues. I am grateful to be in this circle!

To be able to invite pain to join in my experience and not have to control my life to avoid pain is such a freedom!

– Christina Baldwin

We may spend a lot of time and money trying to avoid pain and suffering. Sometimes we use narcotics and/or alcohol to numb ourselves against some of life's harsh realities, like this death of our loved one. Or we may travel to some distant place hoping that our pain cannot follow. But, of course, it will.

What would happen if we invited pain to become a travel companion? Something to welcome?

To do this would require a shift in our attitude. One of my older male friends likes to say that when he wakes each morning he doesn't wonder if some part of his body will ache, but what part of his body will hurt that day. He has made a mental shift in his thinking. He no longer thinks of a painful experience as being an aberration, but as a normal everyday occurrence.

Would we suffer as much if we could accept the death of a loved one so readily?

I will consider inviting death to become my travel companion. Then, when it arrives, I will not be caught off guard.

JULY 29

To be alive, we have to deal with a loss of control.
Falling in love is a loss of control. When we die
or someone we love dies, it's a tremendous loss of
control.

        – Natalie Goldberg

Many of us are take charge men. We are in control and love to have that power. We are proud to be the decision makers. Perhaps in the workplace we manage other employees. We are the go to men there, the problem solvers, in the seat of authority. We are in charge and proud of it. Others follow our lead. We're the boss.

Then, along comes death, the great unknown. Suddenly, we are no longer the captain of the ship. The death of a loved one may send us into an unknown world for the first time in our lives. The old order has disappeared. We have arrived in a strange land. The road signs are written in a language we do not understand. We feel lost. Out of control. No one turns to us for help. Instead, we turn to them. What's going on?

We are no longer in charge.

A former colleague, an important member of our administrative team in a position of great authority, who lost both his wife and daughter in a car accident once said to me, "When I'm at work, everything is okay. I can do my job. But, when I get home, I'm lost and don't know what to do. That's when I struggle."

Gracefully losing control takes practice. This is hard work. It takes a lifetime.

Pain so profound that any man
would hide;
Where is consolation
when death steals loved ones from our side?

– Clifford Denay, Jr.

After the funeral, when the numbness begins to subside, we tend to want to run and hide. Putting our feelings out there on the table is not in our nature. Maybe it's our cultural training to "suck it up and be a man." Maybe we were never given permission to cry.

Still, our thoughts endlessly circle around our raw wound.

And yet, in the face of such a profound loss, where can we stuff these feelings of grief, anger, even rage, over the death of our beloved one? Where, we may wonder, is the one who is in charge of this experience we call life? We are stunned. Why was it our loved one who had to die? We are dazed, in shock. Lost. Scared. Some of us are thinking about suicide to end the pain of this loss. Please, no.

Perhaps some still, small voice from somewhere deep within may be whispering to us to choose hope. Choose hope? Is it possible that God is at our side and we do not know it? Can we hope that our loved one fulfilled his or her mission on earth and simply went home? Can we accept that there will always be far more questions than answers?

I do not understand death. Still, I will choose to hope. And ask for help if I need it.

Don't walk in front of me... I may not follow. Don't walk behind me... I may not lead. Walk beside me – and just be my friend.
                                        – Albert Camus

One of the profound surprises to absorb after the death of a loved one is the reaction of some of our friends whom we expected to be there for us and share our sorrow, prop us up, offer hope, perhaps even cry with us. They are often nowhere to be seen. They avoid us for fear of saying the wrong thing. Their silence hurts, of course, and we may eventually have to be the one who re-establishes contact with them if we value their friendship and hope to keep it alive.

On the other hand, a few guys, even some we weren't necessarily close to, may have fearlessly walked into our grief-struck heart and stayed steadfastly at our side. They had no fear. They simply saw a broken man and decided to help by offering friendship. They realized that words weren't important. Their presence was.

We all grieve differently.

Some men just don't know what to say to us or how they should act around someone who has suffered a major life loss. We can choose to tell them how much their friendship means to us and let it go at that. Some will reach back. Some won't. We can take comfort for having tried to nurture the friendship in such difficult circumstances.

AUGUST

AUGUST 1

My grief is great
Compared to none
Yet smaller when
Compared to some.

– Clifford Denay, Jr.

We men may wonder if our grief sets a new record for sorrow. We may be tempted to compare our grief with other guys who have also suffered a loss. Surely my pain is worse than his, we may think. We may be right or we may be wrong. Who knows? And, in the end, does it really matter? Both of us are suffering mightily.

We are both stunned, both suffering ourselves from what feels like a near-death experience.

Losing a loved one ranks right up there as one of life's most significant losses. And if we have lost a child, well, that loss is most likely the worst one of all. When my son died, I thought the grief would be similar to what I felt when my parents died years earlier. I was wrong. When my son died, a part of me died with him. I was devastated beyond words. I was certain that my sorrow was unexcelled in the history of the world. Surely other grieving fathers feel the same.

What matters most, it seems, is our shared humanity. We all suffer when a loved one dies. Who suffers more or who suffers less quickly becomes irrelevant. That we all suffer is what we recognize.

I am not alone in my sorrow. In the midst of my own incredible pain, I am aware that men are suffering the same loss as me at this moment around the world.

*Life's unfairness is not irrevocable; we can
help balance the scales for others, if not
always for ourselves.*

– Hubert Humphrey

The death of our loved one may have turned our sense of fairness inside out. The one we have lost may have just been hitting his or her stride or come into a sense of peace with life circumstances. How could this person die so quickly at this unexpected moment?

And who made up the rules about who lives and who dies?

Maybe "fair" or "unfair" are not the right adjectives. Perhaps "lucky" or "unlucky" are more appropriate. As we survey the landscape, we see others who have been dealt a tougher hand than we as well as those who seem to have had it made from the start. All of us struggle to some extent, but some struggle more than others. Humphrey's words were for those who struggle the most.

My mother-in-law died at age 62, just months after her retirement. And two years after my father-in-law remarried, his second wife died as well. What are the odds of losing two partners so close together? And my brother's granddaughter died at the age of seven years following a long struggle with a cancerous tumor in her stomach. Why is one so young taken at such an early age? Who knows?

Our work is to reach out in love to those who suffer...we can help balance the scales for others, if not always for ourselves.

Life is not fair. It just is. Our work is to help others not suffer alone...to help balance the scales.

AUGUST 3

We find a place for what we lose. Although we know that after such a loss the acute stage of mourning will subside, we also know that we shall remain inconsolable and will never find a substitute. No matter what may fill the gap, even if it be filled completely, it nevertheless remains something else.

– Sigmund Freud

We may find we are making progress along this road of grief when, out of the blue, a shaft of sorrow intrudes on a beautiful August morning. Where did this come from?

And why now?

It was commencement day for my son-in-law, the capstone of four years of hard work. Many families had traveled long distances to share in the joy of this cool California day. Colorful caps and gowns dotted the stage. Photographers were everywhere. Short speeches praised the graduates' accomplishments and thanked the families for faithful support. Then, unexpectedly, I recalled my dead son's graduation, the excitement of his celebration, and his considerable photography skills. He should be here now. I glanced at my wife and caught her looking at me. She raised her eyebrows and shrugged her shoulders. She was thinking the same thing. Tears filled our eyes. Why sorrow in the midst of this happiness? And why now?

Even as I celebrate a joyful occasion, I can be pulled back into grief. Still, it is only a temporary setback.

AUGUST 4

In this universe nothing is ever wholly lost. That which is excellent remains forever a part of this universe. Human hearts are dust. But the love which moves the human heart, abides to bless the last generation.
— Ralph Waldo Emerson

When the one we love is buried, we may be inclined to think that the end has arrived. But Emerson's words tell a different story. The body may be missing, but the love remains.

Always.

Our loved one may be physically absent, but his or her love endures. We can feel it... nothing is ever wholly lost. One morning after my mother-in-law's death, my father-in-law was shaving upstairs when he clearly heard his deceased wife call to him from the downstairs kitchen. He was startled but still answered her. There was no reply. He was hesitant to tell family members about the incident, but in the end decided they needed to know... love... abides...

Stories abound about how those who have died continue to influence events in the lives of those who remain. Perhaps we have such a story to share. Our stories can provide hope for others who grieve.

Nothing is wholly lost. Love remains. Forever.

AUGUST 5

The morning after a loved one dies everything looks bleak.
— Jami Blaauw-Hara

After a loved one dies, the world looks paste white. Washed out. All is still.

The silence is deafening.

Perhaps our earliest impulses may include "cleaning house," gathering the belongings of our missing one to give away to a charity. Indeed, some family members do just that. The clothing or other personal articles remind them of their painful loss. Still other survivors go to the opposite extreme by turning their loved one's space into a memorial of sorts. They leave everything exactly as it was while their loved one lived.

After my father's death, I walked into his bedroom and took several of his well-worn t-shirts from his dresser drawer. I put one on and felt immediately better. I continued wearing his undershirts for many years, until they finally became paper-thin. Wearing his clothes helped me survive his death. We all grieve differently. We have the right to grieve our way.

I shall not put my love away. Instead, I shall, as John Shelby Spong writes in his book Eternal Life: A New Vision... love wastefully... until the end of my days. After all, I have an endless supply.

Turn your face to the sun and the shadows fall behind you.
— Charlotte Whitton

When someone we love dies, we live in the shadows for a time. Some of us stay in the shade for the rest of our lives. Others move into the sun prematurely, pushing grief aside as if it were no big deal.

But grief is a big deal.

And it will take a lot of time to heal from this loss. We have to be patient with ourselves. Perhaps we need to treat ourselves like we would treat a best friend suffering the same loss. We have to recognize the hardest part of grief is to resist the urge to turn away from it. Yet every time we turn away from something, we eventually must turn back again. Why not face grief head on?

After my son's death, I was hesitant to accept invitations from guy friends for coffee or companionship. I wanted to be alone, to stay in the shadows so I could tend to my sorrow. But one friend was particularly persistent. His encouragement and warm personality tugged on my heart. We agreed to meet once a week for breakfast and continued the plan for several months. Our breakfast meetings helped pull me out of my cold despair and back toward the warmth of the sun, of life.

What would I do without my friends? They are waiting for me to rejoin them in the dance of life.

AUGUST 7

It was missing a piece,
And it was not happy.
So it set off in search
Of its missing piece…

> – Shel Silverstein,
> *The Missing Piece*

This is a story told by an anonymous writer:

I am standing upon the seashore. A ship at my side spreads her white sails to the morning breeze and starts for the blue ocean. She is an object of beauty and strength. I stand and watch her until at length she hangs like a spark of white cloud just where the sea and sky come to mingle with each other.

Then someone at my side says:

> "There she is gone!"
> "Gone where?"

Gone from my sight. That is all. She is just as large in mast and hull and spar as she was when she left my side and she is just as able to bear her load of living freight to her next destined port.

Her diminished size is in me, not her. And just at the moment when someone at my side says:

> "There, she is gone!"

There are other eyes watching her coming, and other voices ready to take up the glad shout:

> "Here she comes!"

And, that is dying.

Can I have faith that my loved one is safe in a new harbor on some other shore that I cannot see?

AUGUST 8

Grief is not through with me – it may never be completely through with me – it still catches me by surprise from time to time.

– John Carnutt

After some months, or perhaps a few years – each of us grieves at his own pace – we may feel we have control over our grief. And most of the time this may be true. We are functioning again and could even feel like our old self from time to time.

Then something catches us by surprise.

A song. A line from a book we are reading. The smell of baking bread. A call from a friend we haven't spoken to since before our loved one died. Children at play. A birdsong. Almost anything can remind us at a moment's notice of who we have lost.

A short stretch of dialogue from a novel I was recently reading while sitting in a bakery near my home stopped me cold. In the story, one character reading from a letter said to another, "My father died..." The other responded, "Yes, I know. I was watching your face." I was instantly transported back in time to my own dying father's bedside, his hospital room filled with children and grandchildren, his body hooked up to machines that were fighting a losing battle against death. How he looked so peaceful in spite of the commotion. Tears after all this time, I thought. I was surprised.

Perhaps there is no such thing as completed grief. Maybe we learn to live with our losses and choose joy as often as we can.

AUGUST 9

*People bring us well-meant but miserable
consolations when they tell us what time will
do to help our grief. We do not want to lose our
grief, because our grief is bound up with our
love and we could not cease to mourn without
being robbed of our affections.*

— Phillips Brooks

Time will eventually bring a healing of some sort. But we can be impatient. We look for a solution to our grief as if death is a problem we have the power to solve. It is not. We hold onto our grief to stay close to the one we have lost. Miserable consolations are just that. Empty words from those who cannot understand.

And we fear forgetting the one who has died.

But wait. How can we lose a part of ourselves? Like the air we breathe, the love we shared with our loved one is quilted into the fabric of our lives. In a sense, we became a part of each other through shared life experiences. And losing a part of ourselves may be the most painful loss. How could we not cease to mourn without feeling robbed of our companion, and our shared hopes and dreams for the future?

I have a right to my grief. Time may heal, but it will take time for me to accept this loss. Who knows how long? Today I take comfort in knowing that _____ is a part of the fabric of my life. Though physically separated, our love for each other will always remain.

Worry never robs tomorrow of its sorrow, it only saps today of its joy.

– Leo Buscaglia

Some of us are prone to excessive anxiety, and the death of someone we love can make this tendency worse. We chew on worries we can do nothing about, fretting over our future, and we are anxious about tomorrow, today.

We wake in the middle of the night and stare at the ceiling.

But regardless of our worry, our sorrow remains. The energy we spend spinning our wheels keeps us stuck in the past. After death we worry that everyone will die, that every goodbye will be the last one. We give up the possibility of joy today for the probability of sorrow tomorrow.

Perhaps we can choose, instead, to dwell on the lives of those who have weathered a similar loss and found healing in a future they also once considered bleak. How did they do it? Who helped them survive? To whom did they turn in their darkest hours? We can read their stories of horror, turned to hope, and, eventually consider a new kind of happiness in spite of their losses. To do this requires a decision only we can make.

I will push the "stop" button on the anxious messages I keep listening to. Instead, I will read stories of hope and healing from the lives of those who have suffered before me.

Life itself is very much like climbing a slippery glass hill. We climb, and we slip; we climb a little more, and slip again. We all slip! Everyone has sorrow, disappointment, tragedy, frustration! But the measure of a man – the measure of you – is not whether you slip, but what you do when you slip.

– Murray Banks

Some of us will eventually heal after this death, and some of us will suffer endlessly for the rest of our days. If we choose the healing journey, it will be painful. But if we choose the suffering journey, it will also be painful. The difference is that the healing journey will have an end but the suffering journey will not.

Which road will we take?

The healing path teaches us to reach out for help from others who have been on this journey before us. They know the way and will share what has helped them to heal. The suffering path teaches us to retreat from those who would help us. We try to make it on our own, ignoring the wisdom of the ages. But Ernest Hemingway wrote, "No man is an island."

He was speaking to us.

My loved one is dead. I have fallen off my slippery glass hill again. This time I will reach out for help.

AUGUST 12

The cut worm forgives the plow.

– William Blake

If our loved one died from "natural causes," surely no one is to blame but nature itself. We are time-limited creatures. Our bodies are built to last for a certain time. We may eat properly, exercise, develop loving relationships, and care for one another. Or not. Still, in the end, we all die just as our loved one has died.

There is no escape from death.

If our loved one is dead because of "poor judgment," "human error," or, worse, was murdered, who shall we blame? The victim or the perpetrator? In the case of poor judgment, the victim was the perpetrator. Was anyone sorrier for misjudging the situation than the one who has died? If human error was involved, and if the one who made the mistake is still living, is there any worse punishment than knowing you caused someone's death? And if our loved one was murdered, how do we approach the murderer? With vengeance, or a forgiving heart? Only we can decide.

William Blake's words offer wisdom worth considering. Forgiveness. We are logical men. We can argue a strong case for retaliation or for redemption. It is up to us to decide. And our decision will likely determine our happiness the rest of our days.

I forgive everyone involved in this death.

We are, and in a breath, are not. If the man may become shadow, may not the shadow become man?

– Jack London

What may amaze us is how quickly one can leave this world. One morning our loved one is alive. Later that day or perhaps the next, gone permanently from our sight. Vanished forever from the world we know. We are left alone, perhaps without our touchstone, the one who walked at our side.

What happened?

Our bodies are marvelously made. Still, we are not invincible. We live in a small range of body temperature. Too hot or too cold, we die. Our flesh and blood is vulnerable to the forces of nature. A falling tree or speeding car can stop us forever in our tracks. We have multiple body systems to help prevent disease. Still, cancer cells can develop and destroy.

So we live. No one can predict how long. Then we die. Man becomes a shadow. What, we would like to know, is on the other side? Jack London's words suggest that our relationship with the dead is ongoing. Even in death, the shadow of our loved one remains. And we develop a new relationship with him or her, one that can never be destroyed again. This may be a comforting thought for most of us.

This death reminds me how quickly I too, can die. I will be prepared to leave at any time so I will not be caught off-guard.

AUGUST 14

Hope is the opposite of despair...

– Skye Jethani

The death of a loved one may send us into despair. And the circumstances surrounding the death may determine the depth of our grief. If the death was expected, as in the case of an elderly family member, our grief may be less traumatic, our despair less debilitating. But if the death was sudden, as in the case of a child, we may be tossed into a cauldron of chaos.

Where is hope when we are in the throes of despair?

Everywhere if we look for it.

But we have to look. Hope is in the warm touch of the nurse at the hospital. The look in the eyes. The quiet way of taking care of business while being respectful of your family's needs. Hope is in the hug the hospital chaplain offers, the deference to your wishes, the availability, kindness, and respect. Hope is a multitude of friends who quickly and quietly show up, and stay. Hope is the funeral director who understands. Hope is the cemetery sexton who is flexible with the burial wishes of the family. Hope is those who send flowers years after the death. Hope is those who send cards, week after week, month after month, year after year. Hope is those who call. Hope is those who visit. Hope is those who sit with us quietly and without expectations.

Hope is those who can never understand but still love us.

I am filled with despair but still choose to hope.

The supreme happiness of life is the conviction that we are loved.

— Victor Hugo

Grief and loss are travel companions on life's journey. And they often show up when we least expect them. Or want them, for that matter.

They can be an unwelcome interruption to an ordered life.

Yet these two intruders often bring with them a surprise gift: new friendships. The success of grief recovery groups is that they bring together those who have lost loved ones. Looking into the eyes of someone who has suffered a similar loss creates an instant bond. The other knows, understands. There is no need to explain. And, there is the opportunity, once again, to tell our story. We take turns listening. Friendship blossoms. We feel at home in the presence of this "family" member. We know we are loved.

Shortly after my son's death, I met another family who also lost a son. We rushed to each other's sides and held one another for several minutes. Our devastating losses quickly became an instant bond. We were strangers no more.

I will look for friendship, understanding, and love in the eyes of those who comfort me.

AUGUST 16

No despair of ours can alter the reality of things or stain the joy of the cosmic dance...

– Thomas Merton

As devastating as this loss is, we will never forget the joy we shared with the one we loved. No one can take our memories away.

Or our stories.

Perhaps we have all seen by now pictures of the earth taken from the moon. The image of our colorful and breathtaking planet puts human beings into greater perspective. We are creatures of the universe inhabiting this flying sphere. We are mysterious. Complex. Awe-inspiring. Loving. Grieving. Still, we are indeed part of the "cosmic dance" that Merton refers to above. In spite of our loss, the fact we exist at all is beyond wonder. We cannot change the reality of our loss, but we can, in time, accept with open arms the miracle of our existence. We can choose to celebrate that we have survived, and we have more time to share life experiences.

Many weddings end with an opportunity to dance. Friends and relatives join the bride and groom on the dance floor in celebrating the newly formed union. Joyful gestures of every making bring laughter and surprise to the faces of all present. The fact that the end will eventually arrive for all of us does not prevent the joy of the moment. And neither will this death keep us from dancing. Or from telling stories of weddings long since passed.

Here I am, broken-hearted. Still, I choose to dance.

Life, after unspeakable loss, becoming poetry again... yes, yes, yes.
                                        – Gregory Boyle

In the midst of unspeakable loss, it may be hard for us to imagine a time in the future when life can become poetry again. Still, we can hope.

Why not?

After the sudden death of his wife, a friend finds comfort and consolation with his beloved tennis court companions. Soon he is invited to join a mixed doubles team. He is paired with a long-time friend whose husband is also out of life's picture. They find a common bond on the court and begin to share off-court time together. Their friendship blossoms as they share stories of children, grandchildren, travel dreams, work, and retirement plans. Wedding bells soon herald a new life for the two of them.

Poetry... yes, yes, yes.

Before his own death, my father always said to me that life was for the living. It seemed a cruel thing to me to leave the dead behind. Now I understand what he meant. We are leaving no one behind. The dead we have with us always. The living still need us. Here. Now.

My beloved one will be with me always. Today I turn my attention back to the poetry of the living.

AUGUST 18

...wringing useful memories from one's subconscious produces unpleasant self-absorption. It puts you in contact with long-dead friends, good buddies, people you have loved, who have been kind to you, whose death left a vacuum.

– Tony Hillerman

The death of someone we have loved always leaves a vacuum. The place this friend occupied in our lives is forever empty. Who will take his or her place?

Actually, no one.

And the thought of replacing a loved one may be appalling. None of us can be replaced. We can only hope for new relationships that slowly coax us back into the land of the living from the wasteland of self-absorption. Still, in the early days of great loss, our eyes are focused on ourselves. Lifting them up to scan the seemingly new landscape often takes more effort than we can muster.

So, what can a grieving man do? We can relish the goodness of enduring friendships, celebrate the faithfulness of those who stuck with us through the tests of time, embrace the love they shared with us (and still do, from where they are now), and bask in the kindness, compassion, and care they extended to us while they lived. In short, we can celebrate their lives and the love they brought to this world. And, especially, to us.

I celebrate both recent and long-dead friends. My life has been abundant because they lived.

AUGUST 19

We need a friend, a confidante.

– John Powell

If we have ever needed a friend, it is at this moment. There is no time to lose. Call, email, or text a friend. Or go to his or her side. Or ask the person to come to you. Today. Now. Make haste.

We cannot grieve alone. None of us can.

We need help. We need someone to hold our heads above the raging seas of loss. We need a lifeline successfully tossed to us above the waves. We need someone to answer our cries of distress. We need calm reassurance in the face of this storm. And we need hope after the worst is over. Only friends can help us with this. We cannot hope to survive on our own strength.

When my son died, the line of mourners at his funeral service stretched beyond sight. I had no idea how much love for me and my family existed in our small northern Michigan community. I learned all of us are important within our own circle of friendships. This is treasure greater than all the world's gold, silver, and diamonds combined. Help is ours for the asking. And the answer is love.

I will ask for help in grieving this loss. One day soon, I will be asked to repay the favor. Guaranteed.

AUGUST 20

When the day returns, call us up with morning faces, and with morning hearts, eager to labor, happy if happiness be our portion, and if the day be marked for sorrow, strong to endure.

– Robert Louis Stevenson

The thought of morning faces may seem strange. Yet, putting on "a good face" may not be a bad idea under present circumstances. After all, feelings follow actions. Acting strong in the face of death may stir feelings of strength.

I returned to my workplace two weeks after the death of my son. Some colleagues felt I had returned too soon and suggested I take additional time off. For me, though, I believed the structure of my daily work routine would help in the healing process. This turned out to be true. And an unexpected bonus was the love and support for me from several colleagues who had also suffered major losses. But not all men would find this idea helpful. For some of us, a longer period of recuperation may be in order. Each of us grieves differently.

And we all hope for the strength we need to say goodbye to someone we love. Saying goodbye may be the hardest thing we will ever do.

*It does not matter where his body lies, for it is grass;
but where his spirit is, it will be good to be.*

– Black Elk

All cultures develop a pattern for spiritual interaction. Perhaps we should be aware of what a spiritual world means to us. Instead of despairing over the death of our loved one, perhaps we should look forward to a grand reunion with them there.

Scientists have long argued our rational minds struggle to fathom what we do not see. Yet we do not argue about the reality of the wind, the beauty of love, the strength of despair, the sense of an idea, the stillness of death. Do we debate the existence of each? Why would our spirits not seek out the home from which they came? That sense of longing we all feel? Where does it originate?

Our bodies do become grass. And flowers, trees, shrubs, fruits, vegetables, and eventually every living thing on earth. But our spirits? We sense they are here. But we also feel their presence, everywhere... it will be good... wonderful!

Although I long for the bodily presence of my loved one, I know this is no longer possible. Now I look forward to our spiritual reunion. It will be good.

AUGUST 22

The stars seem a little closer lately.
I'm no longer afraid to die...

– Jim Harrison

The earth and the sky take on new meanings after the death of a loved one. We no longer see what we once saw. There is a new earth and a new sky that confront us. We do not recognize them. Just where am I, I wonder? Where am I?

What has happened?

We are stunned. Lost. Many of us no longer care if we live or die. No one tells us this is a temporary feeling and it will pass if we give it some time. But we have learned it here in these pages. Wanting to die at first is normal. But this feeling passes. We need our friends to help us believe this. Thank goodness for our friends who help us survive the first days, weeks, months. Sometimes years.

Then, a surprise follows. We are no longer afraid to die. This is true especially if we have lost a child. Or if we have been in battle and watched a loved one be blown away next to us. We have suffered the worst loss a human can endure. What can death possibly do to us now? Nothing. It is not as if we survivors seek out death. Some men do, but most of us do not. We simply are no longer afraid of it.

And, yes... the stars seem a little closer lately. I even recognize a few of them.

Although I am in no hurry to die, I no longer fear death. And, I have a new world to explore.

AUGUST 23

...I came to see that if I can't have the one I miss, or enjoy the life I knew, then I must learn to love the one I'm with, and to live the life I'm given. And I have.

– Suzanne Redfern

In time, we may come to this way of thinking, perhaps not today, but down the road a bit. The only other choice is to give up on life. But this glorious existence offers too much to walk away from.

This grand adventure of living, of breathing and loving, is too enticing to miss.

When someone we love dies, our first inclination is to withdraw. Our world contracts. Our vision narrows. We may not notice those waiting nearby and their need for us. In time, though, we begin to understand we are living in a new world. The old one has passed away. And this new life is calling our name. Hoping for our love.

And because our supply of love is without limitation, we can love anyone we choose, near or far. Amazing, isn't it? The more love we give away, the more we keep. We never run out. Love calls us to love. And we do.

I cannot have the one I miss, but I can love the one I'm with. And I will.

Be careful, lest in casting out your demons you exorcise the best thing in you.

– Friedrich Nietzsche

When a loved one dies, one of our feelings may be that of abandonment. We have been left behind by someone we love. A parent, spouse, child, lifelong friend, an aunt or uncle, a grandmother or grandfather. A colleague at work.

And we are still here. Alone. Adrift on a sea of loneliness.

When my son died, my mind raced to the unfinished work he left behind. Soon, I started mulling over the ways in which he was my helper and friend and how I was now left to fend for myself. I was overwhelmed. I felt abandoned, my solitude forced, my anger rising.

Soon I was filled with both sorrow and rage. My heart was broken and I was angry with him for leaving so quickly, without warning. Yet I was ashamed of my anger, that I could possibly blame him for what was, by any definition, an accident. Eventually I came to realize that I was allowed to feel both my anger and sorrow. And by denying my anger, I would also be denying my sorrow. How could I have worked through grief if I had denied both?

I will be careful not to deny any feelings about the death of my loved one. I have a right to them all. They will enable me to work my way through grief.

Our demons are protecting our most bruised self.

– Jane Denay

The death of a loved one can stir up memories from our past. We men are good at putting our demons in a safe place somewhere in our memory. Death sometimes draws those experiences from the shadows and into the light.

This can be an opportunity to make peace with them.

Our demons are not always rational. One of my demons has been the fear of being left behind, of being abandoned by family and friends, by those I love. And when my son died, my sense of being abandoned returned. Of course, he did not choose to leave me. As a middle school child, I was fearful my sick mother would not return from multiple hospitalizations. And when my first marriage ended in divorce, once again I felt left behind.

When we look for our demons, we will find them. Perhaps this death is a chance to see if they still have a hold on us. Our most bruised self has a better chance of healing if we are able to set our demons aside so they no longer control us. Perhaps a non-judgmental friend or a professional counselor can help. We do not have to suffer any more.

What demon is protecting my most bruised self? Who can help me heal?

AUGUST 26

When grief is new, its sadness overwhelms, and the mind latches onto the loss and yearns to turn back the clock. But with the passage of time, it is easier to remember happy days and celebrate memories that will make us smile, or even laugh.

– Anne Logan

New grief is like a fresh wound. Painful. Stinging. Bleeding. We may be overwhelmed by the loss of someone so dear to us. We review the circumstances of the death in a vain attempt to change the outcome. We cannot.

We are not yet thinking clearly.

Still, slowly, painfully, time passes and a scab of sorts begins to form over the open injury. Even as the healing begins, some part of us feels like we are betraying our lost one, even if just one comforting thought comes to mind. We are not. So we dare to allow a few more joyful memories into our days and find, to our surprise, we feel a little better. Photographs of our loved one become more precious and less painful. The voicemail messages on the telephone may still be waiting, but we start to sense that one day we will look forward to hearing the familiar sound of the missing voice. We find we are smiling again and laughing once more. Our healing journey continues.

My grief is new, so I will be patient with my sadness. I need time to heal. I am confident I will laugh again.

So my Uncle Robert's death, which had looked from a distance to be an all-consuming tragedy was, close-up, the story of a man finding release from his pain...

– Will Cohu

There are times when our grief is stitched into a quilt of relief. Death has finally taken our loved one to a peaceful place. All who loved and sat watch are relieved that suffering is over. No more treatments. No more chemotherapy. No more tubes. No more machines. No ICU. No more decisions. Only silence. Tranquility. The beating of our own living hearts.

Life for our beloved has ended. And we are sad, and glad.

As my father lay dying, several machines monitored his body's attempts to stay alive. For five days he fought the good fight. We guessed his eighty-one-year-old heart could not keep up the rate it had set in its fight with infection. How long can this go on? Not long enough it turned out. Late on a Wednesday afternoon, after several days of being non-responsive, his blood pressure began to drop and his heart rate fell. Soon, he gently and quietly stopped breathing. His battle had ended. He was free at last. He was released from his pain. And those family members who watched him die were forever changed.

I have seen death. It is not always something to be feared. Sometimes it is a gift.

AUGUST 28

When his wife was at his side, she was also in front of him, marking out the horizon of his life. Now the horizon is empty; the view has changed.

– Milan Kundera

Perhaps most of us grieving men are used to following our spouse's lead. After all, isn't this what a wise man will do? But now our compass is gone. Who will lead the way?

Us?

Well, yes. The death of our spouse provides an opportunity to create a new future. Oh, not that this was an opportunity we sought. Not at all. On the contrary, we likely took the words "for better or worse" seriously. Yet, death finds us when it will. Ready or not. We fought for life, but death won.

After the death of a friend's wife, he approached a colleague, a single mother, for a date. She was recovering from a painful divorce. She answered in no uncertain terms that she had no interest in men. Still, over several months and with perfect patience, he asked her several more times. Finally, she agreed to have a cup of coffee with him so they could get to know each other better. Listening to each other's stories helped both of them understand what the other had been through. Slowly but surely, trust entered into their budding relationship. Their views had changed. Marriage followed shortly afterwards.

Dear _____, I miss you and will always love you. Now, my view of the world has changed. Do not worry about me. I will find my way.

For some reason we human beings seem to learn best how to love when we are a bit broken, when our plans fall apart, when our myths of self-sufficiency and goodness and safety are shattered.

– Kathleen Norris

We sometimes rail against death. After all, death is seldom a welcome guest. And often it seems to arrive when we least expect it. Sometimes death shows up in the midst of great joy, or a celebration, or soon after one who has been struggling for direction in life has finally found his or her way.

How ironic.

Many of us have heard of those who have "five year plans" or "ten years plans." Some of us have friends who have discussed their plans openly and often. In a recent discussion with a financial planner, he drew a rectangle and divided it into ten equal parts. He explained that each of the ten smaller rectangles represented ten years of a person's life. Then he drew an "X" through the squares that represented the decades of my life that have ended. Also, he drew an "X" through the ninth and tenth decades as they were typically years of declining health. The "picture" he drew was a startling message. "This is how much quality time you have left in your life." He was pointing to the two empty spaces. "How do you want to spend it?"

My dead son lived a life-long series of "one day plans." Oh, sure, he had long-range plans as well. But his goal was to drink in as much life as possible each day. And he did.

I want to drink in life. Who knows how much time I have left?

May you allow the unresolved hurts, frustrations, and fears from the past to seek their release in the present and thus be healed once and for all time.

– Isaac David Garuda

One of the "gifts" that death presents to us is to stir up "unresolved hurts, frustrations, and fears" from our past. How can this challenge be considered a gift? Well, perhaps now is the time to put them to rest. After all, we have no idea how much longer we will live. And these issues weigh more with each passing year.

Maybe this opportunity is the going-away gift from our loved one who has died.

Professional help may be in order. We guys often resist the idea of using the health care system. We put off annual physicals, skip dental appointments, and delay seeing a health care provider even when we think something may be wrong with our bodies. We are afraid to find out for fear of what a health problem might entail. We can be like an ostrich who sticks his head under the ground at the first sign of trouble. And a mental health care provider? Most of us would never consider the possibility.

Our reticence to seek mental health assistance may be a mistake. The death of someone we love is like experiencing a fall and breaking a leg. We need help setting the broken femur. And we also need someone to help "set" our broken heart. A mental health practitioner is an excellent listener who will care about our stories and help clarify our hurts, frustrations, and fears from the past. And with clarification, resolution is possible. And freedom.

I want to be released from old unresolved hurts, frustrations, and fears. I hope for the courage to seek help.

I often wonder, when listening to the news, did the person who died in the auto accident on his way home from work remember to tell his family how much he loved them?

– Richard Carlson

Men can be guilty of not saying the words "I love you" often enough. We assume our loved ones know. But other than the sound of our name, hearing "I love you" may be the sweetest sound on earth. And today, we may wish we had said it more often to the one who is now gone.

Why hold these words back?

We are courageous in many areas of our lives. We take risks in our workplaces, hobbies, and financial dealings. But taking a risk to speak our love is a special challenge. Perhaps we fear rejection. But when all evidence points to a person who has long loved us, why not risk speaking that love in return?

Somewhere in my early thirties I began telling my father I loved him at the end of each telephone call. We both knew we loved each other before this time. But it seemed that saying the words out loud made a difference in how close I felt to him. And it seemed to make a difference to him as well. When he lay dying in his hospital bed, I repeated those words countless times. It has been said that our hearing is the last function to fail before we die. I wanted to send him on his journey with "I love you!" ringing in his ears.

Dear _____, I love you!

❧ SEPTEMBER ❧

SEPTEMBER 1

I am a more sensitive person, a more effective
pastor, a more sympathetic counselor because of
Aaron's life and death than I would ever have been
without it. And I would give up all those gains in a
second if I could have my son back.

– Harold Kushner

The "price" we pay for our wisdom can be high. In Kushner's case, and most likely for all of us men who have lost children, the cost of our wisdom came too high. Likely all of us would trade the lessons learned to have our child back.

And I would, too, in a second.

In an attempt to loosen rusted bolts holding our aging television antenna in a less-than-effective direction, my son scurried up to the top of the thirty foot tower without hesitation. My skin crawled with fear, and I asked him to be careful after climbing so high. Without looking down at me, he quickly replied, "Don't sweat it, Dad. I'll be climbing a lot higher than this when we build your new house." Plans were underway to start constructing our retirement home and he was the designated contractor. He and one of his friends died a few weeks later in a boating accident on Lake Michigan.

I would give up any gain, anything at all, to have my loved one back.

SEPTEMBER 2

With the real (person) gone, the dialogue cannot continue. Not only have you lost the real (person); you have also lost the interplay that has enriched your internal life.

– Barbara D. Rosof

This loved one we have lost left a gaping hole in the fabric of our lives. We can feel the absence. The telephone no longer rings on the usual day. We miss the warmth of the voice. And the sound of the front door opening that used to announce our loved one's arrival is deafeningly quiet.

The real person is gone.

And here we are, left behind, to cope as best we can. Perhaps we have saved the voicemail messages. Some of us have been able to listen to them, an attempt to soften some of our grief. Others of us have not been able to work up the courage to listen to the now-absent voice that brought so much love and laughter into our world. We'll listen one day, we tell ourselves. Perhaps we will.

What I miss the most is the banter I once enjoyed with my son. We loved to tease each other and to share puns. He liked to groan in a display of artificial agony whenever I came up with a humorous use of a word with a double meaning. Then, happily for me, he started manufacturing his own puns in the few years before his death. I miss, beyond words, this interplay we enjoyed.

Dear _____, I miss our conversations. I miss your voice. I miss you!

SEPTEMBER 3

You prepare for one sorrow,
but another comes.

– Derek Walcott

Perhaps we were expecting a different sort of sorrow rather than the loss of our loved one. Maybe we were thinking that a relationship problem, rather than the death of someone we love, would rear its ugly head. Death is much uglier. We may feel caught off guard. Off balance. Dizzy. Wounded.

Death is likely more than we bargained for.

Why is that? We all know death is on its way. We have known this truth for a long time. Still, until now, death seemed to happen to other people, to someone else's family. Not ours. Not us. Why is something clearly expected, so awful? Today, though, death has knocked on our door and we must answer the summons. We may have prepared for a different sorrow, but life has handed this one to us.

So we face an uncertain tomorrow, a future that does not guarantee our own presence; perhaps we should take comfort in the realization that we are alive today. We are breathing. Our body is functioning. We can move when we choose to move. We are thinking clearly. We are mourning deeply.

Today is a gift. Who knows what tomorrow will bring?

My heart is broken at the unexpected loss of my loved one.
Still, I am grateful I exist today.

SEPTEMBER 4

*...there is no more ridiculous custom than the one
that makes you express sympathy once and for all
on a given day to a person whose sorrow will endure
as long as his life. Such grief, felt in such a way, is
always "present," it is never too late to talk about it,
never repetitious to mention it again.*

– Marcel Proust

Perhaps we have already been on the receiving end of uncomfortable stares, hesitant words. Those we hoped would help us through our loss may or may not have been able to join us in our grief. Others whom we have not known or known only from a distance may have stepped unafraid into our shattered world.

We are grateful someone came.

But few suggested our sorrow could endure and long-term support might be needed. I recall standing in the receiving line at our son's funeral, hoping that some of those who came to greet us would return to share their stories. Some did. Most did not. This may be the norm.

I once had no idea what to say or do for the grief-stricken. I remember greeting a friend whose mother had died recently. My tongue was tied. I had no idea what to say, so I said nothing. Since then, I have learned to simply say... I am so sorry for your loss. I have also learned to say it repeatedly.

I am grateful that some people mention my loved one regularly. My pain and sorrow feel timeless. I drink in their words like a thirsty traveler.

SEPTEMBER 5

If there is no wind, row.

– Latin Proverb

For most of us, the death of our loved one may feel like someone let the wind out of our sails. We may feel adrift with our grief on the calm water, without strength to propel toward a landmark. We may have forgotten the emergency oars stowed below deck.

With luck, we remember them just in time.

Even though our hearts may be broken, we still have the power of choice. We control our attitude even when we have no control over our circumstance. We cannot change the reality of this death, but we are in control over how we respond to it. The first few hours or days or weeks following our loss may possibly feel like we are free-falling without a parachute. Sooner or later, though, we come to realize that we are in charge of the direction our grief takes. We can try to make something positive out of our loss or we can give in to endless despair. The choice is ours.

We can dig out the oars and row, or wait for the wind to take us where we may not want to go.

Though seeing the world through grief-clouded eyes, I recognize I have choices in how I grieve the loss of my loved one. I hope for the strength to make helpful decisions.

SEPTEMBER 6

I wouldn't mind dying young... I've had a full life already.
— Mary Hickman, Age 16

The idea of a premonition of death may fly in the face of our rational thinking. Yet we have likely heard such stories about men and women who, for inexplicable reasons, feel they will die sooner rather than later.

Who knows how some of us seem to know?

These words were spoken by the sixteen year old daughter of Martha Hickman, the author of *Healing after Loss: Daily Meditations for Working through Grief.* Mary died in a horse-back riding accident shortly afterwards. Martha ponders that those of us who lose loved ones often look back for signs the death was approaching. If we had known, could we have prevented the death?

Unlike Martha's daughter, if my son had any thoughts of an early death, he kept them to himself. He enjoyed adventurous activities as many young men do. Mountain climbing, riding motorcycles, bicycling, hiking, camping, traveling, and every water-related activity were on his daily list of things to do. Some could argue these are dangerous pursuits, but perhaps most of us enjoyed them as well. And still do.

This I know: my son packed enough adventure for three normal men into his brief twenty-seven years. Did he know he would die young? I'll never know.

As a man, I am often challenged to accept information about death and dying that I do not understand. This is tough for me to do. I hope for the courage to consider all possibilities.

SEPTEMBER 7

If you love me, let me go.

– Source Unknown

Perhaps letting go of someone we love is the hardest thing we men will ever do. We tend to keep our emotions tucked away safely inside. We may feel broken hearted, yet present to the world a stoic face.

Our challenge is letting our feelings out.

Whenever my son would set off for another adventure with his friends, I shared only one admonition with him: please come back safely. Come back home when you are finished. I'll be waiting. Come back to your family. He always smiled, gave me a man-hug, and assured me that he would indeed come back. Once while crossing the Bay of Honduras on a German sailing boat in a bad storm, he told of how he hung onto the railing of the boat while waves crashed repeatedly over the vessel. At some point, he explained, he wanted to give up. Exhausted from the effort it took to maintain his grip, he wanted to let go. "But," he said with a smile, "I could hear you telling me to come back. So I held on and here I am."

Still, life offers no guarantees. When we let go, we have to turn and walk away with our memories. It is that simple. And difficult. Sometimes gut-wrenching.

I will let go of those I love. And they will let go of me. What else can we do?

SEPTEMBER 8

Laugh and cry does live in the same house.

– Trinidadian Proverb

For broken-hearted men, it may be difficult to consider the wisdom of the words above. Still, upon reflection, we might recall the phrase, "…he laughed until he cried." There likely have been times in our lives when we did the same. Our joy reduced us to tears.

And now our sorrow has done the same.

It may be odd to think that two such different emotions can live in the same house, our hearts. Yet tears free us from our interior lives. Tears free us to share the joys and sorrows of the world. And laughter does the same.

I once attended a workshop on the value of laughter for therapeutic purposes. Our filled-to-capacity room was silent. Soon, a woman walked into the room and stood at the front. Then, she began to laugh. She continued laughing, louder, with deep guffaws. Some of us smiled at the scene and at each other, wondering what to do. Quickly, a few bouts of laughter broke out. In short order, the entire packed room was laughing. No one knew why. Many people started to cry, and tears were streaming down many faces.

Then the presenter suddenly stopped laughing. It took several moments for our laughter to subside. Then, she spoke. "You can laugh because you are happy, if you are sad, or for no reason at all. Laughter makes you feel better." It was an unforgettable lesson.

In the midst of my tears, I have reasons for joy. I will not disregard them. My loved one wants me to re-engage in life. And I will.

I knew I couldn't bring people back from the dead. I got that part of it. But I also knew that if I was with someone who had lost somebody, I might be able to make them feel better.

– Whoopi Goldberg

We cannot change the reality of the death of our loved one, but we can seek out those who might understand our grief because they have been through a similar loss. Finding someone like that may help.

And having a traveling companion through grief will soften our sorrow.

When my son died in a boating accident, I was soon face-to-face with a woman who specialized in working with people who had suffered traumatic loss. As I walked in to meet her, I could tell by the look in her eyes that somehow she understood. I was taken aback. This woman whom I had never met until that moment understood the depth and breadth of my loss. How, I wondered, was this possible?

When someone we love dies, we incorrectly believe that no one has ever suffered such a tragic loss before us. Yes, our loss is unprecedented. This is true. Yet similar losses have been occurring since the dawn of humans. She had walked into the lives of many others who had suffered the same fate as my family. She understood my sorrow unlike anyone else before her. We may likely find it helpful to locate someone who understands.

I will look for someone who understands my loss so I can work through my grief in a healthy way.

SEPTEMBER 10

Inside this new love, die.
Your way begins on the other side.

– Jalal Al-Din Rumi

We mourning men, like sorrowful men of ages past, wonder endlessly where the spirit of our loved one has gone. Rumi's words suggest one possibility, to a new love on the other side. We were not intentionally abandoned. Life as we know it ends in death as we know it. But we know very little about death. Practically nothing.

The adventure of life may continue somewhere where we cannot yet follow.

But we will follow one day. We will know. In the meantime, we can take clues from the natural world. All forms of life on this earth are subject to the same life cycle as we humans. All are born, live, and die. There are no exceptions. And death creates the opportunity for new life.

There is no harm in guessing as to the possibilities inside this new love. Why not consider that the other side holds endless joy and adventure, not unlike some of our favorite activities here on earth. Why would a new world be dramatically different than the world we have come to love? Perhaps there are streams, lakes, and oceans waiting for us to explore. Why not mountains to climb, wilderness trails to explore, perfect campsites and no mosquitoes? Why not clear blue skies and dramatic lightning and thunder? Flowers to amaze? Strawberries and raspberries and blackberries for homemade pies?

And, perhaps best of all, why not everyone we have ever loved waiting to welcome us home?

I do not know what awaits me on the other side. No one does. If it is new love, then it may be more spectacular than anything I have ever imagined. One day I will know.

SEPTEMBER 11

...be gentle to yourself. You are a child of the universe, no less than the trees and the stars and you have a right to be here... be at peace with God, whatever you conceive Him (Her) to be.

– Max Ehrmann

Now is *not* the time for us to berate ourselves for some aspect of this death or to focus on some weakness we think may have had something to do with our loved one's departure. There will be time enough to ponder missteps, if any occurred. When our time comes, all of us die. It's that simple.

And what will assigning blame accomplish?

We men are all children of this universe. Each of us is important in the grand scheme. Consider our loved ones and the positive impact our presence has made in their lives. How much the world would have lost without us! If we do not feel this way right now, we can start fresh before nightfall. We can call a loved one and speak our love. Change can start that easily.

And we can be at peace with the ultimate puzzle of the universe as well: is there a God? We can't really know until we die, but we can keep the garden from overflowing with weeds, speak kindly to the cashier at the grocery store, say "please" and "thank you" as often as we can, and act kindly to all whom we encounter each day we live. And we can thank this lost loved one for his or her life and the richness it added to our own.

I will be gentle to myself. I am a child of this universe and have a right to be here.

There will come a time when you believe
everything is finished. That will be the beginning.

– Louis L'Amour

We may find it hard to consider the end of a loved one's life as the beginning of anything new. It is, in fact, the beginning of a world without the one we have lost. No wonder we may feel so devastated and alone. After all, we have been left behind to fend for ourselves.

And how can we create a new life alone?

This can be the overwhelming question that faces us when someone we love dies. In the early days following the death, we may imagine rebuilding our lives by ourselves. But we are never alone unless we choose to be. Individuals and organizations are waiting to help whenever we are ready for them. We simply need to take the initiative and reach out to them. This may be hard for us men to do. Perhaps we can take lessons from the women in our lives who love us. See how easily they call one another, make plans for coffee or lunch, take walks together, go to the movies with one another, help each other with household chores, or simply stop by because they were in the neighborhood? We men can do the same.

We often suffer needlessly because of our unwillingness to reach out to others for help. We can change that today. Who will we call for coffee and conversation tomorrow?

With this death I thought my life had ended. Now I see it has a new beginning. I am sad, but I will survive.

SEPTEMBER 13

In spite of everything, yes, let's!

– Vincent Van Gogh

We can take lessons from Vincent Van Gogh. His life was filled with trials, tribulations, and troubled relationships. Yet, he kept painting.

And in spite of the death of our loved one, we can choose to do the same.

We can say... yes, let's... to life in spite of this death. Maybe not today, or this week, or even this month. But, eventually, we can affirm the beauty, glory, and the extraordinary fact of our existence in this world and re-engage in the activities of life as soon as we are able. This is most likely what our lost one would want for us.

After my son's death, I started to re-engage slowly. I read a lot of grief recovery books, started seeing a professional mental health provider, but kept my distance from friends who struggled to pull me back into day-to-day activities. I wasn't ready at the time. I also held off writing in my journal. One morning, however, I picked up my pen and have not stopped writing since. Writing is not a cure-all, but it does help get feelings out of our stomach and onto a "table" of sorts. A piece of paper is a great receptacle for all kinds of pain.

My heart is broken, but I will not give up on life. In spite of death, I still say "Yes!" to life, to loving, and to learning about this remarkable existence.

SEPTEMBER 14

...I awoke at three, feeling terribly sad, and feeling rebelliously that I didn't want to study sadness, madness, melancholy, and despair. I wanted to study triumphs, the rediscoveries of love, all that I know in the world to be decent, radiant, and clear...

– John Cheever

What seems unique about Cheever's quote is that he is feeling rebellious and sad – he is not weary of it. He wants to tell it to go screw itself. There will come a day when we will move past this dark grief and into the light of a warm Indian summer afternoon. It happens gradually, not all at once. We can take our time.

Feelings change.

The writer Roger Rosenblatt arrived at a similar conclusion about a year after his daughter Amy's death from an unusual heart condition. In his book *Making Toast* he writes of growing tired thinking and reading about death and talking with others about death. Then he states... I grow weary of my anger.

If we are struggling in the depths of despair and our anger is fresh and raw, this may not be the time to consider the decency, radiance, and clarity of the world. But know when we begin to grow weary of sadness, madness, melancholy, and despair, healing is starting to take place. And when we tire of angry outbursts toward innocent bystanders, it may be time to shift our attention back to the wonders of love.

I will pay attention to where I am in the healing process following the death of my loved one. If I need help with this task, I will ask for it.

SEPTEMBER 15

The only intrinsic evil is lack of love.

– John Robinson

Some of us may have struggled within our love relationships. And this death may have left some of us with unfinished business. It is not too late to share our love in a letter with the one who is gone or to forgive this person if he or she withheld love from us. We can take our note to the burial site.

Sharing love and offering forgiveness are essential in every relationship. We still have time to act.

One challenge I often present to my students is both simple and difficult. I ask them to call three people they love and tell them before going to bed that night. For those who make a habit of expressing love, the assignment is easy. But for those who struggle with the "love" word, the homework may prove daunting. Still, the assignment is their homework.

One student told me he called his father when he got home from class. When his dad answered the phone, he blurted out the words, "Dad, I love you. I know you have always known, but I wanted you to hear the words." The silence on the other end of the line was scary at first, he said. But then his dad cleared his throat and slowly said, "Well, I guess I love you, too. We don't say it enough, do we?"

I will share my love with those I love. And I forgive those who have withheld their love from me. Perhaps no one taught them how.

Being human is difficult. Becoming human is a lifelong process. To be truly human is a gift.

– Abraham Heschel

The death of someone we love can be a wake-up call. It can be a tap on the shoulder, a reminder that we do not live forever. Are we human now, or in the process of becoming human? What does that mean for us? Being authentic? Not holding back? Listening to our small, inner voice?

If today is not the day, then when?

Listen to Thomas Morgan: "I was a 42-year old investment banker. I'm the least likely guy in the world you would ever expect to tell this story. I've never been a social worker or even socially engaged... I just wanted to make more money – all I thought about was the money." Thomas quit his job, sold his large home, and started working to help alleviate the plight of homeless people. His decision has taken his life in a "truly human" direction.

Yet becoming human doesn't require such dramatic change. It can simply be a change in our attitude. We can become more kind, sensitive, and compassionate. Perhaps this death is our gift, our invitation to a new world. After all, how much time do we think we have left?

I want to be human in every respect. The death of my loved one may be my wake up call. I still have time to change.

September 25, 2000, would not be the day I died by suicide. This would instead be the day of my awakening...

– Kevin Hines, Suicide Survivor

Perhaps this death was a suicide of a family member or friend. If so, chances are this person was a man. We kill ourselves at a dramatically higher rate than women.

Why?

We humans are herd animals. We need each other. We are not meant to live in isolation. Think about the worst form of punishment, short of death, that can be administered in a prison setting: solitary confinement. We punish people by forcing them to live alone. Yet living alone is precisely what many of us choose to do, even those who are a part of a family. Instead of isolating ourselves, we can choose to reach out.

We need to remember we are men of value. There are those who love and need us.

Life can get tough and reaching out when we first feel those dips of despair can be helpful to stave off a real crisis. Calling a twenty-four hour suicide hotline can be our salvation. So can a friend, a spouse, mother, father, neighbor, someone willing to listen and care. We are not alone.

Whenever I start thinking of suicide, I will use my courage to ask for help.

*...love was offered me and I shrank from its
    disillusionment;
Sorrow knocked at my door, but I was afraid...*

– Edgar Lee Masters

Many of us know by now that sorrow knocks on all doors sooner or later. Mourning our loss may be a painful reminder of this truth. Surprisingly, we may be afraid of sorrow for now, but perhaps, in time, we may make friends of it. What do we have to lose by trying?

Holding hands with sorrow takes its power away.

And cutting ourselves off from love because of its imperfection only puts more pain into our toolbox. We may recall the phrase...there is no perfection this side of heaven? This implies, of course, that there is such a place where perfection exists. We wonder. But, by keeping loving relationships at arm's length, we prevent the possibility of knowing someone intimately. True, we suffer no disillusionments when we choose not to love, but we also deprive ourselves of the possibility of unspeakable joy that can grow between two people in a loving relationship.

So, shall we take a chance on love? Shall we invite sorrow to a permanent place at our table? We may shrink back from either. Perhaps other options seem more appealing. The power to choose is still ours.

Dear _____, your death has caused me to consider how I want to spend the rest of my life. Thank you for this wakeup call.

Don't worry about losing... nothing good gets away.

– John Steinbeck, on love,
in a letter to his son

Perhaps our greatest fear has happened: the loss of our loved one. Is there anything of greater value that we can lose? And what of our previous fears of losing lesser things of this world? How do they compare?

But let us consider this "loss."

What exactly have we lost? We lost the physical presence of the one we love, but we did not and can never lose the spirit of our beloved one.

Please don't get me wrong. There is no greater loss for us human beings than the physical disappearance of someone we love. After my son died, I looked for him everywhere. I still do. I searched all the familiar places where he hung out with his friends. I endlessly called his name in our barn where he spent countless hours working on car and motorcycle projects. I looked for him in the small cabin next to the "children's forest" where he and his childhood friends played when they were young. And now, several years after his death, I still look for him in crowds or watch young men who have similar gaits thinking he might be my son. Absorbing the physical loss of our loved one is the major cause of our grief.

But my son's spirit will be with me always. I speak with him at will. He walks with me, still laughs at my bad jokes, shares puns, and commiserates with me when I am having a hard day. He is as close as my next thought. And so is your loved one.

It is true. Nothing good gets away. Even those we "lose."

SEPTEMBER 20

Hope is a risk that must be run.

– Georges Bernanos

In the face of this horrific loss, hope for us remains. When our days are bleak and our nights are sleepless, hope remains. When our agony feels endless, hope remains. When life has lost its luster, hope remains. When death seems to have been victorious, hope remains.

Hope is the thing with feathers... as Emily Dickinson declared.

And why not hope for a brighter tomorrow? When we men are in the throes of despair, looking up from a dark well, why not hope to reach for the sunshine we can glimpse at the surface? When every step we take seems to falter, when we stumble and fall, why not hope that someone will reach down and help us to our feet again? When the cold stars lose their sparkle and the night sky seems unfriendly, why not hope that the morning light will warm our troubled thoughts and chase our blues away? And when our tears flow like raindrops, why not hope for a friend who will watch the rain with us?

Is hope the look in a child's eyes? The twinkle in the playground laughter? The smile from across the room? The hug from a friend? The brush of the fingertips from the cashier? The warm rain on a chilly summer evening? The birdsong coming from the white pine? The singing of the waves against the rocky shoreline? The sound of our loved one's voice on the answering machine? The familiar smell of home?

I hope for a brighter tomorrow. Today I will pay attention to the many reasons I have for hope.

...every person's life is a story of passion, with its moments of joy and happiness, of tragedy or sorrow. And each person's story is different, one from the other.

– Stephen Breyer

What do we do when we meet one another after a period of absence? We tell each other stories. And in our sorrow over the death of this loved one, perhaps we have spent time doing the same. Each person lives a life full of adventure and love. And, almost always, laughter.

Each life is a story worthy of telling.

On a short walk last evening, my wife and I encountered a mutual friend whose mother had died an hour earlier. Both he and his wife were distraught. We shared tears, offered condolences, and talked of the importance of parents in our lives. Soon, however, we started telling stories about his mother and our encounters with her through the years. We talked of her positive attitude, her ability to encourage others even hours before her death, her contagious smile, and her fighting spirit in the face of multiple health issues. We laughed as we remembered and honored her while standing on the sidewalk under a cloudy fall sky. Her life had been a life of joyful passion. Wonderful!

I want to live a life of joyful passion. The death of my loved one is a reminder that I need to start today.

*Angels whisper to a [mourning] man when he
goes for a walk.*
                            – Raymond Inmon

Whether we believe angels exist or not, taking a walk in the
woods on a warm fall day is food for our sad spirit. A kaleidoscope of colorful leaves – green, red, yellow, orange, and
brown – surrounds our suffering; all beckon us to lay down
our sorrow for a while and enjoy a forest rainbow.

And something whispers to us.

Where does that still, small voice inside come from? Each of
us gets to decide. Nature holds the potential cure for most any
ailment, including grief. When we do not know where to turn
for relief from our pain, a walk among the trees is a good place
to start. Trees are friends to all. They do not ridicule, criticize,
or judge. They stand tall in the face of adversity, teaching us
the power of friendship. They wait patiently for our companionship, and seem not to suffer in between our visits. They are
always happy to see us and invite us to sit on their branches
and sway with them in the breeze. Who cannot return from
a walk in the woods with at least some relief from a painful
experience?

*I will take a walk in the woods today. Perhaps the trees will
whisper healing words to my broken heart.*

*The turning point in the process of growing up is
when you discover the core of strength within you
that survives all hurt.*

— Max Lerner

Perhaps we thought we were already "grown up." Likely we are grown up physically, but growing up emotionally and psychologically happens in stages and we do not always pay attention to where we are in our growing journey. The death of a loved one is most likely an unwelcome and painful teacher.

None of us would ever ask for this lesson.

Regardless of our age, we have suffered and we have lost. And comparing losses is useless. What is the point of guessing who suffers more or who suffers less? When we lose, we hurt. Each loss, though, has served us. We have grown in our ability to withstand the pain of loss and carry on with our lives. This may be a reassuring surprise in the face of this death.

Before my son's death, I suffered the deaths of both parents, my mother-in-law, a variety of aunts, uncles, nieces, and grandparents from my own family as well as that of my spouse, work colleagues and their families, and the deaths of community members and their children. Now, the death of a child is the worst loss ever. Yet each previous death prepared me in unexpected ways for my son's death. The most important lesson? When he died, I knew I could not handle his death alone.

*I have a core of strength within me that will survive all hurt.
Still, I need the love and affection of family and friends to help
me through each loss. This need is not a sign of weakness. It is
a sign of my humanity.*

My mother was dead for five years before I knew that I loved her very much.

– Lillian Hellman

Perhaps like other friends we have not always had fulfilling relationships with our parents. In fact, some relationships have been painful and filled with terror and rage. Some of us may have been abused at the hands of our parents.

The parent-child relationship is not always pretty.

If today we are mourning the death of a mean-spirited parent, we may be relieved that our suffering is over. Still, we may also be confused, even perplexed. Perhaps we have been told repeatedly that we should love our parents. But how can we love a parent (or anyone) who has withheld love from us? Who has, in fact, harmed us during our formative years? This is a tough call. Perhaps we might remember that forgiveness is, first of all and most importantly, a gift we give ourselves. Whether we choose to forgive or not is a personal decision. Professional help may be needed. For those who do forgive, freedom awaits.

And we mourning men deserve our freedom.

I will let go of something bad that happened to me in the past rather than continue carrying it. There are many things in life I will never understand. This may be the biggest one.

*The mind is its own place and in itself can make a
hell of heaven or a heaven of hell.*

– John Milton

Perhaps we know other guys who always seem to have a black
cloud hanging over their heads. They look on the dark side of
life. And mourning the loss of our loved one is hard enough
without their declarations that they could "see this death
coming from a mile away."

How could they think these words would bring comfort?

Our attitude dictates our happiness. And we choose our attitude. If we choose to see everything in life as a problem, then
everything becomes problematic. If we choose to see our daily
experiences as a grand adventure, then life, and yes, even death,
become grand adventures. It is this simple. So the manner in
which we grieve the death of our loved one will most likely be
the manner in which we approach our daily lives. We will temporarily be overcome by sorrow and despair. When someone
we love dies, we have a right to those feelings. But we will not
allow despair to rule the rest of our days.

And our "black cloud" friends will have to take their perspec-
tives elsewhere.

*I will try to make this hell of a death into a heaven. I will do
this to honor the life of my loved one.*

SEPTEMBER 26

Twilight and evening bell
And after that the dark!
And may there be no sadness
of farewell
When I embark...

— Alfred, Lord Tennyson,
"Crossing the Bar"

In Tennyson's "Crossing the Bar" he bids farewell to a life well-lived and a world of wonder at sea. Perhaps we men can embrace the concept and hope that our loved one left this world in a similar state of gratitude and lack of regret.

After all, isn't this the way most of us would prefer to die?

In a recent conversation with a dear friend, she told the story of how her dying mother recited this poem just four hours before her death. And after reciting it once, she began a second time and was able to finish just half of the lines before she died. Then, her daughter's eyes dancing in the telling of the story, she said her mother's friend in the next bed picked up on the poem where her mother had left off and finished it for her.

Is there a greater tribute?

When I die, may there be... no sadness of farewell... or reason for regret.

...does anyone know where the love of God goes when the waves turn the minutes to hours?

> – Gordon Lightfoot, "The Wreck
> of the Edmund Fitzgerald"

The death of a loved one scrambles our lives like nothing else. Especially if the death was sudden or unexpected, like the death of a child, we are caught off-guard and our "shell" of protection is shattered.

We have had a great fall, indeed!

Our futures, which shortly before looked so solid and secure, may now lie in a crumpled heap of sadness and despair. We look around in a vain attempt to place blame, but the path in either direction is empty. Even if we tried, our fingers could point to no one.

A friend hears a commotion in her adult daughter's room and rushes to her side. She finds her beloved child in convulsions and picks her up to hold and comfort her. Somehow she is able to call for help, but before help arrives, her daughter dies in her arms.

Does anyone know where the love of God goes in such circumstances? No, no one knows. Perhaps one day we will.

The bough which has been downward thrust by force of strength to bend its top to earth, as soon as the pressing hand is gone, looks up again straight to the sky above.

– Boethius

Is there a heavier hand than death? The death of a loved one thrusts us downward and causes our spirits to bend low. How can we remove this heavy-handed intruder?

And will we ever be able to see the sky again?

Thankfully, the human spirit always seeks blue sky. Like cattails blown low by a storm, as soon as the winds shift from a new direction, the cattails stand tall again. This death is a cold gust of wind blowing our spirit downward. We have been caught off-guard, our spirit pummeled low to the ground. Still, almost against our will, we insist on pushing back skyward, rising to our feet as soon as we regain strength. We do not know when that will be, but we hope soon.

And how will we know when the "pressing hand" is gone? When we talk of our loved one's death without crying every time. When we start reading books on topics other than death and dying. When we no longer need daily support and reassurance from family and friends. And when we start helping others who have suffered similar losses.

In spite of my sorrow, I want to eventually look up again straight to the sky. I want my spirit to once more soar. I will ask for help when I need it, and I will offer my help when it is needed.

SEPTEMBER 29

Sorrow that hath no vent in tears maketh the organs of the body weep.

– Samuel Johnson

We feel our loss throughout our bodies as well as in our hearts and minds. Not only are our spirits saddened, but our bodies have suffered severe blows. Some men report looking down at themselves and feeling like the body they see does not belong to them anymore.

This is what unattended sorrow will do to our bodies.

One of our responsibilities (there are so many!) after the death of a loved one is to take good care of our body. This may also be the last thing we want to do. We might have little physical strength for even the smallest of manual tasks. Exercise even seems futile. Useless. Why bother? What's the use? See how quickly death comes?

Yet, there are those who need us. In spite of this death, many loved ones live and expect us to remain a vital part of their lives. We have a responsibility to them and to countless others who also depend upon us. We may have friends in our workplaces, faith communities, civic organizations, township, city, county or state government entities, or a host of other organizations where we volunteer.

So, does our presence in this world still matter? Yes, indeed!

In spite of the death of one I love, my life still matters. I will take care of my body so I can continue to attend to the needs of this world.

SEPTEMBER 30

The first time you go back to anything that once gave you pleasure, you may feel unsure or disloyal. Eating chocolate, going swimming, visiting with friends, watching a movie, making love – whatever you do feels different now.

– Barbara Rosof

Everything is the same and nothing is the same. This is the aftermath of the death of a child. We struggle in ways that may perplex our partners. Their struggles may confuse us as well. We are, after all, two different human beings.

And no two hearts are the same.

So, here is to our differences. Let us honor our partners and the unspeakable loss they have suffered. We, too, have suffered the same loss, but in very different ways. We did not carry this child inside us for nine months. We did not bond in the same way. The mother/child relationship has always been and will always be sacred in mysterious ways that we cannot understand. This is the way of the world.

What we need now is endless love, patience, compassion, tolerance, and someone who cares enough to listen as we repeat the stories of our lost child again and again. We love our son or daughter as much as ever and do not want anyone to ever forget them. We want fearless friends to bring up our child's name in conversations and to ask us how we are coping with their physical absence. We want our friends to stop avoiding us and treating us like we have a terminal illness. We want the same thing our spouses want.

Our child has died. That's all.

My child is dead. I am alive. Please do not ignore my loss.

∾ OCTOBER ∾

OCTOBER 1

*...our gusty emotions say to me that we have
Tasted heaven many times...*

– Robert Bly

When someone we love dies, we naturally turn to our lurking questions regarding the existence of an afterlife. Specifically, we want assurance that there is one. Yet, who knows?

Many spiritual traditions declare an afterlife to be factual, and actual.

Still, we may wonder, and ruminate. Why not, instead, take a look around us and see what may very well be elements of a "heaven" right here on earth. These words from Bly's poem refer to a teenage romance and the object of his affection, a fifteen year old girl. Perhaps we recall the wonder of an early romance of our own. Would we not have described it as heavenly? Consider our first look at the breathtaking glory of the Grand Canyon, Niagara Falls, or the color and texture of a mud pot in Yellowstone National Park. Or the fresh unfolding of red rose petals. Or the feel of a puppy's tongue licking our face. Or our newborn's fingers grasping ours. Or a warm October night sky filled with countless stars. Are these not also heavenly?

A good friend explains, "I don't worry about whether there is anything after this life ends. I try my best to do right by others, enjoy the beauty of this earth, and be a good man. If there is something else after I die, it will be a bonus."

Sounds to me like he gets a taste of heaven every day. Perhaps that is what our loved one did.

I do not know what happens after I die. But this I do know. I will do my best now to enjoy what this world has to offer, and let the future take care of itself.

All the grudges and sorrows have now passed.

– Hafiz of Persia

The death of someone we love closes the door on earthly concerns. For our lost one, all problems, and time as we know it, have ended. For us survivors, former concerns may have faded into the background of our new lives without the one we love. What may have been important before may no longer be important now. And what may have been trivial before this death may now mean the world to us.

Death usually rearranges our priorities.

And our focus may now be on the present moment instead of the distant future or past. If we carried a grudge against the one who has departed this world, well, what shall we do with it other than set it down and walk away? Or if we have been harboring a secret sorrow that somehow involved the one who is dead, is it also time to release that? Grudges and sorrows are heavy. They weigh a lot. We get tired lugging them around. It is okay to release them and walk away, lighter and happier. Free.

One elderly friend said at her husband's funeral, "Well, I guess my work is done. There is no one to be angry at anymore." She died herself fewer than two months later.

Let me take this in completely: all grudges and sorrows have now passed. I am free!

OCTOBER 3

There ain't no answer.
There ain't going to be any answer.
There never has been an answer.
That's the answer.

– Gertrude Stein

The death of someone we love raises more questions about life and death than our minds can possibly comprehend or even attempt to answer. If we were perplexed about life before this death, we may be even more so now.

There will always be more questions than answers.

Perhaps we thought as we grew older, answers to life's questions would become clearer. Likely this has not happened. The questions keep piling up, the answers continue shrinking down. Simple issues befuddle us. After my father's death and while I sat next to his body on the hospital bed, I looked around his room and saw his glasses and set of dentures. I instantly wondered, what will I do with those now? And while I continued to hold his hand and sit gazing outside his room window, I saw a robin, red tulips, yellow daffodils, and the hospital lawn that needed mowing. My voice was barely a whisper. How can everything be the same? My father is dead! How can everything be as it was before he died?

No one answered.

I will always have questions that no one can answer. This is the way of life. I must learn to love the questions themselves.

OCTOBER 4

To see a World in a Grain of Sand
And a Heaven in a Wild Flower,
Hold Infinity in the palm of your hand
And Eternity in an hour.

– William Blake

The death of an infant may be the cruelest death of all. Whether still-born or dead of complications soon after birth, there is faint chance to bond, to get to know one another on this earthly plane. No chance for expressions of joy, no time for laughter, for the interaction we have likely looked forward to since conception. The baby showers, the silent crib, the baby's room empty, quiet. Our aching outstretched arms and unfulfilled dreams. The still rocking chair. Goodnight Moon waiting patiently by the bedside.

We may be looking at Heaven in a Wild Flower if we are gazing upon an infant who has died. Such innocence. Beauty. Infinity! All wrapped up in... Eternity in an hour.

What is a man to do in the face of such loss?

We must be gentle, endlessly patient, kind, forgiving, tolerant, attentive, and love ourselves and our partner like we have never loved before. And tenderly reach out for help.

In the face of this horrific loss, I will love myself and my partner like I have never loved before.

OCTOBER 5

Many heroes are not yet born,
many have already died.

– West African Song

Today we may be mourning the death of a hero or heroine. We each have our individual definition of heroic deeds. Regardless of how this person gained heroic status in our minds, we are grief-stricken at his or her loss.

The world is a lonelier place because of this individual's absence.

Perhaps our hero or heroine is a war veteran recently returned from overseas duty. Or a firefighter caught in a wind shift while fighting wildfires. Or a child, a son or daughter, who served the poor or tried to teach our culture a more earth-friendly way to live. Or perhaps the grocery store bagger who performed her job without complaint and with a smiling attitude week after week. Or maybe the ninety-one year old clerk at the used cloth-ing store who always had a kind story to share and a smile to beam to the world. Or possibly a grandchild who always loved to climb into his or her grandparent's laps for stories and hugs.

Whomever we mourn this day, this world has lost a remark-able human being.

Today I have lost a hero or heroine. They are hard to find. My grieving heart is broken. I will seek out a friend so I have someone with whom I can share my story.

OCTOBER 6

When you were born, you cried
and the world rejoiced.
Live your life in such a way
that when you die, the world cries
And you rejoice.

– Cherokee Saying

The Cherokee people may have a comforting admonition for us. Today we grieve the death of a loved one. Yet this death is a message to us survivors as well: live a meaningful life. If we are pleased with our lives, we carry on. If we are restless or unfulfilled, we still have time to change direction.

As long as we breathe, we can make different choices about how we want to spend our days on earth.

It is likely that when most of us were born, the world rejoiced. Few of us arrived unwelcomed. Then, we set out to discover how we wished to contribute to the world. Our contributions help define us and our place in the greater life drama. What we choose to do with our lives makes a difference to us and to those who love us. We do not want to arrive at death's door thinking our life was unimportant, or, worse yet, unnecessary. We want to know our life matters and that other lives had less pain because we were here to help. We hope the world cries when we die, that we will be mourned and missed.

And we certainly hope we rejoice on the other side where our loved one may be waiting for us when it is our turn to die.

I am listening to the message of this death. I want my life to matter.

OCTOBER 7

We mourning men are often courageous fellows. Oh, yes, we may have our moments of weakness and fear, but who doesn't? We learn to be courageous by making mistakes. And if we live long enough, we also become courageous by experiencing the deaths of loved ones.

Each death we survive means we still live and have more time to grow.

We also realize that we have less and less to lose. The old saying, "When you have nothing, you have nothing to lose" applies. And as we live our lives and survive the deaths of those we love, things begin to mean less to us as well. After my folks died, my brothers and I were faced with the daunting task of what to do with their things. They had a household full of sixty years of accumulation. All of us already had the essential washers, dryers, refrigerators, stoves, furniture galore. What should we do with theirs? As we made decisions and saw their possessions out the door, we realized how unimportant things become. We came to see that our love for each other is what ultimately matters.

And if we have slippers to wear at the end of our lives, well, most likely we'll be pleased to wear them to the other side so at least our feet will stay warm. The rest of our things will have to stay here.

I hope for the courage to stride out with my slippers on when it is my turn to leave.

OCTOBER 8

So will I, softly,
Day long, night long
Change my sorrow
Into song.

– Sara Teasdale

In the early throes of our grief, it may be impossible for us to believe that we will ever smile again. After all, how can we laugh when someone dear to us has died? What is so funny about death?

Nothing.

Yet, will we wish to scowl the rest of our days? The world is still beautiful and the earth turns faithfully on its axis. And, look. The sunrise dries our tears and the sunset coaxes us to sit and rest awhile. Life is still beautiful in spite of our horrific loss. Love reigns. One day we will sing again. Perpetual sorrow is most likely not what our loved one had in mind for us as a going away gift.

On my Uncle Earl's faithful visits to central Michigan, my family home would begin to ring with the sounds of laughter and storytelling. The joy began as soon as he opened the side door and stepped into our tiny foyer and up the stairs into the kitchen. His deep-throated laughter was infectious. He and my parents would launch into the latest family affairs and he always gave us kids a hug. He was determined to sow joy wherever he traveled. On his deathbed, he handed my father the key to his safety deposit box and with a subtle smile said, "You're in charge now, young brother." Even impending death could not change his attitude.

So will I, softly… change my sorrow into song. This will take time. I will become a more patient man.

OCTOBER 9

[Men] who try to drown their sorrows
Should be told
Sorrow knows how to swim.

– Ann Landers

One of our temptations after the death of a loved one is to drink ourselves into oblivion, anything to help numb us from the loss we have suffered. At social occasions we may witness friends filling our glasses beyond normal limits. It is their attempt to help ease our pain. At first we may appreciate their efforts. But the small voice inside us eventually points to the error in our thinking.

Excessive alcohol is not the solution to grief. Consciously working through grief is the only helpful choice.

If we have been in Alcoholics Anonymous, we already know this. So we may call our sponsor more often to help us through any possible temptations to slip backwards. If we are social drinkers and have been able to handle alcohol so far, we may be at greater risk. After all, having a little more to drink can be understood given this death. Friends will most likely tolerate it. But we are the ones who have to live with ourselves and our families. They still need us. They are likely suffering, too. They cannot afford to lose our love and support while we mentally wander away. Unless we work through grief, we will be endlessly treading in sorrow.

Wherever I go, sorrow will follow. Drinking myself silly will only provide temporary relief. And when I awake, I'll be back where I started. Instead, I'll ask friends to show me a better way.

OCTOBER 10

Don't wait for a light to appear
at the end of the tunnel;
March down there and turn
the darn thing on yourself.

– Sara Henderson

Some of us may be waiting for someone to rescue us from our grief. After all, we are the ones who are suffering. And, haven't we helped others through their grief in the past?

Have we?

It is likely that some of us have helped others through grief and some of us have not. Many of us have not known what to do in the face of grief and sorrow. We attend funerals or avoid them, send cards or forget to send them, speak words of comfort, or avoid contact with those who suffer. We may fear saying "something wrong." And some of us feel that others should "have their privacy" when it comes to the death of a loved one. Perhaps all of us have been one of these men at one time or another.

And so if we are waiting for help with our own grief, we may have to wait a long time. It is likely up to us to reach out and ask for help, to turn on our own light at the end of the tunnel. It is possible some brave family members and friends may show up uninvited, but many folks simply do not know what to say or do to help, so they say and do nothing.

I will not wait for a light to appear at the end of my tunnel.
As I work through my grief, I will ask for help when I need it.

OCTOBER 11

I'd like the tears of those who grieve,
To dry before the sun
Of happy memories that I leave
When my life is done.

— Source Unknown

At some point in our grief journey the pain begins to lighten up. It happens slowly, silently, almost unobserved. One day we awaken and we feel different. It is hard to explain. Something is changing. And we may wonder what is happening to us.

Our anguish feels more manageable.

Are we feeling better? If so, what does this mean? What does "better" imply? Forgetting our loved one who has died? No. Forgetting, of course, will never be possible. Nothing to worry about there. How about "moving on?" Others may have asked us if we are ready to move on with our lives. No doubt many of us have been puzzled by the suggestion. Moving on suggests leaving someone behind. We have no plans to ever leave the memory of our beloved one behind. So, how about feeling better for the simple sake of feeling better? Do we intend to grieve forever?

Perhaps we might hear the voice of our loved one recite the above stanza to us. Let's listen now...what do we hear? A wish for us that the rest of our days be filled with happy memories, that the sun dries our tears, that the leave-taking was not intentional.

Dear _____, I cherish your memory and the memories we made together. My tears are slowly drying before the sun. I know this is what you would want for me. Thank you!

OCTOBER 12

How the waters of the world are sweet – if we should die, we have drunk them... we have tasted of happiness – we must be written in the book of the blessed. We have had what life could give... we have been the mystery of the universe.

– Anne Morrow Lindbergh

To have lived at all is the greatest of joys. We often look for more of everything, thinking that more is better than less. But simply to have existed for a while, and still live, is the greatest and most mysterious gift of all.

To breathe, inhale and exhale, what joy!

These words written by Anne Morrow Lindbergh to her husband Charles on July 2, 1944, capture perfectly the nearly inexpressible joy of living even in the face of death. The sweet waters of the world, the tastes of happiness, belonging in the book of the blessed, being a part of the mystery of the universe. And, endlessly more. In spite of the death of our beloved one, the fact of our existence cannot be denied us. And that we existed together will always be our lasting treasure.

What else can this world offer that ultimately means more to us?

Dear _____, Nothing means more to me than that I shared my life with you. Thank you for sharing your precious life with me. I am eternally grateful.

OCTOBER 13

...henceforth Wendy knew that she must grow up.
You always know after you are two. Two is the
beginning of the end.

– J.M. Barrie, Peter Pan

We have known for a long time that there will be an end to life. It is just that the end seemed so far away. But now, here we are. Someone we love has reached the end. What felt to be so far away has arrived.

What a rude awakening.

Before my son died in a boating accident at twenty-seven years of age, he and his wife taught conversational English for one year in a high school in Macon, France. They had sought the cultural experience and to have a chance to become fluent in the French language. And they gladly ate a typical French diet of breads, cheeses, wines, and salads. Near the end of their successful teaching year, our son mentioned with some alarm to his wife that he had gained weight and was developing a small "belly" around his midsection. Although he never personally mentioned the story to me, my guess is that my son, who had previously had a near perfect physique, had gained a new insight concerning the life cycle. You always know after you are two. Two is the beginning of the end.

I know that life has a beginning and an end. This death is a
vivid reminder. I will treasure each day.

OCTOBER 14

At the end of your life you will never regret not having passed one more test, not winning one more verdict, or not closing one more deal. You will regret time not spent with a [spouse], a child, a friend, or a parent.

— Barbara Bush

When someone we love dies, the death may stir up all sorts of regrets. If we chose to list our failures, we may be in for a painful journey. Why not, instead, admit our regrets and then make changes to minimize them in the days to come? Why not spend more time with those who really matter to us?

This death may be an opportunity for a new life.

Relationships matter. How we love and care for those we love counts more than any earthly possession. Why are we grieving this loss? Because this person was someone we love and treasure and now he or she is no longer present to share life with us. We miss our loved one desperately. Our lives may seem empty now. The relationship we had with this person has changed and cannot ever be recovered in the old way. We may wander around, stunned at how fast our life has been abruptly transformed, how quickly death can intrude.

Are there others we love that we want to know better while we still have the chance? How can we make that happen? When will we start?

I want those I love to know it. I will make any necessary changes to make that happen.

OCTOBER 15

I have spread my dreams under your feet;
Tread softly because you tread on my dreams.

– William Butler Yeats

Perhaps a large part of our sorrow is the full impact on us of broken dreams. Especially if this death is that of someone young, we may be suffering the loss of a future devoid of what we had imagined. What we had hoped for. What we had been longing to live.

We mourn for the loss of our dreams, too.

This loved one may have been an important part of our vision for the days to come. What can we do now in the face of this horrendous loss? Perhaps we can consider the possibility, as much as we are able, of living out some of our loved one's dreams for him or her. Not every dream, certainly, but perhaps the spirit of what our loved one had in mind and shared with us in past conversations. Can we capture the essence and make it our own?

There is the old saying that declares, "Imitation is the purest form of flattery." Perhaps adopting our loved one's dreams and doing our best to incorporate them into our worldview may be the best way to honor his or her life. By this I do not mean setting aside personal goals. I mean adopting visions that can comfortably sit side-by-side with our own. Teamwork.

Before you died, you spread your dreams under my feet. Now I will honor your life by making as many of your dreams my own.

OCTOBER 16

Morality only is eternal. All the rest is balloon and bubble from the cradle to the grave.

– John Adams

Even though we may be overwhelmed with sorrow, we can now recognize right and wrong more clearly because what is insignificant has been cleared away. Living a life of integrity is what matters.

The death of a loved one slows us men down and gives us pause for reflection. Sitting quietly in a funeral parlor provides an opportunity to consider the direction our lives have taken. We may wonder Is this the way I wish to live? Many of us might envision our own bodies lying in the open casket. That gets our attention. Could the trembling voice within be nudging us in a new direction?

Since my son's death, I have placed all life options on the table: Work, full-time or part-time; retirement; volunteer opportunities; travel; new hobbies. My wife and I have already built and moved into the new, small retirement home he designed for us before he died. We both worked side -by-side with friends and other work crew members for sixteen months to build the house. This home was his dream for us. Building it was the right thing to do.

I know the difference between right and wrong. I will strive to live a moral life, a life of integrity. The rest is balloon and bubble.

OCTOBER 17

I didn't know myself well, and still don't. But I did know, and know now, the few people I loved and trusted. My feeling for them is one part of me I have never quarreled with, even though my relations with them have more than once been abrasive.

– Wallace Stegner

The death of a loved one gives us a rare opportunity to open ourselves to scrutiny from the inside. We have a chance to reflect on our lives and to review our feelings toward those we love, including the one now gone from our presence.

We have a chance to get to know ourselves better.

Do we like what we see? Many of us do. Some of us don't. Death taps us on the shoulder and reminds us that life is short, and getting to know ourselves can be a long journey. Being truthful to ourselves and others is a readily accessible part of the trip. Being kind, compassionate, considerate, helpful, tolerant, trustworthy, polite, forthright, friendly, and fun to be with also helps. Keeping promises and taking a genuine interest in the lives of others enables us to see our motives more clearly. And serving others in spite of our sorrow can be healing when working through the grief of losing those we love.

Plus we can forgive ourselves for being abrasive with the one now gone. We still love that person. And he or she forgave us.

I am getting to know myself better. This is a life-long journey. I am sorry for the death of my loved one but thankful for this chance for reflection.

Only love heals, makes whole, takes us beyond ourselves... Love gets us There, lets us know Who speaks.

– Marsha Sinetar

Maybe we have always known this. Only love heals. So in our quest for healing after the death of one we love, we are drawn to someone who will love us until we are healed, and beyond. A person unafraid of sorrow. We search willing eyes and hearts. We need someone with the strength and experience to enter pain without flinching. Someone fearless. A person who will stay.

And when we find a healer, the healer rejoices in having found us as well.

Those who have mourned understand the mourner. And understanding helps us heal. Understanding ...takes us beyond ourselves... and back into the realm of hope. We may never have needed hope more in our lives than after the death of a loved one.

Sometimes friends can offer hope. And, at times, even strangers. If we belong to a spiritual community, some members may have excellent listening skills and compassionate hearts. Or we can turn to professional help in the form of licensed professional counselors, social workers, psychologists, or psychiatrists. All can help us find our way through the grief maze and help heal our broken hearts. And all are capable of great love.

My heart is broken at the loss of my loved one. I want to find someone who will teach me how to hope again. And I want this person to have a kind, compassionate, caring, and loving heart.

She's lost her son to an I.E.D. No details yet.
Routine patrol around a dusty village far away.

– David Bottoms

The old phrase "Every man for himself!" has no place in military parlance. The death of one soldier grieves every soldier, and parent, too. Today we may be grieving the death of a member of the military, either from our immediate family, or from our extended military family.

If so, Ernest Hemingway's words may reverberate, "Do not ask for whom the bell tolls, it tolls for thee."

The death of a loved one in a "far away" place, especially if we have lost a military child, may be one of the hardest deaths of all. We likely feel helpless. Alone. And every sinew of our fatherly hearts may be crying out because we were unable to protect our loved one. What is a father to do?

Or perhaps we grieve the death of a beloved friend and fellow soldier who died at our side or in our arms in the field. Perhaps no patrol is "routine" with death lurking around every corner in a distant far away village.

Or maybe we have lost a military mother or father. The call of duty can be the most expensive call of all for a man or woman with children at home. And leaving children behind may be an inexpressible loss for them.

Grief counseling is available. Don't wait.

I will not wait to seek professional help if I cannot make the transition back to civilian life on my own. If I am feeling suicidal, I will call the Veteran's Administration suicide hotline and ask for help.

Some people have the gift of pulling themselves up and out and saying there is more to life than just tragedy. And then there are those who can't, and I'm one of them.

— Maurice Sendak

Perhaps we men reading this book are among those who have the gift... of pulling themselves up and out... after a tragedy. Or possibly we wonder if this ability is a gift given to some, but not to others. Perhaps it is more helpful to think of pulling ourselves "up and out" of grief as a choice.

Thinking this way gives us the power to decide how we want to live the rest of our days.

Should any man judge another man's life? Each of us has our own interpretation of what our life has been and what we might have preferred it to be. No two siblings would describe their growing up years exactly the same. One child may have had a wonderful childhood, the other a miserable one. Same parents, different interpretation of family events.

Some guys walk around with a black cloud hanging over their heads. Others blame Mondays for their grumpy moods. Still many blame their childhood years for the way they have chosen to live their adult years. Perhaps choosing to adjust our "life sails" to take advantage of the ever-changing wind direction might unlock a more helpful and hope-filled journey. It may be worth a try.

In spite of this death, I want to learn how to look on the brighter side of life. If I need someone to help me do this, I will seek help.

OCTOBER 21

Nothing could stop you.
Not the best day. Not the quiet.
Not the ocean rocking.
You went on with your dying.

– Mark Strand

Maybe this brief description also describes the death of your loved one and your inability to effect any change in the events of that day. Such a helpless feeling! We men are used to having a lot of control. But no one controls dying.

And our loved one did the dying, not us.

Our son and his friend died on a glorious April afternoon. The temperatures had been unusually warm for a northern Michigan spring. We had agreed on different plans for that day, but he and his friend changed their plans to accommodate what was to have been a brief romp on Little Traverse Bay in Lake Michigan. My wife and I both protested the change, but he was convinced their outing would be brief and fun and he would rejoin us later in the day. We both asked him not to go, but he insisted. My wife and I kissed him and said goodbye. There were no hard feelings, just frustration in the abrupt change of plans. Our beautiful adult son and his dear friend died later that afternoon after their canoe capsized in frigid waters.

What else can a father do?

Nothing could stop you... you went on with your dying. Oh how I wish I could have stopped you!

OCTOBER 22

I have seen the apples there that toss
you secrets –
Beloved apples of seasonable madness...

– Hart Crane

We grieve so many losses with this death of our loved one! One is the loss of sharing so many of the riches of the earth, including the changing seasons. What a delight it is to anticipate the excitement of each equinox and the favorite rites that accompany the three-month cycles.

And one great sorrow is that our beloved one will not be here to enjoy them with us.

Recently there was an antique car show in our neighborhood. My son loved cars of all kinds, and often purchased "beaters" so he could fix them and sell them for a small profit. So when I saw the signs for the show, I immediately thought of him and lamented, Nate would have loved to go to this show with me. This way of thinking will likely haunt me the rest of my days. And whenever my wife and I encounter an experience that our son loved, we often share comments with each other like, Nate would have loved to see this, or I wish Nate could be here now to share this with us. And favorite foods? Nate was a great cook and often set a place at the table for himself with several plates and bowls so he could enjoy many foods side-by-side. He would have loved to taste his... beloved apples of seasonable madness.

I lament the death of my loved one and the ability to share the joys of living. I will always think of him/her whenever I taste and see the gifts of earth.

Bent with worry, God
paused, to smile.

– Marina Tsvetaeva

The notion that God would worry about us broken-hearted men may be comforting. After all, grieving requires all the attention we can muster. And that God would also smile, well, a smile feels like a father's love, warm and reassuring.

In these early days of grieving, we long to be cared for, to be told that healing will eventually come. At first this message may seem impossible to accept. With time and work, though, we start to understand that healing will likely occur after all. And we may even feel guilty at the notion of leaving our grief behind, like to do so would be to abandon the one we love and lost. These are normal feelings. But the one who is now on the other side wants us to heal.

On a beautiful evening in early July, more than three years after our son's death, my wife and I sat with David, our son's dear friend who has become like a son to us. Together, we watched a low-hanging cloud bank pass over the setting sun. All of a sudden I saw it. The clouds had separated enough to form a smiling human face. Had I seen this by myself, I would have questioned my sanity. But all three of us rejoiced at the wondrous scene. We felt a warm glow about us that this smile was a sign that our son was keeping watch from afar. Just like God paused to smile at us.

I am grateful that God seems to be keeping watch over me. Perhaps my beloved one is also keeping watch from afar. And smiling, too.

OCTOBER 24

For my people...
praying their prayers nightly to an
  unknown God, bending
their knees humbly to an unseen power...

– Margaret Walker

This is what many of us do. We pray our prayers... to an unknown God... an unseen power. We do this so we do not die. We need something or someone bigger than ourselves to be in charge. This may be the first time we recognize we cannot control life alone.

It's a tough lesson to learn.

Margaret Walker was writing about her people caught in the throes of slavery. Perhaps our arrogance has been a form of slavery for us men. Regardless of what we believe about an afterlife, many of us may find comfort in believing in something or someone other than ourselves as the ultimate authority.

Or, maybe not. Some of us are comfortable with the notion that this life is it. We do not need anyone's protection or guidance other than our own. So perhaps our prayers and kneeling are reflexes from our childhood days. Nothing more. And in this book, we simply read how other men have worked their way through the loss of a loved one.

I am working my way through grief the best I can. If I need to pray, I will pray. If I do not need to pray, that, too, is alright.

OCTOBER 25

The dead are dancing with the dead,
The dust is whirling with the dust.

– Oscar Wilde

The image of the dead dancing with the dead may bring some comfort to us. We "see" them having fun with other loved ones who have died and were waiting with open arms to greet them. We feel our dead are not alone.

And, in some sense, we can imagine what an afterlife with a dancing floor might look like.

Why not? It is innocent fun. And who knows what awaits us when it is our turn to leave? Perhaps "Dancing with the Stars" isn't too far off the mark after all. I have often pictured my mother and father dancing their beloved waltz to Lawrence Welk's "champagne orchestra." They faithfully watched his television show and often closed their eyes when a beloved song was being sung. Sometimes, they got up and danced on the worn living room carpet. Their footsteps fell perfectly aligned with each other, the result of years of practice at countless weddings. I still picture them as a young couple, madly in love, from two different cultures, with eyes only for each other.

I still see them in an embrace, moving gracefully in each other's arms, staring lovingly into each other's eyes.

I hope the dead are dancing with the dead! I love them and want them to be happy. I have no interest in a dull afterlife.

OCTOBER 26

Why do I tell you these things?
You are not even here.

– John Ashbery

The dead not here? Who knows for sure? We may only believe what we can see. Still, much mystery remains on this amazing planet. Who knows what we will discover about matter in the years to come? And why do we sense our loved one's presence from time to time? What is that all about?

Why not talk to our beloved dead as though they live? Perhaps they do.

A friend shuts his study door each week and speaks with his dead son. He brings him up-to-date with family news, recent stories from his own life, and, I assume, current world events. A highly educated man, he is perfectly comfortable doing this and has made it a habit over a number of years.

I speak with my own dead son whenever I walk or ride my bicycle and any time I have occasion to be alone. I ask him questions about things I do not have answers for, ask for his help in guiding me to make good decisions, and ask him to give me the courage I need to do my work and protect my family. He always answers me with his irascible smile. I tell him how much I miss him, how I wish he were still here with us, how folks ask about him and share memories of his kindness and good works. I ask him to help me solve mechanical problems, which he excelled at doing and which I have always struggled to do correctly.

I tell him I will always love him.

Why do I tell you these things? Because you may be here after all. And I still love you!

Now that I am without you, all is desolate;
All that was once so beautiful is dead.

– Conrad Aiken

In the first hours and days of our loss, these words may sum up our feelings of hopelessness and dejection. All the beauty we knew seems to have ended with the death of our loved one. What shall we do now? To whom shall we turn for comfort and consolation? And, why bother?

Because we still live.

And perhaps no other reason is necessary. While in the grip of despair, we may mull over every possible reason to live or die ourselves. Those who love and need us hope we choose to live, and, ideally, to love again.

Suicide is at an all-time high here in America. And we men skew the statistics horribly. We kill ourselves five times as often as women do. Why? Primarily because of loneliness and despair. Isolation. We talk ourselves into believing that dying is the only way out of our grief. This is not true. Potential help surrounds us in the form of mental health professionals and organizations devoted to helping the newly bereaved. We just need to reach out and ask for assistance. No one will laugh or make fun of us. No one will think less of us as a man. No one will wonder why we could not stand on our own two feet by ourselves. Here's the secret: no one can. *No one* does it alone. We all need each other.

We men need to remember this. Always.

Not everything that was so beautiful is dead. I live! And my loved one wants me to live!

OCTOBER 28

Looking up at the stars, I know quite well
That, for all they care, I can go to hell.

— W. H. Auden

In the throes of early grief, what can we men do with feelings like these? Put them into words.

I feel like no one cares. I feel like no one gives a damn about my loss. I feel alone and cast adrift in a boat on an open sea. Look, even the stars seem to be looking the other way. No one understands how I feel. I feel like there is no one to talk to, no one with compassion for me. And so on...

Write all your feelings down and then turn them into words. Make a list. Speak them as often as you need to. Hang them on the refrigerator where you can see them every day.

Then make a list of those who love and need you. Write down every reason you can think of why your life matters to them. Write down what you do for them, how you help out, why you would be missed if you were no longer here. Write down how their lives would be diminished if you should decide to leave. Then hang this list next to the other one. Decide each day which list you want to concentrate on. And remember, you are choosing the list that will shape your future.

Living when you want to die can be as simple as this. Words matter.

Looking up at the stars, I know quite well,
They will always care, I can always tell.

— Clifford E. Denay, Jr.

OCTOBER 29

...imagine if I stayed here,
even for the sake of your love...

– Eavan Boland

We might say we would undo this death if we could, bringing our lost one back to life and into our arms again. Yet, would we? If we have lost a child, likely our answer might be a resounding yes! But, wait. How much time has passed since the death? Have others who loved our child healed from the loss, and moved on? How would our loved one feel if feelings for him or her have changed? Or if someone else has taken his or her place?

How complicated would life be!

My wife had a dream about our son who died in 2010 in a boating accident. He left behind his young widow and countless family members and friends who loved him. In her dream, she saw our son return only to find how confusing life had become for him after finding all of us accustomed to his absence. He had expected a grand welcome and instead found us taken aback at his unexpected return. My wife found the dream disturbing and awoke before it ended.

So, if our loved one could stay, even for the sake of our love, what would we do?

Eventually I will learn that moving on with my life does not mean forgetting my dead loved one. The world rolls on just like wounds heal, and that is the law of the universe.

OCTOBER 30

Real grief is not healed by time... If time does anything, it deepens our grief. The longer we live, the more fully we become aware of whom (he/she) was for us, and the more intimately we experience what (his/her) love meant for us... love... makes itself visible in pain.

– Henri J. M. Nouwen

This may not be what most of us want to hear right now. That our pain will last forever is not the helpful message we may have been seeking. Still, depending upon whom we have lost, this message may be speaking the truth to us. The intensity of the pain lessens, but the pain of the loss remains.

Such a loss!

One of the first questions I asked the counselor I had been seeing after my son's death was, "My son isn't coming back, is he?" Looking back, it was a ridiculous question, but still one I felt compelled to ask. "No, he isn't," she replied kindly. "No." She slowly shook her head for emphasis.

So, I have lived with the pain of my son's death. My experience mirrors Nouwen's words. My grief is deeper and wider. But, so is my love for my son. As more time passes, I have discovered countless new reasons why I loved him in life and why I will always love him in death. And my love for him is more intense and intimate than ever. Why should love make itself more visible in pain? It seems a cruel irony that such love is rare when all is well. Maybe that is what we survivors can help change while we still have the chance. Make love more visible now. Today.

My grief may never be completely healed. Still, I will make my love more visible in my interactions with others while I still have the chance.

OCTOBER 31

*So when is death not within ourselves?... Living
and dead are the same, and so are awake and
asleep, young and old.*

– Heraclitus

Some of us may feel that a parallel world where our beloved
dead live exists alongside the world we live in. We cannot see it
but can instead sense its presence. People from many cultures
have reported such a place. It is a comforting world where
death has lost its power. Living and dead are the same.

And everyone we love is there waiting for us.

This idea may either bring us comfort or cause us to feel unset-
tled. Is it hard to believe in something that cannot be seen
with our own eyes. The comforting thought is that our loved
ones who have died before us may be awaiting our arrival. Our
death will be a homecoming. The unsettling thought is that an
entire world about which we know nothing may exist, and we
may wonder how we will fit in there.

Is where we go when we sleep frightening? With the exception of disturbing dreams, the answer seems to be a resounding "no." Why, then, should we fear death? Isn't death simply
endless sleep? By the time we die, perpetual sleep may bring
welcome rest from a busy life. And that may sound inviting,
not scary.

*My death is always just a heartbeat away. I will not fear
death any more than I fear sleep. Why should I?*

NOVEMBER

NOVEMBER 1

*As the living recall the dead, the dead
Are joyless until they call back their lives...*

– Wendell Berry

The notion that our beloved dead are with us always in our memories may bring great comfort to us. But perhaps few of us have thought that our beloved dead might only find joy in their memories of life together with us.

Can we help them?

Will we speak to our beloved dead and remind them of the joys we have shared? Will we reassure them that the happiness we knew together can never be taken from us? Will we recall specific events that brought great fun and lasting happiness to all family members present? And what about the quiet moments, the knowing silence that brought peaceful hearts great contentment? Will we remind them of fingertips touching, taps on the knee asking for backrubs, our shared smiles across the room, the glowing glances that told stories without words, the gentle tributes to pets that died along life's journey?

Will we ask our loved one's forgiveness, or offer ours? Will we speak our love? Will we speak it again and again, endlessly?

I miss my beloved one. I will encourage _____ to remember the good times we shared and the joy he or she brought us.

NOVEMBER 2

I have wrapped my dreams in a silken cloth,
And laid them away in a box of gold...

– Countee Cullen

Perhaps this is the best we can do for the moment – take our dreams of a future together with our loved one and wrap them in a box of gold. Certainly he or she deserves no less.

Doing this would be a tribute to our love.

We may think of military funerals where the flag-draped coffin lies in state. At the right moment, soldiers approach and begin to carefully and lovingly fold the flag up into a neat package of love before handing it gently to members of the family. The flag is what remains of the family's dreams. And the picture boards so common at funerals are another "silken cloth" of sorts. On them we hang memories of days gone by, pictures from every stage of life. We see our loved one laughing, clowning, enjoying existence. We thought those days would last forever. Then, after the funeral? Into what "box of gold" have you laid your picture board dreams?

Wrapping our dreams and tenderly tucking them away is an expression of hope for a new future. This act helps us close one chapter in our lives in preparation for another. This is not an attempt to forget. We will never forget. This is an acceptance of what is. And accepting what is helps us heal.

I accept what has happened. I will wrap my dreams in a silken cloth and lay them away in a box of gold. Then, I will heal.

NOVEMBER 3

*i carry your heart with me (i carry it in
my heart) i am never without it...*

– e. e. cummings

It may be a surprise to us that we now carry the heart of our
loved one with us wherever we go. Death reduces travel time
between two hearts in love to zero. When someone we love
dies, our love lives on, always.

Forever.

Before our son died in 2010, he traveled extensively with his
two friends. The three young men were citizens of the world.
Once, while living near Quito, Ecuador for five months, they
taught conversational English at a local school to earn money
and help improve their Spanish speaking skills. They also spent
time climbing mountains and riding motorcycles. Although I
worried for their safety, often days would pass before my concern grew foremost in my mind and we would call or Skype to
"check in."

Since his death, he is on my mind almost constantly. In my
every spare moment, I see his face, his smile, and I hear his
laughter. I wonder where he is and what he is doing on the
other side of life. I wonder if he sees me and the rest of our
beloved family members. I wonder if he misses us as much as
we miss him.

Yet, I am convinced. Love survives death. And hearts walk side
by side ever after.

Dear _____, *I carry your heart with me. I
am never without it.*

On August 21, 2001, my newborn daughter Ella gave away her heart. It now belongs to an infant boy in Michigan.

– Heidi Hughes

When faced with the impending death of an infant and the decision for the child to become an organ donor, we might ask ourselves, can I love like this? Can we find the strength to help another child live if our child dies?

Our answer would likely be yes.

When our beloved son died, we were asked by the Michigan eye bank if we would donate his corneas so that two other people might regain their sight. When considering the question, I quickly recalled watching him fill out the organ donor section on his driver's license at the kitchen table, authorizing "any and all organs" to be donated in the event of his death. All of us family members made the same decision. He dismissed my gratitude with a wave of his hand saying, "Everyone should do this, dad. It's the right thing to do." I told him I agreed. Now, two women in southern Michigan can see again because of my son's gracious spirit.

And, maybe they know the young man Ella helped out.

Even in my sorrow, my heart is full of hope when I witness generosity like this.

I sha'n't be gone long. – You come too.

– Robert Frost

Perhaps our departed loved one speaks to us in these or similar words. We may be lulled into thinking that following him or her into the realm of death makes a lot of sense. Remember, though, that grieving men are not always thinking clearly.

Be careful about quick decisions.

Check in with non-grieving friends from time to time. Ask them how you appear to be doing. It is true that none of us grieve in the same manner. Still, there are enough commonalities in the lives of new grievers that friends will recognize if we are considering dangerous behaviors. Tell them you need honesty, that you can handle contrary advice. If necessary, create a "non-suicide pact" with someone you trust.

And we male children of grieving parents may have special challenges. One friend tells stories of his broken-hearted dad spending money frivolously. Another friend speaks of a surviving father who is becoming a hoarder, filling his home with food beyond all possible use. A third friend shares stories of his father becoming an alcoholic.

I sha'n't be gone long. – You come too. No one can tell us how long that is, can they?

I have been advised to avoid major decisions for at least one year. So for now, I choose to stay here.

If you are going through hell, keep going.

– Winston Churchill

Some of us have been through hell before, but maybe this particular death is the worst hell ever. Only we can be the judge. Churchill had his share of hell on earth as well. And he knew something we all might want to remember.

This, too, shall pass.

If we are in the early throes of grief, this wisdom may feel cruel. We may be so distraught that we think no one has suffered this much. We may want our pain to end so badly that we see no end to our sorrow. And in the early hours and days after our loss, this may feel true. But with the help and guidance of those who love and care for us, we slowly begin to grasp an important fact. We still live. There is hope.

Or perhaps our sorrow is wrapped around months or years of seemingly endless care for the one now gone. We may be confused by feelings of guilt and feelings of elation. Guilt if we believe we did not do enough, and elation, knowing our loved one's suffering has ended and we have our freedom back. We have gone through a living hell of sorts, and survived. There was a light at the end of the tunnel after all.

My loved one and I have been through a living hell. I am grateful the suffering is over for both of us.

I am obsessed with finding people who have seen the universe bare its ferocious teeth and I am entirely sick of people who seem to live free and easy.

– Natalie Taylor

We crave meeting other men and women who have suffered as much as we have suffered. Not that misery loves company, as some believe, but that misery craves understanding, compassion, and genuine sympathy. Those who have mightily suffered understand. Those who have not deeply suffered do not understand.

They cannot understand, yet.

We have likely been on the receiving end of words that make no sense. Many people fall back onto age old phrases that offer scant comfort to the bereaved and make them feel better for having said something. Have they ever suffered the death of a loved one, we wonder? Still others proclaim certainties from their respective spiritual traditions for the wonder and glory of the afterlife and congratulate us now that our loved one has "graduated" into the next world, free of heartache and pain. Isn't it wonderful, they say, that our beloved no longer suffers? We may think they might question their beliefs if their loved one was dead instead of ours.

I am grateful for those who understand the depth of my loss. I hope for strength to deal with everyone else.

NOVEMBER 8

Books were safer than other people anyway.

– Neil Gaiman

Some of us find greater comfort after our loss in the pages of books rather than in the company of people. Each of us has the right to find our own way through grief. There is no "prescribed" method. Books about grieving and loss abound.

Find the books that speak to your broken heart and the pathway for healing will reveal itself.

Most authors, including me, wrote books about grief and loss as part of their own healing journeys. We write from personal experience and have no agenda other than to share our stories with the hope that we might work through our own grief. One of the many advantages of reading about loss is that we can take our time and go back to the material as often as we need to. "Hearing" the same story several times helps us understand how hard loss was for the writer. We feel less alone and more hopeful. If this person came through it, we think, well, maybe I will as well.

Some writers never expected their "books" to see the light of day. Their work started as simple journal notes. They did not intend to publish them. C. S. Lewis's *A Grief Observed* is one such effort. In books like these we read about the raw emotions of loss and the uncensored sorrow of the one grieving. This kind of book may prove to be the most helpful of all. And maybe we can start one of our own, too.

I find comfort in reading books about grief and loss. I am grateful for those who chose to share their stories.

I began to feel my misery in pallet on floor, listening to music, my misery, that's why I want to sing.

– Allen Ginsberg

Singing may seem a strange notion when we are caught up in suffering from the death of a loved one. Still, many of us have great voices and love to sing favorite songs. Others of us have our "shower" voices and also love to sing, just out of earshot of nearby family members. So why not sing instead of cry?

Singing cannot help but raise our spirits.

We have likely heard various versions of the exclamation "I am all cried out." If this is the point in our grieving where we are now, perhaps leaping into song may be the best next step. And not all singing has to aim at happiness. Strangely, sad songs may also help us heal. Lyrics that help us understand the extent of our loss may clarify the healing path that lies ahead. The work we need to do now. And understanding the depths of our sorrow can help us begin to anticipate the potential heights of future joy.

Men who sing suffer less. Is there a message for us here?

To take a break from my sorrow, I will consider singing one of my favorite songs. Perhaps now.

NOVEMBER 10

...and finally, insane for the light,
you are the butterfly and you are gone.

– Johann Wolfgang Von Goethe

What is the light we seek? What is it we chase? What do we want from this most amazing life? This precious existence? What drives us onward and, at times, to our knees? The death of someone we love?

Or is death the light we seek?

I have always wanted to fly. I watch seagulls turn their graceful arcs, float on warm drafts of summer wind, and I am jealous. I want to float in the air like that. How does the world look from their slow, relaxed perspective? And robins that swoop down in a storm and pull up just in time to settle on the wet grass and start their hunt for worms. I want to swoop and land like that. I also envy hawks that dive from great heights at remarkable speeds to pounce on unsuspecting meals for their young. I want to dive and pounce like that.

And butterflies! What can we say of butterflies? To fly thousands of miles like the swallows of Capistrano and also to flitter inches at a time from one flower blossom to another? To possess fragile yet strong wings of indescribable beauty and wave them for any audience to admire? Yes, I want to fly and flitter and have wings like butterflies do.

Perhaps our loved one flew in death toward a light, a flower of incomprehensible beauty. Perhaps we are all butterflies, we men and women alike, working the flower beds here on earth until it is our turn to fly home.

I imagine my beloved one, insane for the light, as a butterfly on a homeward journey.

NOVEMBER 11

We have set out from here for the sublime;
I have no doubt we shall arrive on time.

– Anthony Hecht

Perhaps we might grasp at the comfort offered in the author's words, that our loved one has set out on a journey for the sublime. Why not? After all, we may wonder where the road ahead leads. No harm in that.

Sublime has a nice sound.

And as for being on time, well, we might argue with the timing of many of life's significant events, death being perhaps the most significant event of all. Many of us might prefer the timing of death to be delayed. Indefinitely. This is understandable. We are likely not sure where sublime is located and what activities, if any, will be available once we get there. No wonder we are in no particular hurry to leave.

Still, some of us can sense the timing of our departures. When my brother and father were leaving our family home on their way to the hospital on the Friday before my father's death, my father stopped just outside the doorway, turned to my brother and handed his wallet to him. Dad never gave his wallet to anyone. "Here," he said, "I won't need this anymore." Dad died five days later.

I'd like to think he arrived on time.

In spite of my sorrow at the timing of this death, perhaps everyone dies on time. I will always wonder.

NOVEMBER 12

This then may be the prayer without ceasing,
this beauty and gratitude, this moment.

– Wendell Berry

It may be almost impossible in the early hours of grief to think of gratitude for the life of our beloved one. We are overwhelmed at the death, the loss, the absence of the one we love. Who has the time or inclination to be grateful?

Not us. Not yet.

But in the days that follow, we start to see more clearly and we begin, once again, to appreciate small things that our loved one said or did or hoped for, or planned for the future. We are lonely and so we reach for memories. And so beauty and gratitude begin to cross our line of vision once more.

In the many years since my mother's death, two examples of beauty and gratitude for her life remain foremost in my mind. The first is a family picture of both parents and we five children. My mother is standing tall and beautiful on our front porch, holding her newest baby, looking radiant and pleased with the new house my father had promised her before their marriage years earlier. The second memory of my mother is that of a farm girl who made sure all five of her children had a chance at a college education. I'll always be grateful that my avid reader mom did her best to encourage us to stay in school and work hard at our studies.

This then may be my prayer without ceasing, this beauty and gratitude, this moment.

NOVEMBER 13

My real dwelling
Has no pillars...

– Ikkyu

So where is our real dwelling, where do we live our lives? Do we live outside ourselves or stay within, in our rich and colorful interior life? And when the death of a loved one arrives, as it has this day, where do we mourn?

Inside or outside? Or both?

Some of us might argue, as Ikkyu has done, that our interior life is our true home. Certainly we tend to live quiet lives on the outside while nourishing our interior lives. We talk less and think more. We analyze until we are blue in the face. So when death knocks on our door, our tendency is to draw even further inward in an attempt to protect ourselves from our fear of sorrow.

Or perhaps Ikkyu is referring to our spiritual home, one without pillars of earth. He may be urging us to keep our eyes on a heavenly horizon and away from the trappings of this world. Many spiritual traditions teach the same theology.

Now that our loved one is no longer with us, we likely mourn in our human manner and with our five senses. We are creatures of earth. This world is the world we know. Our bodies are our current homes. The guardian of the dwelling that awaits our spirits after death will have to be patient.

Death is the greatest mystery. Perhaps death itself is my real dwelling. Perhaps not. One day I will know.

But he had not been dead two months when she lay down and died too, and that may indicate that at that absolute vanishing point they did intersect. They had intersected for years, for more than he especially would ever admit.

There must be some other possibility than death or life-long penance...

– Wallace Stegner

Perhaps the death we mourn this day is the death of a loved one who lived together with a spouse but seemed to exist alone. This is a tough one. We know of couples who have been married many years but who did not seem to "click" with one another. They married and then appeared to live parallel and separate lives under the same roof.

Or did they?

Only the two involved know for sure. Stegner's words imply both possibilities. Our grief may be a heavier burden to carry if we think their years were lonely and full of solitude. Or our sorrow may be a bit lighter if we think that at least at the end of their lives they made a meaningful connection. Why else would they die so close together?

My own parents died just fifty-eight days apart, Dad on May 21st and Mom on July 14th, 1997. When my father died, my mother said to me, "I may as well die, too. My work is over." And it was.

I will never know the truth about this relationship. What I do know is this: I love those who have died.

NOVEMBER 15

How does one hand over everything one possesses?

– Graham Greene

We may wonder what Greene asks. Yet death demands we relinquish all. Everything. We are each one heartbeat, one breath, away from giving up all we possess.

Even those we love.

Today we acknowledge this is what our loved one had to do. And we will one day do the same. Why do we hold *things* so tightly when *relationships* matter more? This may be the intriguing mystery for us to contemplate. Perhaps it is because material possessions are outward signs of worldly success, status, and accomplishments. Loving relationships are interior rewards. No one can see or touch them. We cannot drive around in a loving relationship, or live within the walls of contentment, or win awards for saying "I love you!" the most. No man earns a medal for being faithful. Yet, what matters more?

The author Murray Banks once wrote, "Curling up with a Jaguar on a cold winter's night is a real bummer." There are no outward awards for a relationship built on love and mutual trust. What legacy do we most value? Things or love and trust?

I know I cannot take anything with me when I die except my reputation and the love of those with whom I have shared my life. I will carefully choose how I spend my time on earth.

*A serious moment for the match is when it
    bursts into flame
And is all alone, living, in that instant, that
    beautiful second for which it was made.*

– Kenneth Koch

Koch's poem describes what many lives are like. A lighted match bursting into flame. Perhaps the loved one we mourn this day lived a life in ...that beautiful second for which it was made. If so, we rejoice in the life as well as mourn the death of this unforgettable person. It is no wonder our love for each other was alive!

May our loved one truly rest in peace after a life of fulfillment.

Perhaps our loved one gathered the lonely and broken-hearted around him or her and offered friendship in place of loneliness. Or possibly served meals in a food kitchen for individuals and families temporarily down on their luck. Maybe our beloved gave monetary support to groups and organizations devoted to helping the disenfranchised in our society. Or volunteered time to help friends and neighbors to hospital and medical care provider appointments. Perhaps our lost one was simply a good neighbor, willing to lend tools at a moment's notice or buy magazine subscriptions or candy from children for school fundraising efforts.

Perhaps his or her porch light was always turned on for Halloween. Perhaps their legacy was the same as The Christophers's motto: "It is better to light one candle than to curse the darkness."

Today I mourn the death of my beloved one whose spirit burned with love and service for all.

NOVEMBER 17

I said I wouldn't,
Dammit: No tears.

– Yusef Komunyakaa

Perhaps we mourn a Vietnam veteran on this day, one whose service to our country was vilified, possibly scorned. Returning vets from 'Nam were often airlifted from front lines and transported back to the streets of their hometowns in a matter of days. No chance for de-briefing. Many have spent the years since in silence, drug induced euphoria, or working in jobs where they were able to put their skills to productive use.

For this veteran, though, the war is finally over.

Jesse Carmona. Edward Charlevoix. Robert Benson. Just three of the 58,022 names on the Vietnam Veterans Memorial on the mall in Washington, D.C. My friends from T.L. Handy High School in Bay City, Michigan. Jesse and I worked at Bay City's answer to McDonald's, a place called Mr. Hot Dog. Our specialty was fast food: hot dogs, burgers, fries, malted milks, fried chicken, and on Fridays, deep fried cod. Jesse told me he wanted to go to college and that enlisting was the only chance he had as he came from a large family with slim finances. How many other high school graduates had similar stories?

Edward Charlevoix and Robert Benson. Two members of our Michigan Class A high school diving team. Each a superb athlete. Kind, friendly, out-going. Large smiles and equally large hearts.

Dear _____, I am sorry you died. I want to thank you for your service to our country. I know you were treated poorly when you returned from Vietnam. I apologize.

NOVEMBER 18

How shall the heart be reconciled
to its feast of losses?

– Stanley Kunitz

Not today, perhaps, but one day when we are older we will have to reconcile our... feast of losses. We will add this death to those we have already suffered. How shall we make peace with our losses without appearing macabre?

How about a Deathday Cake?

On first blush this idea may sound strange. However, it is common practice for members of The Compassionate Friends, a worldwide organization that helps parents of children who die to heal from their loss, to celebrate the day of their child's death. Why not extend that practice to the rest of us grieving men?

We can place one candle on the cake for each loved one we have lost. The candles would serve as visual reminders of our survivor status and the strength we possess to so often work our way through grief. Some of us older fellows may be surprised at the candles we have accumulated. And for us younger men, well, let's be easy on ourselves if this is our first candle. Others will follow soon enough.

Perhaps an angel food cake might be in order.

I will make plans to reconcile my losses, whether one or many.
I will ask for help if this idea will not work for me.

Brothers and sisters say that no matter their age, no matter how awful the death, they want to know what has happened. They desperately need their parents to talk straight... They want to be with their parents. Being sent away doesn't feel like protection... it feels like being shut out...

– Barbara D. Rosof

If we have lost a child, it is important to not shut out from the tragedy other children we may have. They need to be included, informed, and connected to you, sometimes literally if they are toddlers. Hold them. Experts tell us to not send siblings away in the hope that we are protecting them from the grief of loss. This tactic creates more pain for them later in their lives.

Sending children away after a sibling's death makes matters worse.

Let's think about a simple example that some of us older men may have endured in our early years in school: being required to sit in the corner of the classroom with our face to the wall. Recall that this was a punishment for misbehaving. The painful aspect of this commonly used technique was the isolation of the child. No problems involving human interaction have ever been solved long-term by isolating anyone. (This includes the still-used "solitary confinement" in our prisons.) Problems are solved through listening, understanding, and compromise.

Children need to be included in decisions that are age-appropriate when a sibling dies. A school counselor or psychologist can answer our questions if we have any doubts.

I will not isolate my other children if one of their brothers or sisters has died.

NOVEMBER 20

The people I've been drawn to have changed considerably...The best way to say it is that I am closest to those people who are connected with their hearts, have agile minds, and are interested in participating in the present moment.

– Van Jepson

Feelings toward others can change after we lose a loved one. This death reminds us how fragile life is and we come to a new realization that we do not have forever to live and that we want to use our time more wisely.

Friendships often change.

We are more likely interested in folks who... are connected with their hearts...than those who are not. We intuitively know who they are. People who are genuine, who do not puff themselves up, who are content with solitude but also enjoy a quiet afternoon's bicycle ride with us. We are more interested in those who take an interest in both sides of any issue. We want to be with friends who live in the moment rather than agonize over the past or fret about the future. We likely understand more clearly than ever that we can only live within each moment. The future is never guaranteed. We want to hang out with those who have no fear of death and are willing to discuss death and dying like any other current events topic.

We want no false assurances. We want, more than ever, to be loved and respected.

I have some new friends since my loved one died. I also kept the best of the old ones. I love them all.

...you have to put it out there. You know things. You have gifts you're not using. You have too much to give to waste it. Don't hide it, and don't be afraid.

– Mimi Redfern

Many of us may have been living our lives under a bushel basket of sorts before this death of our loved one. Perhaps we have been fearful of letting our light shine in the greater world. This may be the day we put our fear aside.

We know things. We have hidden talents to share. And if not now, in the face of loss, when?

Why does it often take a family tragedy to wake up the survivors? We hear stories of "awakenings" for parents and children after a family member is diagnosed with a terminal illness or dies in an accident. It is like a knock on the door that jars us out of a collective lethargy. Time becomes more important. We are getting older. What else do we want to do before we die?

Before my son's death, when asked how much longer I planned to stay in the workforce, I would answer, "Well, I'm not sure. We'll see." Now, I think in more specific terms. 'Well, I'm here today and I plan to be here tomorrow. I also love to write and am working on a manuscript for a book. And I love to travel with my wife."

I will put myself out there as a result of this death. I have one life to live and no time to waste.

How can I go on? How can I ever be happy again? I took the advice of a good friend and counselor. She told me, "Go to the source. Ask your child, 'How should I live?'"

– Stathi Afendoulis

If we have lost a child, it may take some time before we realize our son or daughter is now available to help us. Who would have guessed? After years of taking care of them, they are now able to care for us. Especially when we need advice.

Thank goodness.

Since my son's death, I often talk with him about problems in my life that I need help solving. Seldom would I have done this before his death. Years ago, when I purchased a pair of bicycles for my wife and me, he was offended that I had not consulted him first about the best possible bicycles for the two of us. I apologized. He was right. I should have done so. Since his death, though, I talk with him often about issues large and small. He is always available and ready to assist in any way.

They say that parent/child roles reverse as parents grow older. The parents become like children and the children grow into parents. The death of a child accelerates this process as the surviving parents soon grow to depend upon their departed child's wisdom.

How can we be happy again? Ask your child.

I will ask my child for advice on matters of the heart. After all, why shouldn't I?

NOVEMBER 23

The dead go on before us, they
Are sitting in God's house in comfort...

– Philip Larkin

This is the scene many of us broken-hearted men may want to embrace. Perhaps this is what we were taught as children. To trust that God waits for us and will greet us with open arms when it is our turn to cross over to the other side.

It is a consoling scene, indeed.

And why not take on this gentle mantle if it helps us work our way through the grief of losing a loved one? We could do worse. No two of us see the world in exactly the same terms. We all have the right to choose images that align with our perception of who and what God is. Those who would challenge our pictures of an afterlife do so on the basis of spiritual beliefs not scientific evidence. Every man is entitled to his own spiritual beliefs. Or even no spiritual beliefs at all.

Our next door neighbor when I was growing up was a kind, courteous, friendly, and loving family man who refused to go to his wife's church service on Sunday mornings. She grew up in one tradition, he in another. They each clung to their own beliefs. No compromises. So they spent years embracing their own theology while rejecting that of their spouse.

Were there separate heavens for them when they died?

I do not know what will happen after I die. But I hope to see my loved ones face-to-face.

Life is real – life is earnest –
And the grave is not its goal...

– Henry Wadsworth Longfellow

Longfellow's words encourage us brokenhearted men to focus on the here and now, to make a difference in this world where we are living. As we mourn the death of our loved one, let us consider what we might do to leave our imprint on our beloved planet while we still have time.

The grave is not life's goal.

One act of service that my father always performed before his death was to take his portable "barbering kit" with him whenever he visited friends or customers who were hospitalized. A generous man throughout his life, he gave each sick man a free haircut as a way of encouraging him back to good health. He always told them how much they were missed in his barber shop and how the rest of the guys looked forward to their return. I have to believe that more than one man sprang back to health a lot sooner than he would have done otherwise as a result of Dad's haircut visits.

A popular slogan in recent years goes something like this: Life is not a dress rehearsal. Well, it's true. This is the life we have been given. How can we thank the world for our lives before our own departure?

Today I mourn the death of someone I love. As I work through my grief, I hope to understand more clearly where I am needed in my community.

*I talk always to the man who walks along
   with me;
– men who talk to themselves hope to talk
   to God someday –*

– Antonio Machado

Perhaps many of us grieving men talk to God as we walk through our busy days. Addressing God as "the God of my understanding" has likely saved millions of lives in the Alcoholics Anonymous (AA) program.

Which title is correct? It is up to you to decide.

We can either fight over names of a deity or work through our grief. It may be asking too much of us to do both right now. If we take comfort in speaking with our God, then by all means we should do so. If we find consolation in other ways, then we should follow that path instead. Or we might choose to do both. There are no "grieving rules." Certainly there are suggestions offered by those who have suffered before us, but they are simply that. Suggestions. Stories told from their experiences of loss. Surely there will be wisdom in their words we might use on our journey. After all, we humans suffer similarly.

My dear carpenter friend often talks to himself out loud when he is on the job site. If we are inclined to talk to our God, maybe speaking out loud will somehow speed up healing. Isn't it worth a try?

Sometimes I talk to God, especially in moments of despair and sorrow. Most everyone seems to do it. Someday I hope to talk with God face-to-face. I have a lot of questions to ask.

NOVEMBER 26

*Sweet vale of Avoca! How calm could I rest
In thy bosom of shade, with the friends I love
best...*

– Thomas Moore

Moore speaks warmly of where he hopes will be his final resting place in the shade of a tree next to the River Avoca in County Wicklow, Ireland, with the friends he loves best. Don't many of us mourning men hope to lie next to a friend or lover when it is our turn to lay down forever?

Perhaps this is our plan. And maybe we have the spot already chosen.

Our son died along with his friend in 2010. Both young men were the first in their immediate families to die, so the task of choosing a burial site took both families aback. In the end, both boys were buried within fifteen feet of each other, under the shade of a sugar maple, a tree indigenous to our Emmet County in northern Michigan. Now the boys are friends into eternity. When we visit one, we visit both. And shortly after our boy's death, my wife and I bought burial sites in the same location for the two of us as well. We wanted to be near our beloved son.

When we visit graveyards, it is common to see entire families buried together in the same cemetery "plot." My parents are buried next to many of their brothers and sisters. And a dear friend has chosen a beautiful hillside next to his country home where his ashes will be spread after his death.

How wonderful that we may get to choose our final resting place!

Today I mourn your death. I promise to visit as often as I can.

NOVEMBER 27

*My child's spirit lives on. His spirit lives on not
because I make it so every day, but because
he and other spirits do live on... now he is in a
heavenly body and he is safe.*

– Van Jepson

Many of us may choose to think as the author does. We may be convinced beyond any shadow of a doubt. After my son's death I recall saying to one of his friends, "Now he is safe and I know where he is." I do not remember if I meant he was safe in a heavenly realm or safe in the cemetery.

Either place, he is safe.

In Christian tradition, "safe in heaven" meant actually that; that our beloved dead were safe in a place so beautiful that we humans are incapable of comprehending its splendor. However, for those of us who have stood at the burial site and watched the casket slowly descend into the ground, such a heaven may seem beyond reach. We know where the body ends up. Comprehending where the spirit resides may perplex humanity forever.

Monks are sometimes buried more simply than the rest of us. Trappist monks, for example, are wrapped in a shroud and laid on a board, which is used to lower their bodies into the ground. The board is then retrieved to be used another time. The words, "Remember man, thou art dust and into dust thou shalt return," may sound familiar. For monks buried without a coffin, the becoming dust is speeded up.

Still, where the spirit slips away to may always be the eternal mystery.

I am certain and uncertain as to where my spirit will reside after I die. Until I find out, I will spend my time loving and serving others.

As long as our wounds are open and bleeding, we scare others away. But after someone has carefully tended to our wounds, they no longer frighten us or others.

– Henri J. M. Nouwen

Many folks may steadfastly avoid us grieving men after the death of our loved one. They might think we are jinxed or, worse yet, that we have bad "karma." If they get too close to us, they fear, someone they love may die, too. So they stay away.

This is normal.

I have done it myself. The fear makes no sense, but we humans can still be superstitious. Years ago a recently divorced friend once remarked to me, "Since getting a divorce, no one invites me over anymore. Maybe they think I have terminal cancer or that I will make a move on their wife." The reasons his friends were avoiding him could have included both of these and a host more. "We fear what we do not know," Leo Buscaglia once declared, and we try to keep the odds for personal safety in our favor.

Eventually, as we make progress down the grieving road, our open wounds of loss will begin to heal. I have noticed more people approaching me now that several years have passed since my son's death. I must have finally lost my "deer in the headlights" look. This is a sure sign of healing after loss.

I am grateful that I will become more approachable as I heal from the death of my loved one. I am also glad a brave few did not turn and run after my loss.

*Which is harder for us to believe? That there is a
God? Or that there is life after death?
It's the latter by a long-shot.*

– Ken Untener

From how many angles will we approach the life-after-death
quandary? Ken Untener takes us full-face into the conversation as we struggle with the death of our loved one. Now, we
may be drifting on the sea of unknowing once more. We have
been here before. But now our beloved has departed for a place
far away.

And here we are. Alone and lonely.

The approaching holidays do not help our predicament. This is
the time of year for family gatherings around the harvest table
as we anticipate the winter solstice and the celebrations that
come with it. For many of us, Hanukah, Christmas, or Ramadan are special times of the year. We anticipate seeing relatives and friends while enjoying traditional family recipes. And
if our partner has died, we may struggle being together with so
many couples and their families as a newly single man. They
may appear so happy while we struggle with our sorrow. And
making matters worse, they may not know how to treat us. It
is likely most have no interest in talking about life after death.

What's a newly bereaved man to do in such circumstances?
Perhaps look for eye contact with one brave soul who may walk
unafraid into our bewildering world of grief. It happens. Why
not now? Here?

*I have many questions about life after death since my loved
one died. I hope I can find someone to talk to about them.*

Love is the only thing that we can carry with us when we go, and it makes the end so easy.

– Louis May Alcott

Or at least we hope love makes the end go easy. We will not know until we die. We may be surprised if our journey out of this world is less painful and frightening because we loved and were loved in return.

Love... makes the end so easy.

Perhaps our hope is that those we love will love us always, in life and death. This is certainly my hope. Love is the balm for life's sorrows and enhances the joy of existence. When we gather someone we love into our arms, we often describe the feeling as "heavenly." Why not?

I will always treasure the knowledge that when my son was dying he knew how much I loved him, and that he knew how many others loved him as well. I hope he saw our smiling faces as we waved farewell and that this brought him some sense of peace during his unexpected departure. I hope our love for him made his end easy. I hope he is warm and safe.

Love is all we take with us when we leave. Everything else stays behind. What else matters?

❧ DECEMBER ❧

DECEMBER 1

The drapes at the funeral parlor were slightly frayed where they brushed against the carpet. Her grandfather's hands were folded in front of him, but when she looked closely, she saw they weren't actually resting against his body. They hovered slightly above, spoiling the illusion.

– Mark Salzman

Even in death, not everything is perfect. We have suffered a grievous loss. Our loved one is gone. But those of us who remain sometimes struggle with the details of our farewells. Even funerals can be battlegrounds.

And we may have thought death would be simpler than life.

In this holiday season we may struggle beyond measure with funeral details for our beloved dead. All come to these issues, and there is no "right" or "wrong" way to send off someone who has died. The family gets to choose. But, who is considered "family" under the shadow of death?

Immediate family and blood relatives might be the best equipped to decide. When my mother died, the timing of her burial became an issue. I was thousands of miles away at the time of her death. And when my father died, some family members questioned what would become of the money donated in his memory. Without clear instructions from either parent prior to their deaths, my family was faced with the decision to either bury their bodies or have them cremated. And what clothing should our beloved wear, what casket can we afford, and is the cost of the funeral a representation of how much we loved?

I did not expect conflict over details of this funeral. Perhaps I was naïve. I will remember that relationships are more important than money.

DECEMBER 2

But when I actually started dying, I saw it wasn't so bad. He lay back from the circle, his hands under his head, and looked at the sky. Being dead is profoundly peaceful, he said.

– Alice Walker

Perhaps we do not necessarily think of words like "peaceful" to describe the place where our beloved dead now reside. Yet, why not? Doesn't "peaceful" describe the place where we would like to be after we die?

And isn't "peaceful" a heaven-like sound?

When my wife and I were allowed to enter the room in the hospital where our dead son's body lay after his accidental death, we found a smile on his face. I was stunned. "He's smiling," I whispered to my spouse. "He is smiling!"

What more can a father say? Perhaps all of us would like to find a smile on the face of our beloved dead. And now I hope to leave a smile behind as my going-away gift.

Is there a better gift than a smile to leave behind when we die?

DECEMBER 3

I have begun,
when I'm weary and can't decide an answer to a
bewildering question,
to ask my dead friends for their opinion
and the answer is often immediate and clear.

– Marie Howe

Maybe some of us men think we are crazy. After all, talking to the dead is not our usual activity. Still, it may become more usual than we would have thought possible. The more loved ones we lose to death, the more friends we have on the other side, and talking with them and asking for their help is more common than we would suppose. Perhaps it's more helpful than we could ever imagine.

Just ask a few of your guy friends who have suffered similar losses.

My parents both died in 1997, just fifty-eight days apart. I have been "talking" with them ever since. My folks, perhaps like yours, were full of the wisdom of their years. I often asked their advice while they lived and feel no hesitation to ask them for help since. And my son's death has not stopped me from asking his advice on a variety of topics, especially the proper tool to use on a repair project and also how to create tools from unusual things, one of his many areas of specialty. He never fails to come through for me. My uncle was an expert on humor and I find myself laughing with him as he enters our family home and is walking up the short flight of stairs, his piercing joy ringing throughout the small house.

Friendship never ends with the death of one we love. Why should communication?

I will turn to my beloved dead for help. They have never failed me.

DECEMBER 4

Too often I leave a funeral or the bed of one who is dying and forget that I still have life. I take it for granted. I believe that I will have tomorrow, next week, next year to do all the things I want and need to do.

— Jane Holmes Dixon

We may be tempted during this holiday season to long for Christmas Day rather than to live fully in every moment between now and then. The death of our loved one may be a wake-up call. Tomorrow is never guaranteed. Today is what we have. This moment.

What shall I accomplish while I still have time?

Before his untimely death at the age of twenty-seven years, our son was flying home from Quito, Ecuador, for the wedding of a friend. His flight was due in at 12:45 am. Christmas Day morning. The airport was practically empty as passengers from this last plane in from Detroit for Christmas Eve began to disembark. Then, we spotted him. He was dressed in Santa Claus attire with a long flowing white beard and the traditional red and white stocking hat. A mile-wide smile crossed his face and we could hear his laughter long before we could make out his words. He was holding what turned out to be a nearly empty bag of candy that he had been giving away to children and adults alike on his flights home. "You must have made a lot of children happy," I quickly said. 'Grownups, too, Dad," he answered. "It was a lot of fun."

My loved one is dead, but I am still alive. I will not waste the time I have left.

DECEMBER 5

*Give up all the other worlds
except the one to which you belong.*

– David Whyte

The death of someone we love gives us a chance to clarify our friendships. What relationships are we in for the sake of work-related or social convenience versus love and meaningful friendship? The difference is significant. Our lives are time-limited. We are not here forever. How we spend our time is important because it is a precious commodity.

Just ask people who have been told they have only months to live.

We men know intuitively where we belong. A sense of belonging is not rocket science. We know which groups and organizations genuinely welcome us and those who only tolerate our presence. Shaking hands with someone who is looking in another direction at the same moment gives us a clear message: someone over there is more important than we are. With our limited time on earth, we cannot afford to spend time with folks who refuse to afford spending time with us.

Perhaps no other occasion than death gets our undivided attention. This death provides an opportunity to eliminate extraneous relationships that we suffer through rather than embrace. There is no time like the present to act.

An old song's lyrics remind us, "I haven't got time for the pain." I want to live in the world where I belong.

DECEMBER 6

Peace! Peace!
To be rocked by the Infinite!

– Stanley Kunitz

Perhaps this is all death is: To be rocked by the Infinite. Maybe we thought it would be more complicated than this. We have often messed our lives up by making mountains out of mole hills, as the saying goes. Perhaps we are through with that phase of our lives now.

Peace! Peace! Ah, welcome relief.

When our children were toddlers I loved to rock them in our old oak rocking chair. It had a faithful squeak and had been repaired by a knowledgeable woodworking neighbor. The kids loved to be rocked. So did I. I got to rock with them at the same time.

And as a middle school boy, one of my favorite activities on a windy day was to climb as high as I dared into the weeping willow tree that grew in the side yard. I always took a blanket and wrapped it around me as I gently swayed in the glorious breeze. I often stayed up there for hours and was only coaxed down in time for a meal.

My guess is that my son slept out-of-doors for at least fifty per-cent of his life. He loved most of all the nights when the wind blew. The harder the better. The week before he died, he had slept in the family tent with our small chihuahua on the shore of Lake Michigan. A strong wind came out of the northwest in the night and blew the tent down with both of them struggling inside. He laughed long and hard while telling the story.

To be rocked by the Infinite may be the greatest gift.

DECEMBER 7

First and last, man is alone.
He is born alone, and alone he dies
and alone he is while he lives, in his
deepest self.
— D. H. Lawrence

Perhaps these words ring true at their deepest core. But, not always. The death of our loved one reminds us of our responsibility to each other: to stay in touch, to reach out when appropriate, to alleviate loneliness when possible, to share our lives, to serve others.

To be a friend.

Most of us know other men who create community wherever they go. These rare types invite those living on the fringe of life into the inner circle of shared activity. The lonely hear the invitation and respond in droves. Solitude is good for the soul. Loneliness kills the spirit. We need each other. We thrive when we feel loved and a sense of belonging.

My father was a barber and his shop was a place where his customers felt loved. Raucous laughter and endless story-telling prevailed day in and day out. Regardless of who walked through his doorway, dad always spoke up to make him feel welcome. Dad carefully avoided discussions of politics and religion. He did not want to lose paying customers. Other than those two topics, though, he did his best to create community within his four walls.

We may be born alone and die alone, but while we live, we thrive living in community with others.

I may be alone in my deepest self, but while I live, I will strive to create community wherever I go.

DECEMBER 8

What will we have learned, if at the moment of death we do not know who we really are?

– Sogyal Rinpoche

Perhaps at no other time in our lives do we engage so heartedly in self-examination as when a loved one dies. Ordinarily we tend to fill our days with technology, work-related responsibilities, household chores, and personal activities. The death of someone we love slows us down and encourages us inward where the "meaning of life" questions lay waiting.

We did not expect this.

Set free, introspective questions abound. What does this death mean to me? How will my life be changed? What will happen to me now? Will I have to live alone? Am I in charge of everything? Who am I without the one I have lost? Who am I now that I am free to do as I please? What will I do? How do I make decisions by myself? Who will help me?

And the questions keep coming. Yet they all point to the same ultimate question: How can I discover who I am before I too die?

One pathway is to seek out a good listener who will give us undivided attention without judging our questions and answers. Someone who can share in our life reflections and offer possibilities for discoveries that we may not have yet considered. Someone who will encourage us along the road to a life of deeper meaning. Someone who may be a friend.

I want to know who I really am before I die. I will look for someone to guide my search.

DECEMBER 9

*Fear not that life shall come to an end, but rather
fear that it shall never have a beginning.*

– John Henry Newman

Is there a message for us in the death of someone we love?
Besides the loss of someone dear to us, is this death a "tap on
the shoulder," a reminder of what we have been planning to do
with the rest of our own days? Is this something we have been
putting off "until tomorrow"?

Well, tomorrow has arrived. It is today.

What do we want to do with the rest of our lives? For our loved
one, life has ended. There are no more chances for beginnings.
But for us survivors, we can still choose a new direction. Shall
we continue working or is it time to retire? Do we want to relo-
cate to a new community? Move north, south, east, or west? To
a larger or smaller town? Or simply stay put? Shall we finally
plant the garden? Or the apricot tree? Grapes? Raised beds?
Or is it time to move on from gardening and support the local
farmer's market? Do we want to travel more or less? If more,
where? When? With whom? How long?

*As long as we live, we can create beginnings. But only as long
as we live.*

DECEMBER 10

Some days, although we cannot pray, a prayer utters itself.
                                    – Carol Ann Duffy

For some of us, anything close to a prayer feels uncomfortable. Perhaps little in our upbringing has prepared us for "traditional" prayer. Some spiritual traditions would argue, however, that thinking of praying is a prayer itself.

And in the face of the death of a loved one, we have perhaps thought about praying a lot.

Some of us want nothing to do with religion or anything connected to it, including prayer. Others may have felt betrayed by their religious upbringing and the duplicity they have seen in some of the members of the congregations of their youth. Still others do not believe in a supreme being or any afterlife when this life ends. Many of us, though, likely believe in something. And when someone we love dies, our thoughts may turn to whatever power exists within our individual frame of reference. Perhaps this is what Duffy is saying. "Prayers" can utter themselves, regardless of what name we give them.

My thoughts can be prayers. This is comforting.

DECEMBER 11

*Imagine yourself at your own funeral…
almost universally, when people look back on
their lives while on their deathbed, they wish
that their priorities had been quite different.*

– Richard Carlson

Perhaps some of us know what we want out of life. We are comfortable with our priorities and feel we are living our lives in alignment with our values. Others might not have given these things much attention. Still, if we choose to imagine ourselves at our own funeral, something good may come of it. Be warned, though, we may not be able to go back to our old way of thinking.

Being nudged out of our comfort zone is seldom appealing.

Someone once wrote, "…a mind stretched by a new idea cannot go back to its original shape." Imagining attending our own funeral will most likely nudge us in the direction of change. We may have outgrown our current priorities without realizing it. This death may be a tap on the shoulder, an alarm reminding us that we still live and have time to rearrange things if we choose.

There is a story told about a man who had been hospitalized for two weeks for a heart condition. After extensive surgery and recuperation, he was ready to be released. His wife asked him if he wanted to go home to rest. He scoffed at her suggestion and asked that she take him to his office so he could go back to work.

Are there any priorities we would like to change while we still have time?

I am reevaluating my priorities in light of the death of my loved one. No one lives forever, not even me.

DECEMBER 12

(now the ears of my ears awake and
now the eyes of my eyes are opened)

– e. e. cummings

We mourning men can hear and see with greater clarity because we have lost someone we love and value. This is an unexpected gift in the face of what may be a tragic loss. Our world has changed. And the biggest change is how clear everything has become.

Clear and sharp and bright.

We have awakened to the delicate touch of a snowflake on the tip of our tongue. We hear the northwest winds blowing louder and stronger and bringing brilliant waves crashing into the dark rocks that line the perimeter of the bay. We notice the crunching sounds of breaking ice underfoot, the crackling of the fire in the woodstove, the orange and yellow and red and blue flames dancing inside the firebox, the faint smell of wood smoke. We notice the smoke smudge on the inside of the glass door. We feel the warmth on our face even from several feet away.

And for many of us, people may now be more important than things. We might be surprised at the wisdom on the faces of the elderly, the crow's feet around their eyes, their grey hair, so noble and true. We may notice children at play, their squeals of delight and antics on the playground. Such energy! We may be remembering when we were younger. We may be thinking about life before this death. We may be wondering how all of this could have been going on before.

I can hear and see clearly now. Now I care more about people than things.

DECEMBER 13

*Could heaven be a time, after we are dead, of
remembering the knowledge flesh had from flesh?*

– Galway Kinnell

One of the many things we will miss about our beloved one is
the touch of his or her hand. We have grown used to the feel
of each other's skin-on-skin. Death steals our ability to touch
each other on the shoulder, to "high five" in joy, or to embrace
in emotional moments.

Why not sit back for a moment and imagine a great hand-clasp-
ing reunion in the future?

Endless conjecture about an afterlife abounds throughout
human history. Regardless of our beliefs, let's picture for a
minute a harvest table filled with favorite foods and everyone we have ever loved sitting around this thanksgiving feast,
laughing and talking about the last time we were all together.
We eagerly glance at every smile, each pair of hands that
touched and held us, the lips we so tenderly kissed. All present are healed, every infirmity having fallen by the wayside.
Offenses have been forgotten. Perfect peace fills the room.

Slowly, quietly, as if rehearsed, everyone...remembering the
knowledge flesh had from flesh, stands and reaches for each
other's hands. The children giggle, squeal with delight. Tears
stream down surprised faces. An inexpressible joy descends
and fills the hearts and souls and minds and spirits of all present.

Could this be heaven?

*Is heaven a place, a time, or a state of mind? No one knows.
So, until I know for sure, I'll paint my own picture.*

DECEMBER 14

*Before you know kindness as the deepest
thing inside,
You must know sorrow as the other
deepest thing.*

– Naomi Shihab Nye

The death of someone we love almost always wakes us up to a world we have never known. Searing sorrow stings our consciousness as we feel our way through a black tunnel unlike any we have traveled. And who would guess that such sorrow could become our teacher?

Maybe we have wondered where our capacity for kindness originated.

From losing, it seems. When we lose someone we love, a small window of awareness opens. Through this window we see in the eyes of others the suffering they have also endured. Our capacity for compassion grows and our awareness of the extraordinary need for kindness increases. We see more clearly how quickly life passes. We begin to understand the important role we play in the lives of those whom we encounter each day. We treat them more gently, softly, respectfully, and with a level of kindness that we seldom experience ourselves. We begin to comprehend at a deeper level the universal rule, "...do unto others as you would wish them to do unto you."

Perhaps this is our loved one's parting gift: a reawakened urging to touch the world like a feather.

I want to know kindness as the deepest thing inside me. This sorrow is my teacher. I wish there had been an easier way to learn.

DECEMBER 15

No matter what the grief, its weight,
we are obliged to carry it.

– Dorianne Laux

We men are used to carrying heavy objects. We load ourselves up to prove to the world, or ourselves, we can do it. Others may be watching. No load is too heavy, we say. We can handle it.

Usually.

When we decided to build the house our son had designed for us just before his accidental death, my wife and I became members of the work crew. For sixteen months, we were assigned many of the construction trade's jobs: digging footings to support the basement walls; lugging cement blocks; carrying lumber of every size and description; lifting boxes of nails, tools, air compressors, scaffolding, room fixtures, interior and exterior doors, paint and stain cans, and wheel barrows full of sand and gravel. This heavy work was followed by surgery to my right hand to relieve the pain and numbness of carpel tunnel syndrome. I had injured myself without knowing it until it was too late.

Carrying the weight of grief can be like this, too, with one exception. We want to work our way through our pain and sorrow without causing permanent injury. My hand, though surgically repaired, will never be the same. It swells up from time to time, and now I cannot carry as much weight as I used to. The injury to my hand is permanent. But in the future, I will likely be obliged to grieve more deaths. Just not forever.

This is my grief to carry for now. But, not forever.

DECEMBER 16

...life is filled with sadness when a boy grows to be a man. But as you grow into manhood you must not despair of life, but gather strength to sustain you – can you understand that?

– Rudolfo Anaya

To not despair of life is our primary task for we who have lost a loved one. After all, our first inclination may be to run. But there is no place to run, no place to hide. Grief seeks us out wherever we go. And, it will find us. Can we understand that?

Life is filled with sadness.

But life is also filled with mesmerizing joy. And that is what makes life worth living. Our challenge is to gather joy like a squirrel gathers nuts to help sustain us through our sorrows. It is in our darkest moments that we can recall our greatest happiness to help us remember that sorrow is temporary. Yes, some losses will last a lifetime, as in the case of a child's death. But even the sharp edges of the death of a son or daughter will soften in time and our memories will recall the good times instead of the struggles.

We gather strength to sustain us by strengthening friendships, choosing to be better listeners, taking a sincere interest in the activities of others, and being generous with our time and financial resources. After all, it is in giving that we receive and gather strength to sustain us.

I understand that sadness is part of life. But so is joy. I will do what I can to gather strength to sustain me.

DECEMBER 17

Each life lives unto itself... yet serves eternity...

– Gwen Frostic

Some of us may think the world exists to serve our broken hearts. Perhaps we have it backwards. Perhaps we were born to serve the broken hearts of our world. This idea may seem odd delivered to us now, in the midst of our sorrow. Yet it may help us see our way through the dark forest of grief.

After all, we need a compass to help us find our way back home.

We may wonder what to do with the rest of our life now that our loved one is gone. One idea may be to find some way to serve those less fortunate than ourselves. Volunteer opportunities abound in most communities. The Salvation Army is always looking for donations to its resale stores, and it needs bellringers during the holiday season. Goodwill Industries also serves the needs of the poor through its nationwide resale shops. Area "safe-shelters" for battered women and children need male support on a year-around basis. Most communities have at least one such shelter in need of supplies, staff, and smiles. Food pantry volunteers are in greater demand than ever. And local K-12 schools and area community colleges are always looking for volunteer support for their tutoring programs.

Any of these activities and many other possibilities may help ease the pain of our loss and perhaps give us a renewed sense of purpose. Serving eternity is important work!

To ease the pain of my loss, I will look for ways to serve others. In this way, I can serve eternity. And that makes life worth living.

"Did you see the forget-me-nots?"
"Forget-me-nots? Why do they call them that?"
"I'm not sure, but I think it is because people
used to plant them on graves."
"Graves? Like on top of dead people?"
"Yes, where people are buried."
"Oh, because when somebody dies, you never
want to forget them, never!"

– Exchange between a five year old
boy, Asher, and his Uncle David

One of the many irrational thoughts we have when someone we love dies is that we may forget him or her. Somehow the person will slip from our minds and wander into the fog of our forgotten past.

This is not possible.

This brief exchange between five year old Asher and his Uncle David clarified this issue as only a child's wisdom can. Out of the mouths of babes, huh? Oh, because when somebody dies, you never want to forget them, never!

We humans have a "picture album" of our life experiences stored in our brains. This is why we can recall images of times and places and people with whom we have interacted through-out much of our lives. "Pictures" of our loved ones are firmly and indelibly implanted in that album. We could not forget them if we tried. They are there forever, and we can bring up their smiles whenever we wish. This is why we "see" a loved one's image in our head whenever his or her name is men-tioned. This ability can only be lost in someone with some type of brain damage.

So, forget-me-nots? Absolutely. To help us remember that we will not forget. Ever.

Dear _____, I will never forget you! Never!

DECEMBER 19

When everything is dark, when we are surrounded by despairing voices, when we do not see any exits, then we can find salvation in a remembered love, a love which is not simply a recollection of a bygone past but a living force which sustains us in the present. Through memory, love transcends the limits of time and offers hope at any moment of our lives.

– Henry J. M. Nouwen

When my brothers and I prepared for Christmas as children, we stored a flashlight under the hand-sewn feather and down quilt our grandmother had made. Our unheated upstairs bedroom always encouraged us to stay put. Christmas morning, though, was a different story. We used the flashlight to sneak down in the dark early morning hours to get a preview of the gifts surrounding the decorated tree.

We loved reading the labels to see which packages belonged to us.

As a grown man, I often think of those brightly wrapped packages as warm memories, like the moment my wife and I announced to our parents that she was pregnant with our first child. We had given them key chains with the inscription, "Happiness is being a grandparent." It took several quiet moments for our message to sink in. Then, squeals of delight! Or the day I walked out of the local candy store with chocolate cigars to give away in honor of our son's birth, and again three years later when our daughter was born. Every recipient, without exception, was thrilled.

In dark hours of sorrow, we can find love memories to sustain us. Love is our living force.

In moments of despair, I will turn to my love memories to help sustain me. In them I will find salvation and healing.

DECEMBER 20

Everyone can master a grief but he that has it.

– William Shakespeare

Well intentioned people often offer what they believe to be words of comfort and consolation to us grieving men. Some words help. Others appall us. Still, some words perplex. We can end up comforted, confused, or crushed.

Words can heal or hurt.

Most folks mean well. And, amazingly, some folks do not. Many people may have no idea what to say to someone who has suffered a loss such as ours. The death of our loved one may be beyond their scope of sorrow. So they stumble with their words. We can see the hesitation in their eyes. Perhaps we were once like they are now.

A few themes seem to dominate attempts at consolation. One is the explanation that "...God needed your loved one more than you." Another rationale explains that "...there is a reason for everything that happens. We just do not know what it is." Still a third explores the idea that "...God is in charge and knows what He is doing even if we do not." A fourth is much simpler, "...who knows why these things happen? They make no sense." And finally a fifth that I have heard a lot from a variety of folks since the death of my son, "...only the good die young." Perhaps those of us who have lost children might relate to this last one the most.

I am the grieving one. No one else can understand the extent of my loss. It is okay.

Into Paradise may the angels in whom I do not believe lead thee; at thy coming may the martyrs long decomposed take thee up, in eternal rest, and may the chorus of angels lead thee to that which does not exist, the holy city, and perpetual light.

– William Gibson

Perhaps this is the theme that many of us grieving men would like to trumpet at this season of the year. That this life is all there is. This is it. There is nothing else to come. All has been made up to keep us quiet, toeing the line. Hardly a holiday thought.

And what is a spirit we may wonder?

Still, even convinced of the finality of death, we might ponder the possibility of an afterlife. We may have heard stories about the existence of a "parallel world," one that exists side-by-side to ours, invisible but real nonetheless. This world is earth. That world is heaven. The side-by-side world appeals to our sense of hope and fairness, especially if our loved one died an untimely death.

And ancient stories from many cultures also describe a paradise existence of various sorts. The descriptions may sound appealing: endless light, a divine presence, an end to suffering, a reunion with our loved ones, peace everlasting. Our heartbeat might quicken at the thought. Do we dare hope for such a place? Is it possible that what we believe may or may not be correct? No one knows. It is a mystery to all who still live.

I have many doubts. Yet I also have great hope. Perhaps the two can peacefully coexist until I find out myself.

They say such nice things about people at their funerals that it makes me sad to realize that I'm going to miss mine by just a few days.

– Garrison Keillor

Why not laugh in the face of death? In this holiday season, we have many reasons to celebrate. Of course we are broken-hearted at the loss of our loved one. Our life may be forever changed. God knows the world is overflowing with tears. For just this moment, let us take a brief break and remember our loved one in the fullness of his or her laughter.

Was laughter your loved one's going away gift?

Of course we all miss our funerals by "...just a few days." That's the point of Garrison Keillor's joke. But if we could attend our own funerals, what would we say to our gathered family members and friends? Would we cry with them or would we want to tell them funny stories about some of our life adventures? Our stories define us.

A monkey mask with chubby cheeks purchased years ago for a Halloween celebration has often been brought out for various reasons in our home, including Christmas. Surely Joseph and Mary smiled, perhaps even laughed with joy, at the birth of the Christ Child. Children, teenagers, and adults alike continue to this day to laugh regardless of who wears the mask. Sometimes, when I think of my dead son, I see him wearing that mask and I laugh with him once more. I believe he would want to be remembered laughing rather than crying.

I want people to say nice things about me at my funeral. Most of all, I want them to remember how much I laughed.

DECEMBER 23

I should like to remember my dead to You...all those who once belonged to me and have now left me. There are many of them, far too many to be taken in with one glance.

– Karl Rahner

As we get older, each death gets more of our attention. We know that one day we will also die. For now, though, it is still our turn to say goodbye to another one we have loved. It never gets easy. Once more our hearts are broken. Once more a sad farewell. Once more we are left behind. Once more we are alone in the deafening silence of loss.

How many goodbyes can we suffer through?

An endless number it seems, and... far too many to be taken in with one glance. So we will also commit this precious one into the hands of God. What else can we do? Each one we have loved is sacred. Each one we have loved has been a gift. Each one we have loved has brought something special to this life-feast. And we are thankful that our love for them has been big enough and wide enough and deep enough to embrace them all. Every one of them. Without exception.

Today I say goodbye to another loved one. I remember them all. One day a loved one will be saying goodbye to me.

DECEMBER 24

God gave us memories so that we might have roses in December.

– James Matthew Barrie

It may be impossible today to accept the fact that we have only memories of our loved one instead of his or her physical presence. We don't want memories. We want our loved one back.

But our loved one now belongs to the ages.

We may be filled with rage because of this loss. It's hard to sing Christmas carols through angry, clenched teeth, and impossible to offer hugs with closed fists. Silent Night doesn't touch the depth of our sorrow. Who wants to sing at all?

The first Christmas following our son's death, my wife and I skipped church services completely. We simply could not face the traditional celebrations of the season. But even more importantly, we could not bear to see all of the "intact" families with their children home for the holidays. Our son was dead. Their children were alive. For parents, how more unfair and painful could life possibly be?

Time, though, has softened the hard edges of our grief. Like beach glass smoothed over by the action of the waves, our grief has mellowed to the point that we can see other families in public and not feel as cheated as we felt when our loss was new. Don't get me wrong. We do not kick up our heels in delight at these sightings. But we no longer need to run away.

As long as our memories persist, we will keep our loved one "alive." And these memories truly are like "roses in December."

DECEMBER 25

How is it possible that suffering that is neither my own nor of my concern should immediately affect me as though it were my own, and with such force that it moves me to action?

– Arthur Schopenhauer

Our healing journey after the death of our loved one will likely be possible, in part, by the love and outreaching hands of others whom we never knew before our loss, both men and women alike. Living saints. Angels. Fearless in the face of the ultimate fear.

Certainly faithful friends have seen us through the darkest and most frightening moments. Where we would be without them? Family of the truest sort. Faithful. Unflinching. Ever-present. Fellow travelers down every turn in the dark and unknown road, helping us feel our way toward some sort of light.

But suffering strangers have also unexpectedly stepped into our lives as well. Their actions and words heaped healing balm on our dreadful wounds. Now we call them friends. Who sent them? God? Perhaps many of us would think so.

So as we wrestle with our thoughts and feelings of loneliness on this Christmas Day, let's whisper prayers of gratitude for those who refuse to abandon us and the newcomers in our lives who have joined us following the death of our beloved one.

They who have suffered much, understand much suffering.

DECEMBER 26

What we learn from people who have lost their jobs is to truly cherish our own. What we learn from people who have lost their sight is to truly cherish our own. What we learn from people who have lost their child is to truly cherish our own. What we learn from people who have lost their lives is to truly cherish our own.

– Douglas C. Smith

Perhaps in our great sorrow over the loss of our loved one, the word "cherish" surprises us, sort of sneaks up on us when we aren't looking. The Oxford Dictionary states that cherish means "1... to protect or tend (a child, etc.) lovingly. 2 hold dear; cling to (hopes, feelings, etc.)." Cherish is what we do when we love someone. Even we guys cherish, perhaps without knowing we do.

Possibly we would give anything to be able to still cherish the one who is missing from our sight, especially if his or her death was sudden and unexpected, especially if our loved one was our child. I remember declaring several times that I would gladly give my own life in exchange for the restoration of my son's life.

Cherish!

There is a timeless truth in the declaration that we often don't know what we have until it is gone. We take each other for granted. We think we will have tomorrow for apologies, for family activities, for acts of love and kindness, for speaking our love. For saying goodbye.

I always kissed my son whenever I greeted him and whenever he left my presence for his next adventure. I take comfort in knowing that on the day he died I kissed him goodbye. He knew how much I loved and cherished him.

And still do.

Dear _____, I'll always love and cherish you!

*We are all vulnerable. Anything can happen
to anybody at any time... from small
disappointments... to blows of the heart.*

– Eugene Kennedy

In this holiday season, during sleepless nights brought on by the death of our loved one, we may be reminded, again, of just how vulnerable we are. Staring at the ceiling through our bedroom shadows can take us right back to our fearful childhood, to the monsters that lived under our bed.

Death is the most fearful monster. When someone we love dies, especially perhaps our child, we often feel that we are next in line to die, that our own lives will also soon be over.

Fear of dying is, of course, not traditional "guy think" in our culture. Usually when we talk to other guys we keep the conversation "tough," boasting about our latest exploits in the sporting world, stock market victories, or our new set of wheels in the driveway. Or we speak in "report talk," keeping the conversation wrapped around last night's snow storm or the weather forecast for the coming week. We stay safely away from our emotions. That's women's work, right? Wrong.

Crying is an equal opportunity employer. We have to let our pain out or it will eat its way out from our insides.

Eugene Kennedy reminds us that, "anything can happen to anybody at any time." Life isn't fair. Bad things do happen to good people. Even us. We can recall stories of perfectly healthy people simply being in the wrong place at the wrong time. It costs them their lives. Think the twin towers, 9/11. Strong people. Equally vulnerable. All dead.

Today, in the midst of my sorrow, I acknowledge my vulnerability. Still I choose to walk tall and face my fears with faith, confidence, and hope for a brighter future. I will do this in spite of my loss.

But adversity is what makes you mature.
The growing soul is watered best by tears of
sadness.

– Charles Schultz

Adversity makes us mature? What kind of idea is that? We men are more inclined to think that adversity is something to be conquered, not endured. Adversity is a mountain to be climbed. Just give me time, we often ask. There must be a "fix" to every problem, isn't there? Let me think this one through and I'll come up with a solution. Tears of sadness? I don't think so.

After all, I'm a man.

Except that men do cry from time to time, especially, perhaps, at the death of a loved one. And if our tears are not visible, we are often crying on the inside. Silent tears can claw through a broken heart unless we allow them to see the light of day.

We would never have asked to grow our soul through this kind of sorrow. Yet, is there something about this death that will help us learn more about the value of life? About the value of friendships? About the pure joy of existence? About the beauty of a sunrise? The stunning serenity of a sunset? The love in a child's eyes?

I did not ask for this sorrow, but I hope for wisdom to help me understand how I have matured as a result of it.

*Survivor's guilt, moral injury, feeling betrayed
by leaders... that's what I saw every day... It's
because soldiers have such high standards that
they're vulnerable to moral injury.*

– William Nash

William Nash served as a combat psychiatrist in the Battle of Fallujah in 2004, and is the lead author of the current Navy and Marine doctrine on stress control, according to the December 10, 2012 issue of a Newsweek article written by Tony Dokoupil.

Dokoupil adds, "Now, along with some of the most distinguished psychiatrists in the Department of Veteran's Affairs, he [Nash] believes that moral injury and its sister, traumatic loss, may be...the leading cause of Post-Traumatic Stress Syndrome, depression, substance abuse, and even the military's epidemic of suicide." The article postulates that sadness, loss, and betrayal are the major causes of these problems in the lives of returning soldiers. "The common thread is a violation of what is right, a tear in what people freely call the soul," Dokoupil reports.

Soul wounds can only be healed by time, patience, and the availability of listening and compassionate ears. We men, vets and non-vets alike, need to know that someone cares enough to listen to our stories. On our local community college campus, a veteran's club helps to serve that purpose. "The Center for Soul Repair opened last month at the Brite Divinity School at Texas Christian University. It's a five-year effort to train the nation's religious leaders, as well as the public, to respond to moral injury," Dokoupil concludes.

The wounds of loss are not always visible. Death can happen from the inside out. Soul repair is as much men's work as combat duty. Where do we begin? By listening. And caring.

Who will I call to share my feelings of sadness, loss, or betrayal?

DECEMBER 30

Even if nothing can be fixed, let the vision reconstitute us through a pinhole in time and space – a vision of the lonely God carrying the burden of universal sorrow. Let us take Her in our arms. Let us stroke His temples.

– Deena Metzger

This early winter season, between Hanukah, Christmas, Ramadan and another New Year, can seem endless for those of us who grieve. The daylight hours have shortened, the cold days are settling in for another long winter stay, snow and icy streets may be familiar neighbors once more, and bitter wind may bite at unsuspecting openings in our jacket collars, trying to chill our saddened hearts. Is it any wonder that this particular week can be depressing?

And yet, yet we somehow feel we are not alone.

That even God gets lonely, yet still walks beside us in our loneliness while "carrying the burden of universal sorrow," is intriguing. Perhaps this is the most helpful and healing message of the holiday season for those of us with broken hearts. Can we embrace this heart-warming possibility?

There is a God who understands? We are not forever alone with our grief?

My biggest fear is that I am alone with my grief. Maybe, just maybe, I am not alone at all. This is my holiday prayer: that God walks beside me and shares my pain.

DECEMBER 31

Now it is time for me to lie down – lie down in trust, and be where I am...

– Jane Kenyon

The end of the year. The end of a life. Never the end of love. "Be here now;" the words from the song reach for my attention, "...no other place to be." The music of love plays on and on, oblivious to the clock, the calendar, or the circumstance. Will I trust in the music, in the power that created and sustains the universe, that in the end we will all be okay, safely cradled like a baby in his mother's loving embrace?

When a loved one dies, isn't this the assurance we seek?

A life-long friend Dennis Hensley writes that our beloved high school English teacher, Neil Ringle, has died. Dennis was disappointed that only seventy-three people showed up to say goodbye to this ninety-nine year old man. Pondering upon Neil's love for his students, I believe his tired soul would have rejoiced instead, and embraced Jane Kenyon's simple prayer-like statement and smiled.

Neil Ringle once threw a chalkboard eraser at me in class to get my attention. He missed me, but he did get my attention. He knew the power of the present moment. Happy New Year Mr. Ringle. Happy New Life!

When an old year ends, a new year begins. But love is never ending. Wherever my loved one is now, I know the love we shared lives on.

ACKNOWLEDGMENTS

Endless love and gratitude to my beloved wife, Jane. Her great and gracious love and wise counsel helped shape this book. And, to our daughter, Emily, for her photography skills and constant support for this project.

Also, heartfelt thanks to Jami Blaauw-Hara for her editing skills and gentle encouragement. And David Payne's design and layout efforts enhanced this book's appearance; I will always be grateful for his desire to be a part of this work.

Finally, great gratitude for our family members and friends who have fearlessly walked beside us since the day Nathaniel and Nick died. Please accept our eternal thanks.

PERMISSIONS

Made in the USA
San Bernardino, CA
25 March 2015